184

£4.00

CH00767685

8

THE RACE TO THE
INTELLIGENT STATE

For Jo, Hannah, Elly and Jess

THE RACE TO THE
INTELLIGENT STATE

Towards the Global Information Economy of 2005

MICHAEL CONNORS

Copyright © Barclays de Zoete Wedd Investment Management Ltd 1993

First published 1993

Blackwell Publishers
108 Cowley Road
Oxford OX4 1JF, UK

238 Main Street, Suite 501
Cambridge, Massachusetts 02142, USA

British Library Cataloguing in Publication Data

A CIP catalogue record for this book is available from the British Library

Library of Congress Cataloging-in-Publication Data

Connors, Michael.
 The race to the intelligent state: towards the global information
economy of 2005/Michael Connors.
  p. cm.
 Includes bibliographic references and index.
 ISBN 0–631–19072–4 (alk. paper)
 1. Information technology—Economic aspects—Forecasting.
 2. Information technology—Social aspects—Forecasting. 3. Twenty
-first century—Forecasts. I. Title.
 HC79.I55C67 1993
 303.48'33—dc20   92–44816
                                             CIP

Typeset in 11 on 13pt Times by
Paul Stringer, Watford
Printed and bound in Great Britain by
Biddles Ltd, Guildford and King's Lynn

This book is printed on acid-free paper

CONTENTS

ACKNOWLEDGEMENTS

For the help, advice and encouragement which I received during the writing of this book, I would like to thank: Bill Slakey of Apple Computer, Jerry Taylor of Applied Materials, Paisal Sricharatchanya of the Bangkok Post, Erik Jansen of Alex Brown & Sons, Vatchaporn Mangkonkarn of Leo Burnett Ltd., Fred Moran of Donaldson, Lufkin & Jenrette, Nicholas Valery of The Economist Newspaper, Laurence Heyworth of Robert Fleming Ltd., Ron Altman of Furman Selz Inc., David Gould of Fujitsu America Inc., Gerald Fitzmaurice of the International Institute of Communications, Suchin Suwanacheep of Loxley Limited, Sondhi Limthongkul of the Manager Group, Paul Fox, Krishna Shankar and Tom Thornhill of Montgomery Securities, Jim Mendelson and Steve Milunovich of Morgan Stanley International, Yukihisa Nishimura of Namco Limited, Thanachai Santichaikul of the Nation Publishing Group, Sansern Wongcha-um of the National Economic and Social Development Board of Thailand, Shin'ichi Koike and Nobuyuki Hayashida of NEC Corporation, Hisao Iizuka, Takao Maezawa, Noriyuki Terada and Dr. Mamoru Kitamura of Nippon Telegraph and Telephone Corporation, Satoshi Nakamura and Yutaka Yamakoshi of Nihon Keizai Shimbunsha, Masaru Maeda of Nippon Television, Prasert Mussari and Suporn Aroonpakmongkol of Saatchi and Saatchi, Chirdsak Kukiattinun of the Shinawatra Computer and Communications Group, Yukio Ozawa of Sony Corporation, Professor Ian Gow of the University of Stirling, Olarn Pientam of the Telephone Organization of Thailand, Kyoji Yoshida of Tokyo Broadcasting System, Eric Benhamou of 3COM, Akira Miyoshi of Toshiba Corporation and Professor Nicholas Garnham of the University of Westminster.

Of my colleagues in the Barclays Group, I would particularly like to thank Pradeep Asrani of Barclays Bank in Bombay, Jerry Black, Ossie Law and Mike Richardson of the Economics Department of Barclays Bank PLC, Paul Chanin, Francis Connor, Robert Johnson, Masae Kawashima, Robert Lister, Phongnarin Ratanarangsikul, James Russell-Stracey and Sir Robert Wade-Gery of Barclays de Zoete Wedd, and Donald Brydon, Brenda Jarrett and my colleagues at BZWIM.

Special thanks are due to Manjushri Mitra of the London School of Economics, who tirelessly searched for material and helped me to understand something of India.

Michael Connors

INTRODUCTION

Many of those who today owe their livelihoods to the manipulation of abstractions – academics, managers, financiers, lawyers, politicians and consultants, as well as those directly involved in the more explicitly recognized information businesses – would probably regard as axiomatic an assertion that an information revolution has been taking place during the past three decades. The process of revolutionary change in the world of information may seem axiomatic to some contemporary observers, but it is also as yet not well defined.

We live, we are told, in an information society in an information age. We have information technology, information science and knowledge-based industries. But was this not always so? Certainly it would be quite easy to define advanced ancient civilizations as information societies within the context of their times. Rome was an information society and the Romans, within the confines of their known world, would no doubt have considered themselves to be living in an information age had the idea been suggested to them. Their information technology was in their politics, their language and their mathematics, and their knowledge-based industries could be seen in their armies, their vineyards and everything that differentiated them from their less enlightened neighbours. So, what is it that will distinguish for posterity the intellectual achievements of the late twentieth century from those of the early part of the first millennium or any other period in history? What are the characteristics of our information society that make it more than just a product of the extrapolation of a number of established historical trends?

It could be argued that there is no function which is fulfilled by modern information technology which was not performed by some means or another 2,000 years ago. Radio waves, optical memory and spell-check programs may have at least partially displaced pack-mules and pigeons, books and pictures, and editors and teachers, but there are still places in the world where the mail arrives on a donkey, people everywhere still write and read books in vast numbers, and teachers and editors still wield the red pen. Modern technology provides improvements in speed, convenience and accuracy in our manipulation of language and other abstractions but, unless it causes more fundamental changes to the conduct of our affairs than that (i.e., unless technological change results in some identifiable discontinuity in the stream of history), the notion of an information revolution will be little more than hype.

If an information revolution has occurred, or is in progress, it is an issue of considerable importance and should be treated with due seriousness. Yet we must guard against the temptation to believe our own propaganda and to endow the achievements of contemporary society with a significance which posterity will deem to have been misplaced. Although the pace of change in the world is undeniably accelerating, revolutions worthy of being thus described in the history books do not happen very often and a great deal of evidence will have to be presented in support of the late twentieth century information revolution if it is to pass muster.

The British Industrial Revolution, which our textbooks conveniently bracket into the period 1760 to 1850, is probably the best available model of a fully qualified societal revolution, and it perhaps offers some analytical yardsticks for the evaluation of the information revolution. It undoubtedly marked a great discontinuity in human history, massively accelerating the pace of social change and altering the shape of the world forever. It resulted from political, demographic and technological change and in turn provided a massive boost to those processes of change. If our information revolution has to live up to this as an exemplar, it has a hard act to follow. And yet, the timetable is a comparatively leisurely one – 90 years to transform the world as we know it – and the twentieth century, in its dying years, is still proving to be a fertile environment for global upheavals of all kinds.

While the Industrial Revolution had its roots firmly planted in England and derived from agricultural, technological and social changes in Britain in the late seventeenth and early eighteenth centuries, today's information revolution is a much more global phenomenon, with worldwide change being precipitated by developments in high technology emanating mainly from the USA and Japan. However, although it is tempting to think of the British Industrial Revolution as having been purely driven by technological change, this is an over-simplification. The creation of an agricultural surplus and Arkwright's enlightened approach to factory organization were as important to the process as Crompton's invention of the 'mule' or the mass production of coke. Similarly, the information revolution may be fuelled by intoxicating technology but it is also a product of the political, social, economic and organizational environment of our time.

The Industrial Revolution was about the production of physical goods. The great boom in transport infrastructure – the canals, the railways and the ocean-going steamships – was concerned with their distribution. The investors and entrepreneurs of the time viewed the world in terms of the developing markets for physical goods and the ways of supplying them. This process, coupled with a stream of technological development, created goods and services that had not theretofore existed and, in so doing, transformed the lives of millions. If the information revolution runs a similar course – and there are many who believe that it will – the global market for information and its communication will be its focus.

An information revolution could change the lives of hundreds of millions but it would be managed differently from the Industrial Revolution. The doughty merchants of Manchester were imaginative enough to sell cotton cloth to India and Africa but the goods of the information revolution are quicksilver by comparison. Having established a wealth of economic and commercial techniques for dealing with physical goods in the physical world, we have yet fully to come to terms with our enormous trade in abstractions. The information world is not the world of physical goods and the management of the revolution will require a codified view of the market for information; and yet even everyday traders in information do not, for the most part, see the information world as a systematic entity. If envisaged as an entity, it is ethereal and multi-dimensional; the elements which go to make up the information infrastructure are as diverse as the political climate, the literacy of the citizenry, the price of television sets and the bandwidth available in satellite transponders.

This book is about the evolution of the information infrastructure, which I shall refer to as the 'infostructure', and starts from the premise that profound changes are afoot, that the propensity and ability of mankind to collect, collate, transmit and analyse information has grown to a point from which there is no going back and from which far-reaching change is inevitable in the longer run. It is not, however, the intention here to attempt to make long-run predictions but to describe currently observable phenomena and to draw inferences from such observations as to how the information world seems likely to change in the medium term.

The choice of a time horizon for such predictions is inevitably somewhat arbitrary but the year 2005 has been selected here because some of the government bodies around the world which are charged with making projections of change in relevant areas have made ranging shots into that territory and because the developers of some of the most important information technologies are also setting their sights on targets which are ten or fifteen years in the offing.

The analysis offered here is predicated on the view that the development of the information infrastructures of the world is a process which is primarily technology-driven and which has been going on, at varying rates and in various ways, in all parts of the world since the appearance of man on the planet some two million years ago. Insofar as the process falls within the compass of recorded history, it can be seen to be occurring at an accelerating rate but its results still vary widely as between the world's information-rich and information-poor countries. The nature of the evolutionary process and the extreme unevenness of the distribution of information in the world is described in chapter 1.

The persistence of unequal access to information is a function of the wide differences in cultural and economic circumstances between nation states, in which the pace and extent of change in this area also varies widely. Some Third World nations face enormous difficulties in the development of their information sectors and can only manage slow and patchy progress, while others have proved to be capable of transformation in scarcely more than a decade. Chapter 2 describes the very different experiences of India and Thailand, both of which are relatively information poor, in their efforts to develop infostructures comparable with those of the developed world.

In the creation of a modern infostructure, the central importance of information technology is generally recognized but, although technology is thus cast in the role of the principal propellant of change, the thesis offered here is that it is also the aspect of the information world in which the changes to come over the next decade or so are the most easily forecast. Technology is sometimes subject to sharp discontinuities but research and development are usually so explicitly applied to the achievement of particular goals that the general nature of the changes which they will bring, if not the precise timing and technical details of those changes, is reasonably predictable. It is also often the case that the important new technologies which will be in widespread use in ten years' time are already with us in at least embryonic form. The pattern is not usually one of technical breakthrough followed by instant commercialization and mass implementation. Such cases are the exceptions which prove the rule and the gestation period of many major technology-based commercial products is often surprisingly long. Chapter 3 describes the evolution of some of the key information technologies and offers predictions as to their state of development in 2005 and the implications of the capabilities which they will provide.

While developing nations often utilize the latest technology in their efforts to catch up with the developed world, they are, for the most part, buyers or recipients of new technology rather than creators of it. The development of leading-edge technology falls to the developed nations in general and to the USA and Japan in particular. If the developed nations are concerned with the creation of information technology, they are also concerned with the ways in which it will influence their societies and economies in future. Chapter 4 describes the existing information environments of the USA and Japan, the visions of the information society of the future which are projected by some of their citizens and institutions and the ways in which rivalry between these two information superpowers seems likely to propel the process of change in the next few years.

Much has been said and written in recent years about the ways in which information technology will influence the economic and social structures of developed nations in years to come and the proponents of the notion of the 'post-industrial information society' have become very influential, particularly in the English-speaking world. Chapter 5 examines the way in which the economies of some of the developed nations have become unbalanced in a manner which suggests that this concept has been unduly, or at least prematurely, persuasive and describes some of the institutional and human factors which seem likely to act as major impediments to the development of 'post-industrial' information societies in general.

Struggles over land, resources and political power continue today as they have since time immemorial but the nascent information revolution has added a new dimension to human competition. Individuals, corporations and nation states are today competing with one another for intellectual territory as they never have before. It is, however, territory which few, if any, have yet reached and the competition for it is less a battle over known terrain than a race towards an ideal but as yet unrealized intelligent state. In such a state – and the word could be taken to signify a nation state or a condition – the application of intelligence and a vast pool of readily accessible knowledge to the problems of life are implicitly expected to create a life-style of plenty, ease and spiritual fulfilment. The power of intellect has always been the driving force in human progress and there is a feeling abroad that, with the exciting new information technologies which we now have at our disposal, we can proceed to some kind of 'infotopia'. The destination is ill-defined but the race to the intelligent state is already well in progress.

It would be reckless to suggest that the placings in the race at any point in the future could be predicted with any accuracy but the factors which are likely to determine the course to be run and the pace at which it is likely to be run over the next few years can be rather more readily identified. It will be suggested here that, while developing nations seem likely to derive great benefits from the onrush of information technology over the next decade or so, new problems could be looming for the developed world, which will need to look to its policies and its structures if it is to extract net benefits from the information revolution in the longer run.

If the information revolution is defined as a great leap in the accessibility of information, it is likely that, at least as far as the developed world is concerned, it will largely have run its course by 2005. Such is the ability of mankind to absorb technological change that the undeniably important changes which are under way may not create an information world in 2005 which looks or feels startlingly different from the world of the early 1990s and the much-vaunted information revolution may thus disappoint those who expect it to transform society. There is, however, the intriguing possibility that the information revolution may be the precursor to a revolution in intelligence itself, the implications of which challenge the imagination. In dealing with such huge subjects, a slim volume such as this is inevitably little more than a sketch-map. It will attempt to provide a hazy topography of the information world of 2005 but the pace of change is such and the terrain so complex that, much beyond that, the map might as well bear the legend 'here be dragons'.

1

THE ROAD TO THE
INTELLIGENT STATE

The origins of human civilization are sought in the evolutionary changes
which resulted in the emergence of the genus *Homo* in the early
Pleistocene period. All the genetic forebears of early man, including his
immediate Australopithecine ancestors, lacked the cranial capacity for
the kind of abstract thought necessary for the systematic fabrication of
tools. The Australopithecines had almost made the breakthrough. They
probably used as implements extraneous objects which had some of the
attributes necessary to accomplish the task at hand – a fortuitously sharp
stone or pointed stick. But their brains were a few egg-cupfuls short of
the capacity which would allow them to conceive of how to synthesize
on a routine basis the sharpness and pointedness which they could then
bring to bear on the tasks with which they were repeatedly confronted.
They were therefore, it seems, unable deliberately to fabricate tools.

The arrival of the new breed, *Homo habilis*, with the requisite
cerebral horsepower, coincided with the repeated and deliberate
fashioning of the stone implements which have survived to provide
clear evidence of the event. They made tools and therefore, according
to the *ex post facto* definition, they were human. The capacity for
abstract thought was not just something which allowed these creatures
to satisfy the entry requirements for some arbitrary academic category
later invented by palaeontologists, it was the point at which humanity
began its dominance over all other species.

When and how events unfolded from the time *habilis* made the great
breakthrough, about two million years ago, is far from clear but,
whenever and however the dominant species on the planet came into
being, the seminal events in question occurred very recently indeed in
any palaeontological time-scale. The biological evolution which has
taken place over the 40,000 or so years since *Homo sapiens sapiens*

emerged as the ultimately successful competitor to the Neanderthal *Homo sapiens* has been minimal and it is often said that a time-travelling Cro-Magnon *sapiens sapiens* could turn up in Fifth Avenue or Oxford Street, buy himself an outfit and disappear into the crowd as an unremarkable, if possibly somewhat hirsute, modern man. He could probably also, if suitably coached, graduate from high school and hold down a job in a bank. It is now generally believed, in other words, that ancient man was equipped with something very close to a modern brain and that the distance between the individual crafting of stone hand axes and the mass production of integrated circuits, zip fasteners, soap powder, bank statements and software packages has been travelled as a result of a cultural, and not a biological, evolution.

Important aspects of cultural evolution in prehistoric times are largely obscure. While flint tools and fossils provide clear evidence of some physical accomplishments, clues to cultural development, such as cave drawings and burial practices, tantalize as much as they inform. It is believed that the more advanced of early tool makers had the cerebral capacity for speech, although even the Neanderthals probably had vocal tracts which were inadequate for the forming of complex linguistic sounds. There is, of course, no record of how, or indeed whether, they did speak or how well they could convey complex abstract ideas. It may be that the wide geographical spread of the tool-making culture evidences not only the conceptualization but also the verbal communication of the concept, but all that can be said with confidence is that complex human language evolved between the rise of *Homo habilis* and the appearance of the first written word in Mesopotamia around 4000 BC. The rest is history.

If the conventional picture outlined above is broadly correct, it seems natural to infer that the success of human civilization is a function of the ability of man as an organism and as a social being to generate, transmit, comprehend, adapt and store abstractions. If the evolution of communications media in the broadest sense was what enabled this great leap to take place, it is worth reflecting a little on the process. Communications theorists generally identify three epochs in the evolution of human communication: the oral, print and electronic ages. The three clearly telescope into one another chronologically – in entering the electronic age we did not abandon oral communication and printed matter – and they combine and interact in a manner which reflects their important qualitative differences.

The historical effects of the development of speech upon human life can only be glimpsed dimly but the characteristics of face-to-face verbal communication – either one-to-one or one-to-many – are clear in contemporary life. Unrecorded speech or, rather, speech recorded only in memory, is usually ephemeral, although the effects of oratory, with its undertones of music and theatre, can be very different from the influence of the same words frozen on the page. Speech is also a group activity, to the extent that speaking to oneself is commonly regarded as a sure sign of eccentricity or worse. Speech has an emotional dynamic which other forms of communication usually lack and perhaps a greater tendency to descend into chaos. No political journalist or pamphleteer, no matter how skilled or famous, can match the effect which a skilled orator can have on a crowd, which may itself respond with banal yet emotionally powerful chants. Speech is the medium of here and now and its effects are often immediate and potent.

The written word, although not necessarily devoid of emotional expressiveness, is usually recorded and read in a quiet and solitary manner. It is usually more considered, more measured; and this is true whether the word is hand written or typed in a single copy of a document or reproduced many times. It also differs from the spoken word in that the writer and the reader are rarely together in space or time. Indeed it is this latter fact which gives the written word its power. The abstract concept recorded semi-permanently in writing is the basis of all scholarship and a good deal of science and technology. Those cultures which developed syllabic or ideographic letters, writing materials and the other tools of the written word at an early stage reaped great benefits. The technology of paper-making was brought into the Arabian peninsula from China in the eighth century AD, whereas Europeans were forced to struggle on with parchment until 400 years later. By the end of the eighth century, collections of scholarly works had been built up throughout the Arab world, which extended across North Africa and into Spain, while Northern Europe remained benighted. Europe's technical breakthrough in the sphere came in the fifteenth century, with the advent of movable type, and the world's cultural centre of gravity shifted northwards.

The inventors of typography opened the door on the era of the mass communications medium. Books, pamphlets, magazines and, above all, newspapers became the media through which people were informed of what was going on in the world and through which efforts were made to influence mass consciousness. Printed media continue to perform this role today to some extent but, whereas for three centuries or more print had a monopoly in this function, the twentieth century has seen its leading role being usurped by the electronic mass media. The rise of radio and, more recently, television coincided with the ascent of the USA to superpower status and the most powerful culture of our time has thus been projected beyond its national borders by the most potent technologies which have ever existed for the mass dissemination of information.

The revolution in the mass media which occurred in the first half of this century and which gathered pace in the second has been a very visible phenomenon. In addition, electrical and electronic technology has supported simultaneous developments in the communication of information which is not for mass consumption: the telegraph, telex, telephone and facsimile machine, for instance, each mark points along a linear path of development of what is essentially point-to-point communication. The invention and exponential development in the capabilities of the integrated circuit and its application in computers and their peripherals has, however, marked the beginning of a second major phase in the electronic information era. Indeed, the implications of the development of computer technology for the ways in which we now, and will in future, utilize information are so far-reaching that there can be little doubt that to the generally accepted three epochs of communications technology (oral, print and electronic), should be added a fourth – the computer epoch.

The process of technological development often results in the displacement of the old by the new, but this is far from true of the phenomenon sketched out above. The four technologies developed in a clear chronological sequence but it would be an oversimplification to view them in a simple hierarchical fashion. The great inventions of speech, writing, electrical communication and computers are profoundly complementary; they combine in advanced societies to form information systems of great complexity and power and it is the ways in which the technologies cluster and combine which determine the relative sophistication of the information systems in question.

There is a mass of historical evidence which suggests that the possession of the most sophisticated information systems bestows great advantages upon a society. It is interesting to consider, therefore, how the curious and somewhat chaotic dynamics of history have created a world in which there is a far from uniform distribution in the multi-faceted trade in abstractions and the use of the sophisticated skills and technologies which support it.

There are countries whose people exhibit a high propensity for abstraction. In such countries a majority of the population is engaged in activities which are abstract or cerebral in nature and even manual workers spend a lot of time dealing with abstractions. However, many of these activities are not invested with any great sophistication. A simple laundry list is an abstraction, as is an equation in quantum mechanics, and, given that much of human economic activity is concerned with the simple organization of simple physical tasks, the amount of abstract work to be done in diverse and specialized societies expands almost exponentially as a function of that diversity and specialization. Complexity, it seems, breeds complexity and the generally accepted model of the advanced society is one in which the primary (i.e., agriculture, fishing and mining) and secondary (i.e., manufacturing) industrial bases support an ever growing tertiary (i.e., service) sector with more and more abstract and esoteric occupations and ever more sophisticated information systems.

The opposite case – that of the low abstraction society – is characterized by relatively few occupational categories, concentrated mainly in primary and simple secondary production, and a relatively narrow range of issues with which the population at large typically concerns itself. There are fewer aromatherapists and interior designers in Botswana than in California, with correspondingly fewer related professional associations, magazines, conferences, expenses claims and endowments.

The high abstraction/low abstraction dichotomy corresponds closely with the north–south divide and with the global split in power, wealth and human comfort. The high abstraction state seems, on the face of it, to be typically that to which the governments and peoples of all nation states aspire. The general perception is that abstraction has served mankind well and the abstraction business seems likely to continue to grow, possibly at an accelerating pace.

The general direction of the trends which equate with (at least) the developed world's notions of progress seems, then, to be fairly clear but the geographical distribution of the abstract activities upon which this progress is based continues to be very uneven. And if the key to human material well-being is the creation of a physical environment through informed thought and considered and organized action, it is clear that the efficiency with which a society deals with the abstract activities at the beginning of that chain will be a major determinant of the extent of its success. The rich and powerful nations generally have sophisticated information systems and it seems reasonable to infer that a cardinal prerequisite of a successful modern society must be the access which the mass of its population has to information.

Political factors have always had a profound effect on the nature and volume of information flows in a society and it has long been recognized that control of information can be a formidable instrument of political power. Whatever other constraints may have been placed on the access which people have had to information, whether by physical isolation, linguistic or technical problems, politics has always shaped that access to a greater or lesser extent in all societies. Those who seek to exercise political power have from time to time sought to control all the media of communication, including individual speech itself.

The notion of political control of the media in the more modern sense perhaps first emerged in China in the late years of the T'ang dynasty, towards the end of the tenth century AD, with the invention of block printing, which for the first time raised the possibility of uncontrolled mass information flows. Although this innovation was enhanced by the introduction of movable type in China *circa* 1040 AD, the reluctance of the ruling classes to see such a potentially dangerous technology popularized greatly inhibited its early development. When the technology reached Europe (the Gutenberg Bible was printed in 1453) it soon proved to be a politically potent force which spawned mass communication media with tolerably wide circulations by the early seventeenth century.

Substantial freedom of expression, including a high degree of freedom of the press, was established at an early stage in Europe and this principle, which has as its obverse the notion of free access to information, is taken for granted by most people in the developed world. But it would be a mistake to assume that total freedom from political control exists in the communications media in Europe or anywhere else. Censorship of the press and other media takes many forms, from murder and crude physical force, through formal editing routines to peer group pressure and other subtle forms of coercion.

In countries where democratic principles are undeveloped or are in abeyance, government ownership and control of the media are common. Censorship is more often exercised through warnings, confiscation and withdrawal of rights and privileges than by pre-publication editing. Licensing and controls over transmission or distribution are also common, as are restrictions on the entry of foreign broadcasts or publications and requirements that stories be obtained from, or cleared with, a government news agency. It is quite common for all electronic broadcasting media in a country to be owned and controlled by the state and, in many, the use of these media to bolster the political status quo is quite flagrant. Where the media are not under direct political control, vaguely worded ordinances concerning the national interest, defamation or libel are sometimes invoked to achieve the same effect.

In democracies such as the USA and the UK, formal censorship of the media is either absent or strictly limited. The UK has the Official Secrets Act, under which guidelines, known as 'D-Notices', are periodically issued to the media in order to inform them which specific areas are currently deemed to be off-limits. The USA has no such legislation and the press is ostensibly free to report what it will, provided only that it does not intrude upon the National Security Agency, whose codes and other secrets are protected under law.

The most common form of restriction on the mass media, and hence of public access to politically sensitive information, in democracies is the practice of self-censorship. This usually occurs as a result of the relationship of mutual assistance which exists between the media and the government or, perhaps more pertinently, between the representatives of the media and government officials. The government uses the media to disseminate its information and views and the media men depend upon reliable sources in government for the timely information which earns them their daily bread. It is very easy, in these circumstances, for officials and politicians to exert subtle pressure on the media, provided only that they do not go beyond tacitly accepted bounds.

It can be said with some confidence that non-democratic regimes tend to be more restrictive, and more crudely restrictive, of information flows than do democratic governments. There is similarly little doubt that such restrictions have an invidious influence on the broader information environment, as censorship itself is usually but part of the story. Overt censorship and/or more subtle forms of political control over information flows exist everywhere; they form a variable backdrop to aspects of the information scene in any country and cannot be ignored but, across the world as a whole, the limitations on information flows and the access which the citizenry has to even the most utilitarian of information services are usually much more a function of the state of economic development than they are of political manipulation. The development of the information infrastructure of a nation is, in turn, fundamental to its success in the modern world.

Information is, by its nature, a dynamic commodity. Although it can be frozen on paper, magnetic tape or silicon, its existence can have no functional meaning until it is transferred. It seems reasonable, therefore, to measure the information power present in a nation by examining the volume of information flows or the potential for such flows to take place. Information-rich environments – the advanced nations with their preoccupation with abstractions – are full of equipment for the communication of information and people who are willing and able to use it. In information-poor environments – essentially the Third World – people lack either the equipment or the ability or both.

Travellers flying from London to New York are showered with information from all sides from the moment they leave until they arrive at their destination. Reading newspapers in the taxi, they are sub-consciously aware of the sound of the driver's radio. Glancing out of the window they read the more interesting of the advertising hoardings. Painted signs, electronic notice boards, boarding cards, telephones, loudspeakers, television sets and in-flight entertainment systems continue to bombard them with information, amusement and entreaties all the way. Illiterate Afghan hill farmers, on the other hand, may be left to their thoughts from one day to the next.

The rigorous measurement of an environment in terms of the access to information which it affords its inhabitants would be a formidable task, as data on the wide range of variables which determine the intensity and quality of the information environment are difficult to collect on a genuinely comparable basis. The nature of the phenomenon being measured ironically contributes to the difficulty insofar as, in information-rich environments, the scope, volume and complexity of the data is too great to be susceptible to accurate and consistent measurement whereas, in information-poor environments, there is simply too little information available altogether. Some relevant statistics are, however, available on a world-wide basis and, by using these, it is possible to assemble a crude, and admittedly incomplete, index of the accessibility of information in most of the countries of the world which offers at least some perspective on the issue.

Governments and national boundaries are always subject to change and so the political map of the world is not entirely constant. One recent count (prior to the unification of Germany, the dissolution of the Soviet

Union and the rift in what was Yugoslavia) put the number of nation and city states and semi-autonomous colonies and dependencies in the world at 189. Agencies such as UNESCO provide basic infostructure data on about three-quarters of these.

The statistics which readily present themselves for the construction of our index cover items such as literacy, newspaper circulation, radio and television stations, radio and television receiver ownership, magazine titles, advertising expenditures and telephone installations. No comparable data are available which give any indication of the access which the citizens of different countries have to computers or data networks and some of the figures which are available cannot meaningfully be used. Advertising expenditure and magazine title figures, for example, are not available for many Third World countries, while the figures for radio and television stations are distorted in some countries by the use of transmitter numbers in place of station numbers.

The home-grown index offered here, which will be referred to as the 'Information Access Index', therefore incorporates only figures on literacy, newspaper readership, radio and television ownership and telephone installations, some of which are in themselves revealing. The Index, and the raw UNESCO and other data upon which it is based, are shown in full in the appendix.

Any index which is intended to compare data from countries as diverse as the USA, Indonesia, Brazil and Singapore can only be based on per capita figures and so all statistics used here are calculated on that basis. The Information Access Index takes per capita data for each item and then indexes them around the arithmetical average score for the item. The indices for each item are then added and the totals indexed around the arithmetical average of the totals. Thus a country in which the literacy rate is high, newspapers widely read, radio and television receivers widely owned and telephones widely installed will have a high score and countries where none of these conditions prevails will have a low score. The index focuses on the accessibility of basic information through conventional media and says nothing about the level or diffusion of modern information technology or new media in the countries.

The use of simple addition and averaging means that, although an unusually high, low or distorted score in any one area will produce some distortion in the index as a whole, the distortion will at least be arithmetic rather than geometric.

From Burkina Faso to Bermuda

It is curious that the state which, according to our Information Access Index, enjoys the richest information environment (per capita) in the world is an island in the Atlantic Ocean measuring 53 sq. km, while the most isolated people in the world, in terms of access to information, live in a landlocked country a little larger than the UK.

Bermuda may not be the first place to spring to mind when contemplating the notion of the high information state but, according to our simple index, it tops the table with an impressive score of 373, forcing the odds-on favourite, the USA, into second place with a mere 326. Bearing in mind that the global average in the index is 100, a score approximated by the United Arab Emirates with 99 and Venezuela with 96, the gulf between Bermuda at the top and Burkina Faso, which sits at the bottom of our league with a score of 5, is vast. The numbers which form the basis of the index do indeed illustrate starkly contrasting situations.

The 60,000 people of Bermuda have a literacy rate of 98.4 per cent and a GNP per capita (in 1991) of $27,516. They have over 60,000 telephones – more than one for every man, woman and child – and 57,000 television sets. Their 83,000 radios give most of them a choice of receivers on which to listen to the broadcasts of their two commercial radio stations. They are, however, perhaps more avid viewers and listeners than they are newspaper readers, as every thousand Bermudians share only 321 copies of local daily newspapers. Bermuda's surprising position in the index ranking is almost certainly a reflection of the huge presence of foreign insurance companies on the island. In 1990, 270 foreign companies had a physical presence in Bermuda, which is said to have the largest concentration of qualified accountants in the world. This combination of general affluence and the presence of an information-hungry offshore industry was sufficient to win the top slot.

The people of the République Démocratique Populaire de Burkina Faso live in a more austere world in which 91 per cent are illiterate, GNP per capita is a modest $310 and there are only two telephones per thousand people. There are five daily newspapers, one weekly and one monthly, only one of which (*L'Observateur*) is independent of political control. Total newspaper circulation among the population of nine million – and a literate population of around 800,000 – is tiny, amounting to about one copy per thousand people. There is one state-run radio station, which broadcasts on FM and short wave to around 230,000 receivers nation-wide. The national television station broadcasts (in colour) for five hours per day to a tiny audience which owns about 45,000 receivers.

The specifics of Bermuda and Burkina Faso reflect the general patterns at the top and bottom ends of the scale. The top ten scores in the index go to: Bermuda, the USA, Switzerland, Japan, Denmark, Sweden, Finland, Norway, Canada and New Zealand. The bottom ten are: Burkina Faso, Mali, The Central African Republic, Nepal, Benin, Mozambique, Niger, Bangladesh, Haiti and Burundi.

The average literacy rate for the top ten countries in the index is 99 per cent, for the bottom ten it is 23 per cent. Daily newspaper diffusion in the top ten averages 420 copies per thousand people. In the bottom ten, the figure is less than 1 per cent of that.

The top ten countries typically have 675 telephones per thousand people while the bottom ten have just two. Television is similarly associated with rich countries (569 per thousand as compared with three) but, whereas telephone installations fall off very steeply from a point just below the median index score, television diffusion falls sharply somewhat lower down the rankings.

Radio receivers achieve diffusion rates in excess of 100 per cent in the top ten countries, with an average of 1,122 units per thousand people. The important role of radio in the Third World and the resilience of radio diffusion in even the very poorest countries is, however, illustrated by the comparatively high figure of 49 per thousand for radio diffusion in our bottom ten.

Discussions of development in Third World countries, or in those countries which were for many years part of what became known as the Second World and are now undergoing upheaval in their institutions, are usually predicated on an implicit understanding of the direction in which development should proceed. The implied picture is generally one of more or less rectilinear progress towards a state similar to that which prevails in some parts of the developed world. It would perhaps be an oversimplification to say that perceptions of the desired state differ only in detail but, with the decline of world communism which has been seen in recent years, such major ideological divides as once existed in the developed world have now largely disappeared and the role models of modernity have become, if not homogeneous, at least more narrowly focused. The citizens of developing countries typically aspire to the living standards of the rich countries and, while they may wish to avoid some of the problems encountered by them along the way, they are often largely uncritical, believing that, in accepting such a life-style, warts and all, they would, in the worst case, not be inheriting any worse a case of warts than they already have. The developing world, in other words, has a fairly clear idea of where it wants to go, and this idea is, if anything, reinforced by the effects of the export of western, especially American, mass culture.

The correlation between our Information Access Index and GNP per capita for the countries included in the list is +0.565 (where 0.0 indicates a purely random relationship and 1.0 a perfect and invariable correlation). Given the number of values in the series, this is a tolerably reliable-looking correlation and one which rather confirms the prejudice that high information states tend to be rich and low information states to be poor. Causation, however, is another matter and, while correlation is necessary for any proof of causation, it is not sufficient evidence in itself. However important the role of communications media may be in political, economic and social development, their scope extends so far into the sphere of entertainment and leisure that a measure of media accessibility must of necessity be no more than a very crude proxy for their application to serious business. One observer, describing the role of the mass media in social change, goes as far as to suggest that the

> ... mass media have proved to be a string of rattling tin cans offering disinformation, educational irrelevance and noisy nothingness. (Fugelsang, quoted in Sussman and Lent, 1991, p. 9)

Whether or not they can fairly be described a 'noisy nothingness', it cannot be denied that much of what is purveyed by the mass media is of the nature of a mass-consumer good, and does little, if anything, to promote productive activity as a quasi-capital good.

The role which the availability of information in general and the operations of the mass media in particular should play in economic development has been the subject of considerable debate, a debate which highlights some of the important issues relating to the unequal distribution of information around the world. The history of systematic development aid began after the Second World War, with the creation of agencies such as the United Nations, International Monetary Fund and World Bank, and most of the body of theory relating to international aid has been formed over the past half century.

Of the work relating to the role of mass communications media in development, perhaps the best-known and most representative study of the 1950s was Daniel Lerner's *The Passing of Traditional Society* which was published in 1958. Lerner's work is frequently cited as epitomizing the strongly prescriptive approach to Third World development which was taken by the US government after the war and seems to have reflected the dominant thinking of the time.

It was generally believed that the communication of information about the thinking, practices and achievements of the developed world to a receptive minority of potential opinion formers in the developing nation, supported by the development of a mass media system to disseminate the ideas of change, would set in train a self-reinforcing cycle of literacy, technical innovation, economic growth, urbanization and industrialization – in other words, of 'modernization'. This view is probably still quite close to the popular perception of the subject in the developed world but it has been widely criticized by specialists in the field for a number of reasons.

Lerner, a professor at MIT, had studied propaganda methods and had carried out a project on audience potential for the *Voice of America*. Establishment figure that he was, and writing, as he did, at the height of the Cold War, he unsurprisingly purveyed something akin to the official line. Whatever the merits of his argument, the reputation of his work suffered as the extent of the covert propaganda operations and general skulduggery which supported the *Pax Americana* became apparent. The backlash which sprang up against the approach which the western establishment took to Third World development in the 1950s and 1960s emerged because this approach increasingly seemed to be founded more on self-interest than on enlightened altruism and because it was becoming increasingly apparent that it was not working.

The UNESCO initiatives in the field of development communications in the early 1960s were also criticized as being out of touch with Third World realities. The Organization recommended that developing countries should seek to achieve certain minima of media availability which would enable the virtuous process of self-enlightenment and self-help to get started. The minimum standards recommended were:

- ten copies of a daily newspaper per 100 persons;
- five radio receivers per 100 persons;
- two cinema seats per 100 persons;
- two television receivers per 100 persons.

The advent of the cheap, battery-powered transistor radio has enabled all but a very few nations to achieve the recommended diffusion of radio receivers, while television has reached two receivers per 100 persons in about 70 per cent of the world. Recent figures suggest, however, that the recommended figures for daily newspaper diffusion are approximately at the median levels actually achieved in recent years, indicating a relative under-performance of the UNESCO standards. Although radio here appears to be a success story, it is believed by some observers that the UNESCO standards for radio were insufficiently ambitious. Radio, they argue, is a highly effective Third World information medium and should be encouraged to fulfil its natural potential. Daily newspapers, on the other hand, are deemed by the critics to be of little relevance to isolated communities, where they are always well out of date by the time they are read and where weeklies and other periodicals are more useful.

But if the western establishment went into its development communications programmes with questionable motives and ill-considered policies regarding the physical media through which the message was to be transmitted, the ineptitude, according to the critics, extended to both the content and targeting of material. Much of what was on offer, even in the more specifically educational and advisory programmes, did not get through to those most in need. The potential opinion-formers on which the 1950s' model depended to spread the word tended to be unrepresentative of the majority of the population being addressed. Those who were most likely to seek out and learn what was on offer were usually literate, relatively well-educated urban residents with little in common with the illiterate, uneducated agriculturists who were the real targets of the message. And the message itself was often couched in terms which were unlikely to be understood. Unfamiliar weights and measures and even calendars, however wide their currency in the developed world, often serve only to confuse those who speak no language but their own and are bound tightly by the constraints of their traditional culture. Little wonder, then, that the one transistor radio in the Third World village, which could act as a conduit for valuable practical advice, has often been permanently tuned to a popular music channel.

The problem, then, was that the messages which were being conveyed from the rich nations to the poor were being transmitted by people who had little or no understanding of the conditions which prevailed in the recipient states, were being delivered in an inappropriate form, were often abused and distorted and sometimes served only to make a bad situation worse. In particular, the dissemination of images of the prosperous west did not immediately give rise to a 'revolution of rising expectations', as Lerner initially suggested, but rather to a revolution of rising frustrations, as it proved impossible to deliver anything like the life-style to which the people were being encouraged to aspire.

Similar, although partially contradictory, claims are sometimes made that western intervention in Third World mass communications, well-intentioned or otherwise, has usually given rise to political problems in the recipient states as it has served to increase the unequal distribution of power and wealth by raising both the aspirations and the productivity of the more privileged information-consuming segments of society and increasing the competitive disadvantage of the have-nots.

The counterblast to the western establishment view which prevailed in the 1960s came in the report of a UNESCO commission in 1980, chaired by Sean MacBride. The MacBride Commission report reflected the pressures of the Non-Aligned Nations Movement (N-ANM) and the frustrations of many development communication theorists and practitioners. The report recognized many of the problems inherent in the approach which UNESCO itself had previously taken and joined the N-ANM in calling for a 'new world information and communication order' which would recognize the particular problems of the Third World, guarantee the rights of its citizens to communicate, and take action to right the acknowledged imbalances in the ways in which international communication was run. Although the views expressed in the report were on the whole quite close to what has become the accepted wisdom among development communications specialists, it met with widespread disapproval at the time, from right-wingers for being too radical and from left-wingers for being not radical enough.

Development communications specialists have subsequently proposed models for the transfer of information and knowledge to the Third World which are rooted in a more realistic assessment of what can be done in the shorter term. In particular, they have sought to overcome what they consider to be fundamental conceptual flaws, such as what they refer to as the 'pro-literacy bias', which can be detected in the world view of most people in the developed world, who are accustomed to the ideas of near-universal literacy and compulsory primary and secondary education.

However, although the raising of literacy rates may now not be the first priority in enhancing communication in the most underdeveloped infostructures, there can be little doubt that illiteracy, and the lack of educational infrastructure which allows it to persist, are the most common impediments to a broader access to information on a global scale. Fully one-third of the adult population of the world is functionally illiterate and, in some countries, illiteracy rates are over 85 per cent. The north–south divide in access to information is nowhere more evident. Western Europe overall boasts a literacy rate of 97 per cent, an average brought down by Portugal's 79 per cent figure, while Africa as a whole does no better than 47 per cent, the Middle East 55 per cent and Asia 59 per cent. It is worth noting, in this context, that the UNESCO literacy figures quoted above are not based on any single objective standard of literacy. Such is the difficulty of measuring literacy on an objective and truly internationally comparable basis that UNESCO defines a functionally literate person as one who

> . . . has acquired the knowledge and skills in reading and writing which enable him to engage effectively in all those activities in which literacy is normally assumed in his culture or group. (Wagner, 1987, p. 5)

Differences in the total 'stocks' of literacy between countries are therefore probably understated, as the literacy standards demanded in the developed world, where the diffusion of literacy is high, are higher than those used to define functional literacy in countries where it is relatively low.

The crude statistics included in the Index attest to the differences between the information-rich states and the information-deprived states of the world in general terms but, in every case, they mask the complex of circumstances which surrounds and defines any information environment. Identical daily newspaper readership figures for two countries may, for example, be the products of wholly different combinations of factors. Local custom and practice can vary to such an extent that high or low numbers can lack much sociometric significance – low newspaper readership in Spain, for example, reflects historical political factors as much as anything else. Hence, figures which ostensibly reflect wealth or deprivation may not in reality do so.

The data and analysis provided by UNESCO and the development communications specialists nonetheless serve to illustrate not only the extremely uneven distribution of information and the means of its transmission and processing but also the likely persistence of the unevenness. The potential role of information transfer in development aid and the mechanisms by which it can be efficiently applied are becoming better understood but, as the picture becomes clearer, the magnitude of the task also becomes evident. Whatever may have been the motives of the development communications theorists of the 1950s and 1960s, it is clear that they greatly underestimated the scale of the problem and overestimated the pace of change in the distribution of information in the world's most information-poor areas.

The problem for the countries at the very bottom of the league table is believed by many to be greater now than it was. The putative information revolution which has taken place in the developed world over the last 30 years has widened the gap. The encroachments of the western media may have served to instil in the citizens of poor primary producer nations a desire to travel the western route to the high abstraction society and the wealth which it seems to offer but the pre-conditions which must be met before the journey can commence have in some ways become more rigorous. It was possible in the 1950s and 1960s to envisage a convergence of living styles and standards resulting from a transfer of what passed for information technology at the time. Today, when even the developed nations are struggling with the implications of the forces which have been unleashed by the explosion of the information business, many worry that some of the existing members of the rich countries' club will be unable to avoid relegation from the first economic and political league.

From the standpoint of a country in which adult illiteracy is in excess of three-quarters of the population, access to even basic information is denied to the mass of the population and the average income is little more than the cost of a box of floppy disks, the notion of entry into the modern information society looks not only daunting but also largely irrelevant. The journey from Burkina Faso to Bermuda cannot be made in a single leap.

2

BUILDING AN 'INFOSTRUCTURE'

If the global information environment is to some degree a product of parallel evolutionary processes in society and technology, it is also a product of some more revolutionary developments in technology and major social upheavals. Major inventions and the mass migration of peoples and ideas have been as important in this particular history as the steady progress of learning and technology *in situ* but, from the standpoint of the developed nations (in most of which the story has unfolded over an extended period of about 2,000 years), the process gives the illusion of having been one of relatively steady accretion.

It certainly does not seem such a gradual process in those countries which have been excluded from the techno-economic mainstream for much of the period since the beginning of the Industrial Revolution in Europe and now find themselves significantly disadvantaged in relation to the developed world. The political and business leaders of these nations are often faced with the necessity of creating an information infrastructure ('infostructure') virtually from scratch, as they can no longer survive without communicating and competing with the outside world, which constantly intrudes and projects its values and life-styles. These nations are the latest to be affected by the kinds of disruptive forces which have, in fact, been the norm throughout history and it is they who now feel obliged to respond to socio-economic systems which have established considerable momentum elsewhere and cannot be ignored.

Few things, however, wreak more havoc with existing social and political arrangements or have a more profound impact on the nature of political and economic control than an upheaval in the information environment and the comprehensive upgrading of an underdeveloped infostructure is always extremely expensive. The accelerated development of a modern infostructure is a multi-faceted and daunting process and is seldom seen as a monolithic objective. Rather, the inadequacies of existing arrangements in education, the mass media, telecommunications and data processing are often tackled in piecemeal ways which reflect the problems and priorities of those who are empowered to manage such things.

The two short case studies which follow are intended to illustrate how two developing countries have progressed with the building of their infostructures in the face of very different internal and external pressures.

Development and Communication in India

The history of the Republic of India as an independent state coincides quite closely with the post-war era of systematic economic and technical aid to the Third World and the development of the country's communications infrastructure has been influenced accordingly. The pattern of development has also been a product of India's geography and its ethnic and political make-up.

The Indian Constitution came into effect in January 1950 and the newly independent nation chose to take a non-aligned path, with a brand of democratic socialism, a mixed economy and a substantial degree of state planning and control in areas deemed to be of strategic significance. The Planning Commission was established in 1950 to oversee the strategic planning process and the first of the Soviet-style Five-Year Plans was launched in the following year. It was evident to the government of the time that, if the dirigiste approach implicit in this and subsequent plans was to succeed, it would be necessary to mobilize and augment the existing media of communication in order that the plans might be widely understood and acted upon. The main thrust of the government's policy with regard to communications in the early years after independence was therefore necessarily concerned with the fostering of a system of mass communication for development purposes.

India is one of the largest countries in the world and is predominantly rural, with three-quarters of its more than 800 million people living in the estimated 550,000 villages and fully two-thirds dependent upon agriculture for their livelihoods. Life-styles differ widely, between the modern urban populations of the large cities, the more or less traditional communities of the small towns and villages and the ancient hill tribes of the central and north-eastern parts of the country. There are 15 basic language groupings, with 1,600 or more distinct dialects. Hindi is the official language of the state but it is the native language of the majority in only six of the 22 states. English, the 'associate' official language of state, although spoken only by a well-educated minority of the literate 40 per cent the population, is fairly evenly distributed nationally and functions as a 'link' language in that stratum of society.

Early development activities associated with the Five-Year Plans depended heavily on verbal, face-to-face contact between the local clients, specialist extension workers who served blocks of 100 or so villages and generalist village representatives called *gam sevak* or 'village servants'. The first plan recognized the importance of reaching the mass of the people in ways which would be comprehensible to them and which would provide central and state government with a feedback mechanism which would facilitate the planning process. The second plan placed more formal emphasis on the utilization of the mass media, most particularly the press, for the purpose. Subsequent plans involved broadcasting and, finally, an integrated multiple-media approach to the problem. But if, in the early years, the government was concerned to use the existing media infrastructure to encourage development, this is not to say that it was well-suited to the purpose. Nor, indeed, was the purity of the government's pro-development stance on the media maintained, as social, commercial and political pressures combined to compromise it in later years. The story of communications media in independent India has been one of idealism, dissent and compromise, with the strands of planned development, profit-oriented capitalism and power politics interwoven to create dynamics which are particular to India, however representative India may be of Third World information-poor environments in general.

The Press – A Traditional Watchdog

The first newspaper in India, the weekly *Bengal Gazette*, started publication on 29 January 1780. The proprietor, one James Augustus Hickey, while claiming a lofty impartiality for the paper, in fact used it as a vehicle for personal criticism of the East India Company and the Governor-General. Several of the early newspapers, published in English and of interest to the British community alone, were set up by former employees of the Company who, like Hickey, delighted in critical and often irreverent treatment of it. These and the other newspapers of the late eighteenth century were parochial and often scurrilous but they established a kind of press freedom, and an adversarial style which set the style for the English language and vernacular press in the nineteenth century and beyond.

The press in India, as in most countries of the developing world, carries with it much of the intellectual baggage of the colonial era, an era which spanned the first 167 years of its history. By the time independence was achieved and the nation had moved into the post-war development phase, the editorial identity of the Indian press had long been established. It was urban, elitist and political in its focus and, particularly in Calcutta, adversarial in style. Mahatma Gandhi made very effective use of the press in support of the independence movement, continuing the adversarial tradition. This tradition again proved its worth during the state of emergency imposed by Mrs Gandhi's government in 1975–7, as many newspapers, notably the *Indian Express*, fought with some success the censorship which was imposed on them and emerged more determined than ever to take an investigative and, if necessary, confrontational line. It was the *Indian Express* which subsequently exposed the Bofors scandal during Rajiv Gandhi's premiership.

Whereas the broadcast media in India have always been government owned and controlled, the press has remained in private hands and there has been a marked divergence in approach between the print and broadcast media. The broadcast media have been more pro-government and have played a more important role in the development aspects of journalism, while the press has, by and large, restricted itself to a political watchdog role. The divergence reflects differing proprietorial interests and, as far as the press is concerned, an established journalistic tradition similar to that which now prevails throughout most of the developed world. Few editors of western newspapers would pass up a scurrilous titbit concerning the activities of a famous politician or film star in favour of a more worthy piece concerning irrigation or contraception, and Indian editors are of the same mould. The experience of the 1975–7 emergency heightened the political vigilance of editors and made them less receptive to the government's entreaties that, in the interests of the nation, they should devote more space to reporting on development activities, but there is clearly ambivalence in the press community with regard to the issue.

Some influential members of the journalistic community have criticized the press at large for its overwhelmingly urban orientation and accuse it of being out of touch with the majority of the population for this reason. As more than 90 per cent of the circulation of the dailies, at least, is in urban centres with populations larger than 100,000, it is clear that they reach fewer than 10 per cent of the population. Nor does this low figure merely reflect a preference for weeklies, although it is recognized that daily newspapers are often not the most appropriate printed information medium for isolated communities and that weeklies are more effective. It is estimated that as many as 75 per cent of villages do not see newspapers or magazines of any kind. The accusations of pro-urban bias strike home but the problem is self-perpetuating, as the large-circulation dailies, catering to an urban readership, lack editorial staff who are knowledgeable in rural affairs. Editorial policy could be changed but the problems faced by the press in any attempt to redress the balance of its impact and to increase its relevance to the population at large are formidable.

A rural reading habit simply does not exist. Widespread illiteracy, low incomes, transport difficulties, shortages of equipment and trained manpower and a lack of market feedback combine to make the expansion of newspaper distribution in villages very difficult. Despite these problems, a rural press does exist, although the small independent rural newspapers lead a hand-to-mouth existence. Advertising revenue for a small-circulation newspaper serving a poor rural area is, understandably, hard to come by and many survive – although they are not, in any purely economic sense, viable – either because their proprietors are committed to serving their communities or because the Ministry of Information and Broadcasting, when selecting newspapers to receive government advertising, gives preference to small rural outfits with a suitably developmental editorial bias.

Local newspapers with circulations of fewer than 15,000 copies, account for three-quarters of the titles in India but for less than one-quarter of the total circulation. They have no access to news agencies and tend to act as local discussion forums. Reporting as they do local concerns, problems and successes, they provide a valuable source of local feedback for the central planners. They do not, however, reach the important stratum of urban opinion-formers, a readership which remains the preserve of the large-circulation dailies. In general terms, the large-circulation press emphasizes political issues while the local newspapers play an important role in rural development, with neither type having easy access to the information sources or readership of the other. There have, however, been cases in which large-circulation newspapers have dealt with rural and agricultural issues effectively and to considerable public acclaim. The most celebrated example of this was the series 'Our Village Chhatera' which was for many years run by the *Hindustan Times* (New Delhi; circulation 286,000) and which was credited with having raised significantly the consciousness of the paper's urban readership of rural issues.

The limited success of efforts to involve the press in development journalism and to extend its rural reach reflects some fundamental problems inherent in the physical and intellectual infrastructure which remain, for the time being at least, largely insuperable. The problems associated with the regular distribution of large amounts of paper on the back of a rickety physical transport infrastructure to the scattered villages of a huge and ethnically diverse country, beset with high levels of illiteracy, give rise to the thought that there must be some easier way. And it has become clear over recent years that broadcasting offers that easier way. Whatever pressures the print media in the developed world may be experiencing as a result of the rise of broadcasting, those operating on the Indian press are of a different order of magnitude. The natural advantages of broadcasting technology as a means of reaching the rural masses look likely to restrict the role of the press in India to that which it has performed so well in the past. The newspapers have been valuable guardians of democracy and brokers of informed opinion in the cities where political power is wielded. It seems unlikely that this will change at any time soon.

Reaching the Villages

It is not unusual to find armed tribesmen in the remote north-eastern parts of India, tending their sheep and listening to transistor radios hung around their necks. The ubiquitous, cheap, battery-powered transistor radio has brought an efficient form of mass communication to this remote part of the world but, in doing so, it has created a broadcasting battlefield. The Indian government, conscious that some of its citizens are geographically and ethnically closer to Tibet than to Delhi, has installed high power transmitters in border regions to combat interference and propaganda from Tibet and China. Radio can encourage national unity but it can also be used to undermine it. The medium has always been subject to state supervision and control and, sometimes, to use by other states as a vehicle for propaganda and political destabilization. All India Radio (AIR), established in 1927, was controlled by the British prior to independence and has been used quite consistently as an instrument of the state since. As the government, in the early years after independence, was inevitably preoccupied with the idea of statehood, it used the radio as a means of encouraging a national identity and, as so often happens, rather overdid it. For example, in striving for a pure cultural identity, AIR in the early 1950s emphasized broadcasts of Indian classical music to an audience which preferred film music. This popular film music, although usually Indian in origin, was usually played on western instruments which were not on AIR's culturally pure approved list and the state broadcaster declined to give it air time. Radio Ceylon took advantage of this situation – rather as Radio Luxembourg profited from the overly serious attitude taken by the broadcasters in the UK in the 1950s and 1960s – and earned good revenues from commercial sponsors by transmitting film music and other popular fare across the border. AIR was eventually forced to take a more pragmatic attitude and, in 1957, set up a separate light entertainment network which proved to be very successful.

The pro-development bias of the government's mass communications policy in the early years after independence was reflected in the programme content of AIR. Community listening was the rule in the 1950s and early 1960s, before the spread of the transistor radio, and early experiments in development-oriented programming centred on the 'Radio Rural Forums' which were established in more than 20,000 villages across the country. As private radio ownership increased among the more affluent segments of society and the commercial implications of radio as an advertising medium became evident, the relative importance of the development message in radio declined sharply.

Radio is the developing world mass communications medium *par excellence*. It offers considerable geographical reach for what is, in reality, a modest capital outlay. Receivers are now cheap and efficient and do not depend on mains electricity, which is still not available in many parts of developing countries such as India. Many proponents of radio in India maintain that it is the most cost-effective medium for the transmission of political, developmental and commercial messages. The audience is large and the cost of reaching it, in terms of rupees per listener, is extremely low. None of this can, to the same extent, be said of television and yet it was television which became the growth medium of the 1970s and 1980s.

Doordarshan – A Power in the Land

The first television broadcasts in India took place in Delhi in 1959 under a UNESCO-funded educational experiment and a limited regular service, broadcasting for 21 hours a week and serving schools and urban teleclubs, was established in Delhi in 1965. In 1967, an agricultural teleclub called *Krishi Darshan* (Agricultural View), which broadcast programmes on agricultural innovation for one or two hours nightly to 79 villages near Delhi, was established by a number of government agencies, including the Department of Atomic Energy. The DAE, which incorporated the Space Research Organization, was to become a very influential player in the broadcasting field. Although there was a steady expansion of conventional broadcasting capacity in the first half of the 1970s, with the building of terrestrial broadcasting stations in Amritsar, Bombay, Calcutta, Lucknow, Madras, Pune and Srinagar, a technical co-operation agreement struck between the government and NASA in 1969 was to give rise to an experiment which would set the technical pattern for television broadcasting in India.

The Indian government had become keenly interested in television as a mass medium from around 1965, when Indira Gandhi became Minister for Information and Broadcasting, and there was a strong desire to expand television viewership nation-wide and to use the medium to enhance the sense of national unity and the authority of the government in general, and, some say, the Nehru family in particular. Vikram Sarabhai, who headed the DAE and the Space Research Organization, was a close political ally of the Nehru family and its second Prime Minister, Indira Gandhi. While AIR proposed a long-term development of broadcasting capacity, spreading over 20 years and utilizing a microwave and coaxial cable network to be provided and maintained by the Posts and Telegraphs Department, Sarabhai was a keen advocate of the use of satellite television to provide educational programming to India's villages. A study jointly conducted by Sarabhai's department and NASA in 1967 suggested that a hybrid system, using direct satellite broadcasts to community antennae in rural areas and to five terrestrial re-broadcast stations in the urban centres, was most suitable for India's needs and that the costs involved would be about one-third of those for a purely terrestrial system. Gandhi did not need to be persuaded of the virtues of nation-wide television, although her motives were almost certainly more political than educational, and, as Sarabhai's satellite scheme seemed to offer a cheap short-cut to achieving this, satellite thinking dominated India's broadcasting technology from the signing of the NASA deal onwards.

Under the terms of the agreement, NASA loaned its Application Technology Satellite 6 (ATS-6) satellite for 12 months, from August 1975 to July 1976, for a project known as the Satellite Instructional Television Experiment. SITE was the most ambitious such project of its time. Antenna dishes and receivers were provided to 2,400 villages in six of the country's poorest states. The satellite was used, as was envisaged by the architects of the project, for educational purposes. For four hours a day, the viewers were sent programmes concerned with public health, birth control, agricultural techniques and general educational material produced by *Doordarshan* (literally 'distant vision' – television), the television agency of AIR, in three centres established for the purpose.

SITE was but one of a number of satellite projects in which India was involved during the late 1970s and early 1980s. All of these projects drew on widespread international co-operation: the Satellite Telecommunications Experiment Project (STEP) was conducted between 1977 and 1979 using the Franco-German Symphonie satellite; Bhaskara 1 & 2, the country's first remote sensing satellites were launched by Soviet vehicles in 1979 and 1981; and Apple, an Indian-built satellite, was put into geostationary orbit by an Ariane rocket in 1981 and served a small disaster warning network for its scheduled 30-month life. The experience gained was used in preparation for the launch in 1982 of India's first multi-purpose satellite, Insat 1A, which was de-activated due to technical problems after only five months, during which time it broadcast radio and television programmes. It was succeeded in 1983 by the similarly configured Insat 1B, which functioned satisfactorily.

Things were proceeding reasonably smoothly in space but the headlong rush into national broadcasting was causing difficulties back on earth. Technical problems were experienced with telecommunications and meteorological functions of the satellite because of a lack of infrastructure and the television broadcasters faced similar problems, in the form of a lack of programme production facilities. The country's chronic lack of foreign exchange, exacerbated by the activities of OPEC, placed constraints on this kind of infrastructure development but television had by now acquired a life of its own. By the end of 1985, 173 of the nation's 179 television stations and 93 AIR stations were in the Insat network and 1,500 direct reception sets had been installed in remote areas. In 1979 there had only been 19 television stations in operation, with signals reaching 150 millions of the population; by the end of 1985 signals from the 179 transmitters were reaching nearly 400 millions. That is to say that 400 million people were within the range of a television transmitter. The actual audience was constrained by the high cost of receivers, which were far beyond the reach of most Indians, but an installed base of 6.8 million sets was estimated to have been viewed by around 60 million people by the end of 1985.

It has often been said that the hybrid satellite/terrestrial television broadcast system which India adopted was the only viable option, although it proved to be more expensive and less effective than its advocates claimed and it was certainly opposed vigorously enough by Doordarshan and the Posts and Telegraphs Department at the outset. There has also been continued criticism, frequently levelled at Rajiv Gandhi during his premiership, of what some have regarded as the use of high technology for its own sake. But any wrangling over the nature of the broadcast technology to be used has been muted by comparison with the debates on more fundamental issues. The questions asked were broadly those raised with regard to television in many developing countries: Is television the most suitable mass communications medium for India today? Can the country afford colour television? Should television be commercial? Who should control it? For whom should television work?

The proposal to introduce colour television prior to the Asian Games, which took place in Delhi in 1982, resurrected questions about the purpose and the control of television and could be regarded as a milestone in government policy on broadcasting. Although it would be inaccurate to describe the advent of colour television as marking the end of the development television era, as programming continued to include the kind of development material which it had done in the 1960s and 1970s, it perhaps marked the beginning of a period in which the television agenda was to have a sufficient number of items added to it that government policy was bound to undergo an irreversible change. The proponents of colour pointed out that other developing countries had made the transition to colour and that monochrome TV was now obsolete. They suggested that educational and development-oriented programmes would have more impact in colour and pointed out that colour transmission equipment would have to be installed in order to broadcast the Games to other Asian countries in any event.

If these arguments sounded thin to those who still regarded the broadcast media as primarily instruments of national development, the notion of national prestige, and the role which television could play in enhancing it, was now on the agenda. New television systems have often been introduced on the occasion of events associated with national pride, such as the Olympics or the Asian Games and, in this, India was merely following a path well-worn by other countries. In fact, two international events which were hosted by India were televised in the first 12 months of colour transmissions: the Asian Games and the Seventh Conference of the Non-Aligned Nations Movement. The first colour broadcast, however, was purely a domestic affair. On 15 August 1982, Indira Gandhi's address to the nation during the Independence Day celebrations in Delhi was televised in colour, giving the Prime Minister the opportunity simultaneously to address the entire nation and to wring the maximum political prestige from association with the new medium, although the majority watched the broadcast on black-and-white sets.

The developmentalists looked askance at the policy on colour television but the government took steps to increase its availability. It cut the prohibitive import duties which had been intended to foster the development of indigenous technology and encouraged foreign manufacturers to import into their Indian joint ventures on a screwdriver or complete knockdown basis. This seems to have been simple pragmatism, as the sourcing of electronic components by that time was becoming ever more centralized in Japan and the USA, the technical and capital requirements of the industry were growing exponentially, and the unit costs of colour sets were falling sharply.

Television diffusion rates have proved to be too fast-moving a target for the statisticians and estimates have varied widely. Official estimates throughout the period of rapid growth in television diffusion seem to have lagged behind the reality which subsequently published figures indicated, and some of the more aggressive unofficial estimates have recently suggested that the number of households owning a television set is approaching 30 million. If this is the case, given the continuing habit of inviting friends and neighbours in to watch television, it may be that viewership is now approaching one-quarter of the population.

The existence of the broadcasting infrastructure and an increased availability and affordability of television receivers alone are not, however, sufficient conditions to create a large viewing public. If television were to achieve a level of popularity similar to that seen in the developed world, it was clearly necessary to leaven the loaf of worthy educational and developmental programmes with some light entertainment content. *Krishi Darshan*, for example, was still being broadcast five times a week in 1982 but its viewership had fallen to less than 4 per cent. The initial response to this problem was for Doordarshan, which had previously produced all its programmes internally, to look outside, principally to the Bombay film industry, for expertise. The result was the highly popular *Hum Log* (We People) soap opera which first appeared in 1984. Modelled on the experience of pro-development soap operas in Mexico, *Hum Log* sought to inform and to influence opinion on matters such as family size and women's rights as it entertained. The series commanded huge audiences in the Hindi-speaking north of the country and was reasonably successful in the south, where Hindi material was generally rejected by most viewers. *Hum Log* was followed in 1986–7 by *Buniyaad* (Foundation), a soap based on the period surrounding independence and the partitioning of Pakistan from India, and *Ramayana*, a Hindu religious epic. At the peak of their popularity, the viewer loyalty which these programmes commanded was phenomenal. Buses stopped, funerals and weddings were curtailed and the country generally ground to a halt when they were broadcast.

Doordarshan had first invited commercial advertising and programme sponsorship in 1976 but the arrival of *Hum Log* and its successors shifted commercial exploitation of television onto a higher plane. The celebrated case of Maggi 2-minute noodles, a Nestlé product with minimal penetration in India, whose sales trebled in three years as a result of the company's sponsorship of *Hum Log*, illustrated that television was reaching a comparatively affluent consuming public and that advertising could turn Doordarshan from a cost centre into a profit generator. The growth in Doordarshan's advertising revenues, which had expanded from $640,000 in 1976 to $16.5 million in 1983, turned sharply upward with the arrival of the soaps and by 1988 had reached $107 million.

The debates surrounding television in India continue but the trends are clear. The move from the command economy of the 1950s, and the rebound from the anti-western policies which coincided with Indira Gandhi's period in the political wilderness after 1978, have been accompanied by a steady liberalization of the government's approach to television as a commercial medium and a dilution of the development message. The influence of multinational corporations in television-related activities and advertising has also increased. Survey data suggest that the majority of television viewers are, as *a priori* logic would suggest, relatively affluent, Hindi-speaking, Hindu urban dwellers. The government, through television, seeks to maintain the support of this elite group, while advertisers naturally gravitate to an audience which has spending power. Whatever vestiges of the development and national unity messages remain, it seems that many Indians outside of the elite group do not feel that television talks for them or to them.

Wiring the Nation

The broadcast mass communications media in India, encouraged by the developmentalists and supported by an imaginative use of satellite technology, have managed partially to escape from the strictures imposed by the rural dispersion of the population and the inadequacy of the physical transport and educational infrastructure. This is in marked contrast with the print media, for which the problems of illiteracy and an underdeveloped infrastructure represent formidable barriers. The persistence of linguistic, cultural, educational and economic barriers to their diffusion into rural areas has, however, meant that even radio and television are predominantly urban phenomena. The shift from the command economy to the market economy which was seen under the Singh and Rao administrations, and the resulting dilution of the developmental element in communications policy, accentuated the urban, consumerist focus.

In telecommunications, efforts to develop rural services have been hampered by a lack of resources and the proponents of ruralization are often daunted by the sheer scale of the physical network required. India has one of the lowest rates of telephone diffusion in the world, having fewer than six telephone lines for every thousand of its citizens, and the pattern of urban concentration which we have seen in the print and broadcast media is even more marked in the telecommunications field. Telephone diffusion is on average 50 times higher in urban areas than in the countryside and, to cite an extreme example, the number of persons per installed telephone line in urban areas of the state of Uttar Pradesh is 90: in rural areas the figure is over 11,000. The scale of the infrastructural problem is breathtaking. The population of India at the time of independence was estimated at 350 million, a figure which has grown at a compound rate of around 2 per cent every year since 1947 to reach 844 million in 1991. The operators of a system with around five million telephone lines are thus being asked to cope with nearly 17 million new potential subscribers every year. Small wonder that waiting lists for installations sometimes stretch out beyond 15 years and many potential subscribers have abandoned hope of ever being connected. Some 90 per cent of the nation's villages have no telephones at all. Even for the privileged urban areas which are connected, the service provided is limited and unstable. In New Delhi, the nation's capital, system failures resulting in incomplete calls are common and the average telephone breaks down altogether three times a year. Such qualitative problems are so endemic in the system that telex has become an increasingly important commercial and administrative tool. The stability of transmissions over Indian telephone lines is notoriously poor and, where telephone calls often fail, telex transmissions almost always get through. As a result, the number of telex subscribers doubled in the three years to 1990.

Attempts to deal with problems of such magnitude can be simultaneously very impressive and wholly inadequate. The Telecom Commission's Five-Year Plan for 1990–5 projected a compound annual increase of 15 per cent in telephone connections over the period of the plan, which, if achieved, would more than double capacity by 1995. Other planned upgrades include the automation of all manual exchanges and the digitization of all crossbar trunk exchanges. The policy is to discriminate positively in favour of rural development insofar as half of the projected expenditure is for rural projects. Given the huge urban/rural imbalance in the system and the considerable emphasis which has been given to the metropolitan areas, this might seem inadequate but, in view of the extreme commercial pressures to improve the urban systems further, it represents quite a bold commitment to redressing the balance. But, even if the planned 15 per cent rate of increase in installations is sustained until the end of the century, the diffusion rate of telephones across the country as a whole will still barely exceed 2 per cent, as compared with current developed world levels of 50 per cent or more.

India's telecommunications network, like those of most countries, is technologically hybrid. The transmission network, as at March 1990, consisted of some 23,000 km of coaxial cable, 30,000 km of analogue microwave, 1,800 km of digital microwave, 4,000 km of optical fibre, and 67 fixed and 17 mobile satellite earth stations. The emphasis in the planned expansion of the network is naturally on digital media and on technologies which facilitate the installation of large chunks of capacity on trunk lines and in centres of very high demand and some skeletal capacity across long distances and in large areas which are currently not served at all. The current Five-Year Plan projects a trebling of digital microwave capacity and a sixfold increase in the optical fibre laid. The number of satellite earth stations is to be doubled.

The use of satellites for telecommunications in India closely parallels their application to radio and television broadcasting. The original ill-fated Insat 1A, for example, carried 1,800 two-way voice channels in addition to its television transponders and telemetry equipment. Three similar multi-purpose satellites have been launched since. The telecommunications counterpart of the community antenna in the SITE programme is the very small aperture terminal (VSAT) used in the Department of Telecommunications' Remote Area Business Network, which uses Insat 1C to provide telex and data links to business users in remote areas. The VSAT is simply a small, low-cost transceiver dish suitable for remote installations where large-scale earth stations and the infrastructure to support them would be uneconomical. VSAT is regarded as a strategic technology for such purposes and it is thought that the network will eventually extend to 10,000 or more such terminals nation-wide.

The extension of the telephone network to India's villages is mainly, however, based on terrestrial technology. Under a long-term project led by the ebullient Mr Satyen ('Sam') Pitroda, who established the government's Centre for Development of Telematics (C-DOT), domestically developed digital switching equipment is being used to connect the villages to a minimalist voice network. The concept is simple. As Mr Pitroda says:

> We are emphasizing accessibility, more so than telephone density. You can say that India has only four telephones per 1,000 people, but that is a western parameter. The question is, how easy is it to have access to a telephone? Is there one telephone in the village that works? (quoted in *Telecommunications*, 26, 3, March 1992)

The Department of Telecommunications (DOT) is accordingly emphasizing the installation of village payphones, with a view to increasing the number of private lines in rural areas later.

Mr Pitroda has for many years been an outspoken advocate of the indigenous development and production of telecommunications equipment in India and his view has held sway at least in the digital switching sector of the market, from which foreign companies have been largely excluded. The Pitroda approach has a persuasive logic. India has suffered from chronic shortages of foreign currency reserves, a problem which reached crisis point in the late summer of 1991, and cannot afford to import even a fraction of the equipment needed. Indigenous development has until recently been hampered by the fact that development and production was conducted in government establishments and consequently suffered at the hands of India's infamous bureaucracy. The recent huge inflow of foreign currency from the non-resident Indian community which has resulted from the amnesties and liberalization announced in Finance Minister Manmohan Singh's 1992 budget could provide the capital base for new telecommunications businesses operating in an environment much more conducive to private and public enterprise. The prognosis for India's telecommunications system, and for its embryonic telecommunications equipment industry, is probably better now than it has ever been. The accumulated experience in the application of technologies suitable to India's situation might, in a suitable commercial environment, be put to use in exporting to markets where similar problems exist, particularly in those non-aligned and former socialist states with which India retains strong links.

The Technopolis Tendency

The concentration of educated people and information infrastructure among the affluent urban population in India is increasingly creating two nations and official policy is showing signs of bowing to the inevitable. Non-resident and resident entrepreneurs have understood the power and commercial potential of information businesses in India and substantial fortunes have already been made in these areas. In the form of the Bombay film industry, India already has its Hollywood (Bombay is sometimes referred to as 'Bollywood') and the sheer size and appetite of the Hindi-speaking audience has made it one of the largest film industries in the world (although, with only eight cinema seats per thousand people, India still falls far short of the two per hundred UNESCO prescribed minimum). It has also spawned related industries, in the form of a buoyant trade in pre-recorded video tapes (one reason for the languishing movie theatre business) and satellite antenna-based cable television networks. Many businesses in both the video tape and cable areas started out as pirate operations and it is only recently that some of the entrepreneurs of the pirate video business have become sufficiently wealthy to have elected to legitimize their operations. The cable businesses feed off overseas satellite broadcasts, some of which thoughtfully provide Hindi material allegedly pirated from the Bombay film makers who, unsurprisingly, have sought government action to protect their interests.

The domestic television set manufacturers saw sales falling sharply, after a surge in the late 1980s, as sales taxes put their products out of the reach of many and forced what the manufacturers consider to be a premature saturation of the market. So, while the masses in the villages are still largely excluded from the media revolution, the affluent urban dwellers enjoy it in a range of new ways, giving rise to new technology-based information businesses.

The focus of India's rapidly growing information technology businesses, the country's answer to Silicon valley, is to be found in Bangalore, the capital of the south-western state of Karnataka, where a large number of both domestic and foreign technology companies have congregated. The reasons cited for this concentration are the agreeable environment, the progressive attitudes of the local population and the availability of appropriate skilled manpower. Of these factors, the last is undoubtedly the most important and, as so often happens when a place becomes 'the place to be' in technology and attracts like-minded people, it seems to have established a momentum of its own. Foreign and non-resident Indian capital has been put into Bangalore in small amounts but the emphasis has been more on software than on fabrication and the capital requirements of such businesses are relatively modest. Texas Instruments, for example, has used its Bangalore facility for the design of application-specific semiconductor memory and other design-intensive products. This strategy brings together Indian talent in such a way that it can interact with the outside world and has helped small venture businesses to establish momentum quickly, a feature reminiscent of Silicon Valley in the early days. Two such ventures, Sonata, a specialist in Indian language desk-top publishing, grew from a standing start in 1986 to a respectable $2.5 million turnover in 1991–2, while Software Mart India Limited (SMILE), a software subsidiary of Zenith Computers reached a similar size in its first full year of operation. Tata Consultancy Services (TCS), which exported $47 million worth of software and technology consulting services in 1991–2, heads a group of five large enterprises (TCS, Tata Unisys, Digital Equipment, Siemens and Citicorp Overseas Software) which represent the heavyweight end of

India's software business. Each of them exported more than $5 million worth of software products in 1991–2.

The country's software industry, whose sales grew from $30 million in 1985–6 to $257 million in 1991–2, with nearly 60 per cent of the latter figure accounted for by exports, could prove to be highly competitive internationally, against the background of a world-wide shortage of software talent. The sheer size of India means that, in spite of the generally low educational levels, the country still has more university graduates than developed countries the size of the UK. The availability of such people for comparatively very low wages, combined with the increasing involvement of highly entrepreneurial non-resident Indians (a group of which Mr Pitroda is a conspicuous former member) could also prove to be a crucial competitive advantage in telecommunications, an industry in which software capability is becoming an ever more crucial element.

The information industry scene in India undoubtedly has its bright spots but formidable problems remain. India's industry and commerce will continue to suffer a significant competitive handicap as long as the nation's communications network remains well below the standards of the developed world. As the DOT and the other purveyors of communications products and services struggle to keep pace with India's growing population, the developed world, with its largely stable population and its obsession with technology could compound its competitive advantage.

It seems likely that the past pattern of uneven development between the urban and rural areas in India will persist and that, ironically, such a concentration of developmental firepower in urban centres will probably be necessary if the nation is to become competitive in a whole range of modern industries. Bangalore and, to a lesser extent, Pune seem likely to emerge as significant 'technopolis' areas, feeding the broader infostructure and generating useful export earnings. However, in a country where the basic telephone system falls well short of required standards, integrated services digital networks (ISDN), electronic data interchange (EDI), point of sales (POS) systems and the other electronic paraphernalia deemed to be so crucial to commercial competitiveness in the modern world must seem to most people like distant dreams. And the rest of the world will not stand still.

Thailand – A Kingdom in Transition

Some 1,700 miles due east of Bangalore, the metropolis of Bangkok is at the centre of Thailand's industrial and information revolutions. The Kingdom of Thailand is similar in geographical area to France and, with 57.8 million people in 1992, has a population of a similar size. Sited on the delta of the Chao Phraya river system, Bangkok has an official population of 5.9 millions but the city has sprawled out into the neighbouring provinces and a more realistic estimate of the size of the conurbation is generally accepted to be in excess of eight millions. Being at the head of the fertile alluvial delta, the capital is also at the centre of the most densely populated rural area of the country. As the rest of Thailand is predominantly rural, Bangkok dominates the urban scene, being about 50 times as large as any of the provincial capitals, such as Chiangmai and Songkhla. Outside Bangkok and its immediate hinterland the population is quite evenly distributed.

As in India, there is a divergence between the fortunes and life-styles of the rural majority and the large metropolitan minority but the gulf is not as wide and, although some outlying areas are notably backward, there is much greater cultural and social homogeneity throughout Thailand than there is in India. Thailand is in fact very ethnically homogeneous by the standards of the region, with 95 per cent of the population being Thai-speaking and Buddhist. The large ethnic Chinese minority which came into Thailand during the years of European colonial influence have been well assimilated and the only persistent source of separatist conflict is with the million or so Moslem ethnic Malays in the south of the country. Some 70 per cent of this population, which is concentrated in the four provinces bordering Malaysia, are Moslems and many older people in these areas speak little Thai.

Primary education in the Kingdom is universal in principle and near-universal in practice. The average number of years of school attendance increased from 4.1 years in 1980 to 5.3 years in 1990 and, although only 40 per cent or so of children were enrolled in secondary education in 1990, it is the aim of the Seventh Five-Year National Economic and Social Development Plan to increase participation in education to nine years for 98 per cent of the population by 1996. It is not, however, considered practical to make secondary education compulsory at that stage and the problem of high secondary school drop-out rates may persist.

Basic literacy is claimed for 93.6 per cent of the population, a figure which has improved from 85.1 per cent in 1985. Illiteracy is more common in rural than in urban areas but 89 per cent of rural dwellers are considered literate and sources in the newspaper industry suggest that Thailand's definition of literacy equates quite closely with the ability to read the mass circulation daily *Thai Rath*. It is the government's intention to eradicate illiteracy in the 14–50 age group by 1996 and, although Thai Five-Year Plans frequently fail to achieve their targets fully, the raising of basic educational standards is an explicit national objective and the ministries charged with achieving these ambitious educational targets have on this occasion been given what they consider to be adequate funding.

Actual enrolments in secondary and tertiary education vary considerably between regions in most developing countries and Thailand exhibits the typical pattern, having a much higher than average level in the capital. This is particularly pronounced in tertiary education, as about three-quarters of Thailand's university students are drawn from Bangkok. Provision of education up to high school level is 85 per cent state-run and 15 per cent private, and objective test scores in the private sector are generally 10 per cent higher than in the state schools.

The Seventh Plan calls, as part of the country's continuing process of demographic planning, for a continuing decline in the birth rate to levels below 20 per thousand which, it is estimated, will result in a 1996 population figure of only fractionally over 61 millions. Population growth in the latter half of the 1980s is estimated to have averaged 1.6 per cent and the birth rate is believed to have declined from 26.7 per thousand in 1982 to 21.3 per thousand by 1990. Put another way, the number of live births to the average Thai woman fell from 4.3 in the latter half of the 1970s to a projected 2.2 for the first half of the 1990s, and is expected by the more optimistic government departments to fall to the 2.1 replacement level in the early part of the next century. The National Economic and Social Development Board (NESDB) takes a more cautious view of likely progress but even they project population growth rates around an easily manageable 1 per cent by the end of the century. The success of Thailand's birth control campaigns contrasts with the relative failure of those in India, where the average woman still gives birth to 4.41 children. The Thai infant mortality rate, on the other hand, is targeted to fall from 37 per thousand in 1990 to 25 per thousand by 2005, reflecting rising living standards.

The Thai birth control policy stemmed from a 1971 study conducted jointly by the Ministry of Public Health, the NESDB and Chulalongkorn University, which projected that GDP per capita by the year 2000 would be 30 per cent greater if these goals were met than if the fecundity levels were to remain unchanged. Thailand has had a coherent population strategy for 20 years and is widely believed to have resolved the problem of population pressure on the nation's resources. The country appears to be heading for near population stability and, with less than half the geographical population density of India (112 per sq. km, compared with 259 per sq. km), over four times the per capita GNP ($1,410 compared with $340 in 1990) and a young (over half the population is under 30 years of age) and increasingly healthy population, Thailand is far better placed to take control of its economic destiny.

Continuity in social and economic policy has been maintained in spite of the *coups d'état* which have plagued the country ever since the transition to constitutional monarchy in 1932 and the signs are that the economic imperatives of the nation are clearly gaining ascendancy over the interests of the various cliques within the military establishment. The moral authority of the monarch has been brought to bear on the civilian and military politicians during several of the emergencies of recent years and this has allowed the life of the country to continue in a comparatively uninterrupted fashion in circumstances which might otherwise have been catastrophically disruptive. These periodic political upheavals are the only way in which Thailand deviates from the classic model of the rapidly industrializing agrarian economy. Political stability is normally a prerequisite for such a transition and the best that can be said of Thailand in this regard is that the rapid growth of recent years has been based on political stability of a rather curious kind.

The latter half of the 1980s nonetheless saw the Thai economy growing faster than any other in the world. Real GDP over the period grew by an average of 8.6 per cent each year, with a peak of 13.2 per cent in 1988. GDP growth is expected to continue at the 8–8.5 per cent level for the period up to 1996. The overall figures mask predictably divergent growth rates in agriculture, which grew at an average 1.5 per cent over the period, and manufacturing, which averaged nearly 11 per cent, reflecting a continuation of the structural shift in the economy which has been occurring at an accelerating rate since Thailand provided bases for US forces during the Vietnam war. Between 1986 and 1990, the percentage of GDP accounted for by agriculture fell from 16.2 per cent to 12.4

per cent, while the manufacturing sector expanded from 23.6 per cent to 26.1 per cent.

The growth of the economy in the late 1980s was reflected in the improved accessibility of information. Calculations of our Information Access Index, based on UNESCO data over this period, show Thailand moving up the league table of nations from 82nd position in 1986 to 74th in 1990. India, over the same period, went from 120th to 116th. The 1990 position reflects newspaper circulation of 87 copies per thousand people, and ownership of 182 radios, 109 television sets and ten telephones per thousand. The accessibility of a basic infostructure in Thailand in 1986, measured in the terms of the Index, was almost exactly half as good as the global average, giving an index of 50; by 1990, this score had improved to 61.

However, the UNESCO figures, which are used in the Index throughout for reasons of consistency, almost certainly understate the progress which has been made in developing Thailand's infostructure – a suspicion which some of the more recent figures quoted hereafter confirm.

Military Men and Mass Media

One of the first strategic objectives of the leaders of any self-respecting *coup d'état* is the control of the radio and television stations in the capital and principal cities. In Thailand, which has had 17 coups since 1932, effective military control of the broadcast media has, until recently, been a permanent feature of national life. Some 200 radio stations are owned by the government and another 288 by the military and the police. All five terrestrial television channels are owned either by the Government Public Relations Agency or the military, and the broadcast media, although they carry advertising and a normal mix of news and entertainment, have been used as mouthpieces of the authorities where political news is concerned. This control has frequently been manifested in blanket censorship; coverage of the large pro-democracy demonstrations of May 1992, for example, was completely blacked out.

As in India, the reading of newspapers in Thailand is predominantly an urban habit. Approximately 60 per cent of urban dwellers read newspapers daily, while less than 20 per cent of the rural population does, giving an overall national adult readership of about 27 per cent. Rural readership is difficult to assess as the majority of rural newspaper readers avail themselves of the 50,000 or so government-provided village reading halls which typically provide one copy each of *Thai Rath*, the popular leader in the circulation stakes, and *Matichon*, the country's third largest newspaper, which is generally regarded as the leading quality vernacular daily with the best political coverage. The sparse rural circulation is more a function of this communal reading habit than of physical distribution, which is not really a problem in Thailand.

The circulation of *Matichon* rose from 170,000 copies to a peak of 600,000 just after the May 1992 disturbances. This reflected the news black-out in the government controlled broadcast media, the urban focus of the newspaper medium and the independent ownership of the press. Press freedom, however, is only relative and the newspapers, on this occasion, were soon told to desist from reporting the disturbances or face closure. The press responded in a variety of ways, with the English language *Bangkok Post* complying but running blank pages in protest and *The Nation* and *Phansetkit* continuing to print in the face of vigorous harassment by the military.

The press in Thailand has generally maintained an independent stance since the first newspapers were published in the country in 1844 but has always run the gauntlet of sanctions for any implied or inferred criticism of the military or for *lèse majesté*, a charge which resulted in the closure of one of the country's first newspapers, produced by the missionary Dan Bradley. In this sense it has performed a role similar to that of the Indian press and still has a predominantly urban, middle-class focus. The rapid growth of the middle class in recent years has resulted in a broadening of the role of the print media. It is estimated that as many as one million people nation-wide now invest or speculate in the stock market and this has been reflected in the proliferation and success of economic and business newspapers and magazines such as those published by the Manager Group, the circulation of whose specialist daily grew to 75,000 within three years of its inception. Economic growth and the diffusion of television has generated interest in a wide range of topics among the growing literate middle class and it is expected that all segments of the press, quality and popular, general and specialist, will see their healthy growth rates of the late 1980s continue through the 1990s. Bangkok is likely to continue to dominate the newspaper scene, although there are some small local newspapers which have had limited success in the Chiangmai area.

The cause of independent broadcasting is likely to be significantly advanced by a cabinet decision in July 1992 to loosen the hold of the military on the broadcast media by approving plans to create five new private television channels, at least two of which were to be genuinely both private and civilian – a distinction which is relevant in Thailand where some senior military men also have considerable commercial interests. Television is clearly Thailand's most important mass communications medium; 75 per cent of all households nation-wide have a television set and 72 per cent of people questioned in a 1991 survey had watched television in the last 24 hours. Although marginally more households own a radio receiver, only 42 per cent of respondents in the same survey had listened to radio during the previous day. Television ownership and viewership rates are predictably higher (97 per cent and 88 per cent respectively) in Bangkok than in the rest of the country. Overwhelmingly the most popular television channel in the country is the army-licensed Channel 7, which is regularly named by 60 per cent of the population as its favourite and which commands a similar percentage of peak-time viewership. This channel established comprehensive national broadcast coverage before its competitors and carries a mix of news, drama and light entertainment, which surveys suggest are (in that order) the preferred viewing of Thais. The miserable showing of Channel 11, the educational channel, which achieves viewership figures only of around 1 per cent, perhaps underlines the difficulties of educational television in developing countries.

Although 24-hour broadcasting is allowed, there are government restrictions on what can be aired and when. The motivation behind prime-time programming restrictions has undoubtedly been partly political. No foreign-sourced programming can be broadcast in prime time and programmes aired during these hours emphasize Thai culture and values and retain some residual developmental content. Advertisements for alcoholic drinks and condoms cannot be shown until after 10.00 p.m. and tobacco advertising is banned completely.

Given the popularity of television, its already dominant position in the Thai media world and the dubious parentage of some of the existing stations, the emergence of an independent broadcasting sector was perhaps inevitable after the Mass Communications Organization of Thailand (MCOT) granted a 20-year concession to International Broadcasting Corporation (IBC), a subsidiary of Shinawatra Computer and Communications, to operate a subscription television network in Bangkok. A similar concession was granted to Siam Broadcasting Corporation a year later. Private ownership of the microwave broadcasting medium does not, however, mean that subscription television escapes the attentions of the censors. Almost all of the programme material used in the network is imported from the USA and Europe and, in the case of IBC, is received via satellite at the Shinawatra headquarters, where it is approved by MCOT officials, who are permanently stationed with the company, and is broadcast after a 30-minute 'processing' delay.

The two subscription TV companies launched competing microwave services with the firm conviction that at least the metropolitan market for independent television had considerable potential. IBC plans to extend coverage to rural areas, using the satellite to be launched for its parent company, Shinawatra, in 1994, although the more dispersed and less affluent nature of the rural market is likely to make such an undertaking less commercially attractive than the provision of services in the capital. Nonetheless, there is a recognized market for low-cost entertainment in the provinces which IBC, and Siam Broadcasting (Thai Sky), together with the emerging commercial UHF broadcasters, will seek to supply. Indeed, projections for subscriber numbers were raised above the level of initial estimates because demand from lower income groups was much higher than expected during the first months of operation of subscription services.

The main thrust of subscription television marketing, however, has been towards affluent urban dwellers and expatriates. Two of the three IBC channels are broadcast in English, although 85 per cent of subscribers are Thais, and the emphasis in news coverage is on foreign news, with CNN enjoying a large viewership. Both subscriber networks suffer from shortages and low quality in programming and it is clear that this will need to be expanded and improved significantly if any substantial fraction of the estimated 1.2 million potential subscribers in the Bangkok area is to be reached. The subscription television operators have aggressive targets for subscription levels (IBC, for example, has a target of 500,000 subscriptions by 1996) which may be difficult to achieve if programming fails to satisfy and/or other forms of broadcast media are deregulated.

Satellite television, in the form of Star TV, a Hong Kong-based operator using the ASIASAT system and Pacific Communications, broadcasting from Darwin and using the Indonesian Palapa satellite, already exists but access to these services has been limited by the high cost of the requisite equipment and the strict regulation of the Post and Telegraph Department, which until recently restricted receiving licences to senior government officials and well-connected individuals in the private sector. Satellite is, however, a very suitable medium for Thai private broadcasters (the government channels started using satellite links in 1988) and the launch of Shinawatra's Thaisat in 1994 is intended greatly to extend the reach of IBC, enabling it to compete in the Thai rural market and to expand its business beyond Thailand's borders. How far Thais themselves will be allowed to benefit from the technology remains to be seen and it may be that, until the regulatory environment changes, satellites will only legally be used for uplinks which could widen the footprint of subscription community antenna television (CATV) (using local microwave links) and not to provide direct broadcast programming for viewers with satellite receivers. There is some evidence, however, that the regulations regarding the use of satellite receivers are already widely ignored.

The initial demand for subscription television has led the companies involved to conclude that there is room for two major competitors in the metropolitan market, and that there is little risk of 'crowding out' as a result of the growth of competing media – for the time being at least. This situation reflects a considerable pent-up demand for information and entertainment and also the rapid growth of the broader economy, which has raised disposable incomes and also created substantial advertising revenues for the mass media as a whole. Advertising billings were growing at annual rates around 30 per cent during the late 1980s, with television taking around 60 per cent of the total and newspapers around 30 per cent. Growth rates have continued to be sufficient that a loss of advertising market share need not result in a diminution of revenues, which is just as well for the newspapers given that they derive the bulk (anything from 60 to 90 per cent) of their revenues from this source. Newspapers, in fact, have remained a strong advertising medium, particularly for the booming real estate sector, which uses them in preference to all other media.

In summary, it can be said that the mass media in Thailand appear to be in a phase of rapid transition from the state-owned and/or highly regulated model typical of the Third World to the much more open, commercial and hybrid structure seen in most of the developed world. Progress in this direction will continue to be subject to political factors as long as the government or the military consider control of the media to be essential to their grip on power but the political climate changed markedly with the incumbency of the Anand (2) and Chuan administrations, censorship appears to be loosening and most trends in the industry seem to be very much in the right direction. Perhaps the most outstanding feature of change in the mass media environment, however, is the way in which television has emerged as clearly the most powerful agent of change in Thai popular culture.

Communications and Commerce

Thailand's frenetic economic growth has continued to place considerable strain on its telecommunications infrastructure and fears that the foreign corporations which have been so important in enriching the country would be deterred from operating there by communications difficulties caused the authorities to take steps dramatically to increase capacity. The waiting list for telephone lines is estimated to have grown from around 300,000 in 1986 to 1.33 million in 1991 (a figure perhaps inflated by a thriving black market in telephone lines), at which time the total installed base was only 1.43 million lines. As in India, the metropolitan telephone system is comparatively good, with 12.7 lines per hundred people in 1991, while rural areas have around 0.6 lines per hundred, with only 300,000 lines serving a provincial population of some 47 millions. Projections by the Telephone Organization of Thailand (TOT), the domestic telephone monopoly, forecast demand for over 10 million lines by the end of the century and nearly 20 million by our horizon year of 2005.

Budgetary constraints on the TOT and the state-owned international carrier, the Communications Authority of Thailand (CAT), have meant that network expansion on the scale necessary is deemed to be impossible on a publicly funded basis and it has been decided to issue concessions to private companies for the installation and operation of the system. On this basis, the plan is to achieve an installed base of five million lines by 1996, raising the ratio to 8.5 lines per hundred people. The manner in which the initial concessions were granted, however, caused considerable controversy and allegations of corruption surrounding the deal giving Charoen Pokhpand (CP) – an agribusiness group with no telecommunications experience – responsibility for installing three million telephone lines ostensibly triggered the 1991 coup. The CP concession was subsequently scaled down to cover two million lines and the company was excluded from tendering for one million (potentially more profitable) rural lines, which were awarded to a newly formed consortium, Thai Telephone and Communications.

The first phase of the rural network expansion plan is mainly concerned with nine provincial cities in the eastern and southern development areas and another national scheme for the installation of an additional six million lines is expected to be launched in 1996. The system is already 80 per cent digital and suffers from a lack of capacity rather than inadequate quality. Optical fibre trunk links are being installed along main highways and railways between Bangkok and the eastern seaboard development zones, and Thailand's first telecommunications satellite is due to be launched by the end of 1993. In the meantime, gaps in the systems are partially covered by the use of cellular telephones, subscriptions to which grew from a standing start in 1986 to over 100,000 by 1991. Although optical fibre links can be installed comparatively quickly and the targets for expansion of the conventional telephone system are aggressive by any standards, such is the size of the backlog and such is the flexibility of mobile communications that enormous demand has emerged for mobile telephones. This is as true in the comparatively well-served capital as it is in rural areas because the lack of any viable mass transit system in Bangkok has contributed to diabolical road traffic congestion.

The problems of Thailand's telecommunications system have been attacked using a variety of technologies. VSAT links are being planned for rural areas and international circuits are to be expanded via both satellite and undersea optical fibre links. Some of the enterprises involved in these undertakings may be financially over-extended, and the participation of foreign companies may be more prominent than some would like, but all the signs are that the problem is being tackled with vigour and that the country's telecommunications infrastructure will be transformed over the next decade.

The future of advanced telecommunications and information services is unclear. Initial experiments with videotex have so far proved to be commercially unsuccessful and, although an embryonic Integrated Services Digital Network system (see ISDN in chapter 3) has been installed, its potential customer base is generally perceived to be extremely limited for the foreseeable future. The main thrust of the country's efforts in telecommunications will therefore continue to be in the provision of universal and reliable telephone services. With its stabilizing population and its buoyant economy, Thailand is far better placed than India to catch up with the expanding demand of its people for these basic facilities but the projected pace of demand growth is such that it seems unlikely to be satisfied for a long time to come.

Farangs and Screwdrivers

The government's open-door policy to foreign investment has resulted in the establishment of a nominal bias towards manufacturing in Thailand's information sector which has not sprung spontaneously from the domestic culture. In 1991 Thailand's exports of electronics goods exceeded those of its traditional agricultural staples, namely, rice, maize, tapioca and rubber. Goods exported include integrated circuits, from 13 different companies, a wide range of domestic electrical appliances, computer disk drives and printed circuit boards. This rapid transformation of the export statistics, in which primary products were, until recently, dominant, is due to massive direct investment by American, Korean, Singaporean, Taiwanese and Japanese companies.

Most of these *farang* (foreigners') plants, however, have been built to take advantage of Thailand's cheap labour (the average wage was $100 per month in 1991), low-priced land and convenient geographical position: they are involved in assembly and packaging processes only. Although such 'screwdriver' plants employ large numbers of people and help to expand the local economy, their true value to Thailand's trade is limited because between 60 and 90 per cent of the value of the finished products is imported. Nonetheless, the government has taken a very lenient stance with regard to import tariffs for such companies and has only protected local manufacturers by, for example, requiring foreign electronics firms to acquire much of their plastic materials locally in order to encourage the domestic petrochemicals industry.

Thailand has a comparatively small market for electronics goods and a very small pool of experienced electronic engineers and the government has therefore seen little point in attempting to establish an integrated domestic electronics industry. Rather, the policy has been to welcome foreign manufacturers for the benefits which they bring and not to impose tariffs or other costs which might cause them to go elsewhere. Foreign companies, for their part, find it impossible to source products which require highly skilled inputs in Thailand and, therefore only rely on local suppliers for very simple components.

A small domestically owned electronic component and sub-assembly industry has grown up around the foreign factories and most of the companies involved have chosen to offer only low-tech products which can be manufactured taking advantage of the abundant supply of cheap labour. Some, however, have been pulled along by the technological demands of the industry which they are supplying and are installing modern automatic assembly equipment which will enable them, in due course, to supply more sophisticated products which cannot be produced manually. Although Thailand can be seen, in this sense, as being little more than an electronics entrepôt, by taking this lenient approach, the government has created an environment in which an embryonic domestic electronics industry can be formed and it is possible that, as the general level of education and per capita incomes in Thailand rise over the years to come, this will become a more important part of the economy than it is today.

Although rapid industrial growth has hitherto outrun the infrastructure, ongoing plans to develop industrial zones on the eastern seaboard and improved communications links up to the Laos border represent the first part of a concerted effort to achieve a more balanced development pattern throughout the country. The building of a second international airport in the north-east and the laying of the optical fibre telephone trunk lines along railway lines, joining the region with Bangkok and creating an eastern seaboard 'teleport', are important parts of this scheme. The Thai government has not espoused a technopolis strategy in any explicit form but the plan to encourage 'clean' industries, particularly electronics, and to provide the appropriate infrastructure for them, in Leam Cha-Bang on the eastern seaboard, could result in the development of such a region if and when appropriately skilled manpower becomes available. For the time being, high technology manufacturing in Thailand is likely to remain the preserve of foreigners and the government seems content that it should be so.

Development and Transition in the Infostructure

Thailand has been described here as a state in transition, whereas India has been represented as a nation concerned with more basic development. Although the two countries have started from similar infostructural bases in recent years, the distinction seems a valid one to make because it seems likely that Thailand will, over the next decade or so, make the transition to the kind of infostructure which prevails in the developed world whereas India, at least India as a whole, seems most unlikely to do so. Both countries are more or less consciously building their infostructures and are dealing with some similar problems in similar ways and yet there are differences which make one likely to progress much more quickly than the other.

The two countries are demographically very different. India is a huge, linguistically, ethnically and culturally diverse nation whose population growth is still essentially out of control. Thailand is much smaller, culturally, linguistically and (relatively) ethnically homogeneous, and has its population growth more or less under control. These demographic differences, combined with the much higher literacy and per capita income levels in Thailand, are sufficient to explain much of the difference in the prospects for infostructural development.

Both nations are subject to their own particular brands of political instability and, given the importance which any aspirant to political power always places on control of mass communications, this has influenced the development of the media in both. There are striking similarities between the political roles played by the independent press in India and in Thailand; both have maintained a critical stance with regard to government and both have defied the authorities at times of national emergency. This role can be contrasted, in both countries, with the relative or absolute complicity of the government-controlled broadcast media on such occasions. In both countries, however, the political and ideological role of the broadcast media is being increasingly subverted by commercial interests which are bringing their own particular brands of consumer democratization.

In developing their mass media and communications, the two countries have taken advantage of similar combinations of new technologies to help them to overcome the sheer magnitude of the tasks at hand but, whereas India has continued to be concerned with limiting the participation of foreigners in the process and has opted for the steady development of indigenous industries, Thailand has more readily sought foreign assistance in its rush for growth. And the reciprocal nature of the relationship between economic growth and the development of all forms of communications media is very clear. Whereas Thailand's foreign capital has come largely in the form of direct investment by international corporations, India has attempted to bootstrap its way ahead, with only the sizeable non-resident Indian community as a particular source of overseas funds.

The contrasts, in both countries, between the development of the infostructure in the cities and in rural areas are striking. There is, however, no sign that Thailand will divide ever more sharply into two nations in this regard; the economic boom is a national phenomenon and the scale of infostructural expansion across the country is such that the information gap is likely to be reduced further. Any rush for growth which is likely to occur in India, on the other hand, is much more likely to be a localized affair, with Bangalore, for example, featuring as an information technology centre which shows signs of developing a life of its own, whereas the majority of the population which lives in the villages is likely to see change come about only gradually. Bangkok and Bangalore are both at the centre of information revolutions of a kind but, whereas the Bangkok version shows signs of spreading to the rest of the country, Bangalore is likely to continue to occupy a special position in a country whose real information revolution is still some way off.

3
THE TECHNOLOGY DIMENSION

The impact which the application of modern technology can have upon a society which has been excluded from the technological mainstream of the developed world for an extended period can, as the examples described in chapter 2 illustrate, be quite dramatic. Television and the other mass media, once established, can project images and ideas which change the collective consciousness of a nation in the space of a single generation and set in train radical changes in institutions and life-styles. It is by now commonly accepted that technology can have this effect and technology transfer to developing nations is a recurring theme in any discussion of their economic advancement.

The nations of the developed world are no less concerned with technology; indeed, their citizens are accustomed to the idea that its development has an important role in their lives. They do not, however, have the advantages, which the developing nations enjoy, of being able to select the technologies most appropriate to their needs from a wide range and of being able to purchase the fruits of new technologies relatively cheaply and in fully developed and packaged form. Although these 'advantages' may be regarded as being of dubious value, they can be contrasted with the difficulties which, conversely, the developed nations experience – those of re-orientation in the face of new technologies and of the costs involved in their creation and application. The view which the developing world has of a technological future can be quite clear; most of the technology which it aspires to possess is there for the buying and the learning. For the developed nations, the future is less clear because it is they who are creating the advanced technologies and making judgements about if and how they might usefully be applied.

Because the shape of advanced infostructures is so dependent upon technologies which are still evolving and whose influences are yet to be seen, it is necessary at this point to make a detour from the broader description of infostructural development and to examine some of these key information technologies and to assess their likely future impact. Readers who are familiar with these issues, or who for any other reason wish to avoid the detour, should proceed directly to chapter 4, where we re-emerge into the infostructures of the developed world.

Predictable Progress

The image of Archimedes running naked through the streets shouting 'Eureka' has long since been supplanted in the public consciousness, as a symbol of the scientific breakthrough, by images of the likes of Einstein and Hawking labouring over incomprehensible equations and making equally incomprehensible statements about black holes, the curvature of space-time and particles with 'charm'. Big Science excites awe and wonder but, as far as most people are concerned, the pursuit of understanding at this level has taken on the character of a kind of weird spectator sport – the subject of magazine articles, television documentaries and not a few books, but something which has no relevance to everyday life. 'High' technology has, in many ways, acquired a similar mystique but, unlike Big Science, it does usually have fairly immediate relevance to everyday life and it does not, for the most part, manifest itself in terms of major discontinuities. Rather, it thrives on the steady development of a comparatively limited range of basic principles and techniques. Science may change the world view of a cognizant minority in a sudden flash; technology changes the life-styles of the majority by a process of creeping change.

Thomas Kuhn's book, *The Structure of Scientific Revolutions*, which modified and popularized the use of the word 'paradigm' and itself represents a paradigm for thought on the philosophy of science, defines scientific revolutions as: 'those non-cumulative developmental episodes in which the older paradigm is replaced in whole or in part by an incompatible new one' (p. 92).

Technology, which usually manifests itself as a kind of applied science with most of the controversy removed, seldom, if ever, produces revolutions which would satisfy this definition. And yet technological developments which involve no apparent paradigm shift, but merely extrapolate from what is already known, can from time to time have more far-reaching implications for everyday life than some of the real revolutions of the scientists. It has, for example, been suggested, at least semi-seriously, that the invention of the stirrup, by enabling a lance, broadsword or other heavy weapon to be wielded by an armoured man on horseback, was a kind of medieval Manhattan Project, and resulted in an arms race which, in turn, brought about the rise of the feudal system (see White, 1978). Responsibility for changes in the world order has often been laid at the door of the inventors of the atomic bomb and, if you accept the theory, the stirrup may have played an analogous role in the middle ages. The difference is that the atomic bomb was based on science but the stirrup was pure technology.

Electronic Origins

The revolution which has occurred in information technology since the building of the vacuum valve-based ENIAC computer in 1946 has been founded on a single revolutionary scientific discovery and a mass of technological developments on the theme – including one which has had as dramatic an effect as the scientific breakthrough which fathered it.

John Von Neumann, a Hungarian exile working on the ENIAC project at the University of Pennsylvania, had recognized by the mid-1940s that triode valves could be used to store numbers in binary form and he went on to develop what have ever since been the basic architectural principles of the vast majority of computers. These would never have been applied on any really significant scale, however, if the advent of solid state electronics had not allowed the components of computers to be miniaturized and produced at correspondingly minuscule cost. Computers were awaiting a breakthrough in electronics and electronics was awaiting a breakthrough in physics. The breakthrough came in 1948 in the form of the invention, at the Bell Telephone Laboratories of AT&T, by John Bardeen, Walter Brattain and William Shockley, of the world's first semiconductor electronic device – the transfer resistor or transistor. For this work, which laid the foundations for the modern electronics industry, the three received the Nobel prize for Physics in 1956. Their revolutionary discovery was that the electrical properties of semiconducting materials, such as germanium and silicon, were entirely a function of impurities in the crystals and that, if very pure and electrically 'neutral' crystals were fabricated, they could be used as raw materials for the creation of electrical devices. Areas of the semiconductor, it was discovered, could be induced to act as conductors or insulators by the systematic introduction of impurities into those areas and small electrical circuits could be thus be created within solid bodies.

The first Bell transistors, although seminal in their significance, were large and not very useful and the revolutionary potential of solid state electronics, first in the form of discrete semiconductor devices and later in integrated circuits, was to be realized by others. Among the first to license the Bell patent for transistors, in 1952, was a young man called Masaru Ibuka, co-founder of the Tokyo Telecommunications Laboratory, which later became known as the Sony Corporation. Ibuka was convinced that, although the production yields of transistors which could be used in high frequency applications were, at the time, wholly insufficient for them to be considered commercially viable, these devices could eventually be used in the manufacture of small radios, an application not generally considered feasible at the time. Against considerable odds and, ironically, in spite of considerable obstruction on the part of Japan's Ministry of International Trade and Industry (MITI), he eventually proved his point and the world's first transistorized radio, the Sony TR-55, went on sale in August 1955. The transistor soon became synonymous with the radio and, together with its other solid state siblings, the component became the feedstock of a boom in consumer electronics products.

Discrete semiconductor devices of this kind enabled Sony and its competitors to make a whole generation of sophisticated products, culminating in the video tape recorder, but, as Ibuka and his colleagues were striving to produce cheap high frequency transistors, some colleagues of William Shockley, who had left Bell Laboratories to set up his own company in the early 1950s, were embarking on a developmental path which was to lead to the creation of a new and even more sophisticated generation of components and end products. Fairchild Semiconductors, established under the stewardship of Robert Noyce in 1957, was in many ways the cradle of the Silicon Valley integrated circuit industry and had more alumni (sometimes referred to as 'Fairchildren') among the senior engineers in the industry during its early years than any other company. Texas Instruments filed the first integrated circuit patent in 1959 but Fairchild produced the first commercial version in 1965.

The integrated circuit (IC) was a logical extension of the principles used in the creation of discrete semiconductor devices. If it was possible to create areas within a piece of silicon or some other semiconducting material, which have differing electrical properties and thus to create a single electrical device, it should be possible, if the silicon is treated with sufficient precision, to create a multiplicity of devices, and thus create a more complex functional circuit, in the same space. No paradigm shift was required in the science at this point but the technological problems were daunting and a whole range of fabrication technologies had to be developed, not from scratch but in ways not previously envisaged. The semiconductor integrated circuit, which was to prove to be as revolutionary in its implications as the transistor itself was, like the stirrup, a product of technology, not of science.

Stretching Silicon – Japanese Style

The first integrated circuits offered only a very small scale of integration (SSI) and the individual devices in the circuit were large enough to be visible to the naked eye. They offered only modest advantages over the groupings of discrete components which they replaced but the potential of large- and very large-scale integration (LSI and VLSI) excited the imagination. The magnitude of the fabrication problems involved was just beginning to be understood but the possibility of putting whole computers onto a finger nail of silicon offered to open the door to undreamed-of applications. The transistor paradigm shift started the process of the information technology revolution rolling but it was only with the advent of integrated circuits in bulk and at a low cost that it really took off.

The creation of an integrated circuit requires skills in two broadly separate types of technology: design and fabrication. The design of the circuits themselves, particularly of the microprocessors and micro-controllers which form the logic centres of all microsystems, is immensely complex and involves many man- and computer-years of work and no small amount of intellectual art. It is the quality of these design and software activities which determines the success of any proprietary device in the market and which has established the reputations and fortunes of such companies as the Intel Corporation, the world leader in microprocessors. Intel, Motorola and a host of smaller American companies hold the lion's share of the world market in 'design-rich' devices – mainly logic circuits of one kind or another – and it is generally accepted that the USA has a clear lead in the design of integrated circuits and in the markets for the most sophisticated circuits.

American companies also pioneered most of the fabrication technologies used in the industry but, since the mid-1980s, the world leaders in integrated circuit fabrication have been concentrated in Japan, as have the makers of much of the integrated circuit fabrication equipment. Japan now also leads the world in many areas of fabrication technology and continues to invest huge sums in research and development to maintain this position. This ascendancy has been accompanied by complete Japanese dominance in memory chips and the other most numerous 'commodity' devices which are used in large numbers in all complex electronic equipment. By 1990, Japanese manufacturers occupied the top three, and six of the top ten, slots in the integrated circuit sales league table. Their rise to this pre-eminent position was based principally on their determined assault on the market for the most commonly used types of device, and notably on production of the ubiquitous dynamic random access memory (DRAM) chip in which they had by 1990 achieved a world market share in excess of 80 per cent.

The bulk of the central part of the circuit diagram of a DRAM chip resembles a grid of 'crosswires', with one binary digit (bit) of data being stored at each of the junctions, where a 'gate' is formed. The ability of the device to store data is therefore a function of its size and the number of 'wires' which can be drawn on the silicon. A doubling of the number of lines drawn on each axis results in a fourfold increase in the number of junctions and, therefore, in the capacity of the device. Any major increase in the physical size of the chip would result in an unacceptable slowing of the access time of the device – as the electrons in the circuit would be forced to travel much further – and would also make the components unacceptably large for the purposes of systems design. Therefore, memory capacities can only practically be increased by 'drawing' ever finer lines on devices which remain more or less unchanged in physical size. It is in the application of such techniques in mass production that the Japanese companies have proved to be particularly skilled.

Each generation of DRAM device has seen a quadrupling in memory capacity and a new generation has appeared approximately every two years throughout the past decade. If we take up the story in the early 1980s, with the then state-of-the-art 4 kilobit (4K) DRAM, which held 4,096 bits of data, the periodic halving of the line widths drawn on the chips brought devices which stored 16,384 (16K), 65,536 (64K) and 262,144 (256K) bits of data and so on, through to the 16,777,216 bit (16M) devices available in small quantities at the time of writing. To put this into perspective, the 1981 model could store the text of about eight lines of one page of this book; the latest chip, of similar price and physical size, could store nearly four copies of the whole book. This has been achieved with very little modification to the basic, comparatively simple, design concept (as one industry observer recently commented: 'If you've seen one DRAM, you've seen 'em all.') but the fabrication technology required has changed dramatically. The speed with which the essential 'commodity' circuits have fallen in price and increased in capacity has largely been a function of the desperately (internally and externally) competitive Japanese integrated circuit oligopoly focusing its attack on the most homogeneous segment of the integrated circuit market and driving fabrication technology rapidly along the learning curve. The battle for the commodity segment of the market has, in other words, been a battle for superiority in fabrication, and the Japanese have been winning it for a number of years.

The importance of the availability of these cheap, powerful, commodity-type integrated circuits in influencing the pattern of electronic hardware developments has meant that the whole electronics industry has indirectly been dependent upon improvements in a range of fabrication techniques and equipment. The development of the chip-maker's art (and, if things continue as they are, this means the Japanese chip-maker's art) will be a major determinant of the nature of the platforms on which information systems will be operating early in the next century. At any given time there is usually one area, within the fabrication disciplines, which presents either an opportunity for progress or an obstruction. The critical discipline has most often been photolithography.

The first stage in the manufacture of an integrated circuit is the production of the high purity semiconducting material which forms its base, or substrate. The most common material used for this purpose is silicon, a very common material in the earth's crust, but some more exotic materials, such as gallium arsenide (GaAs), are used in applications where their molecular structure encourages the high degree of electron mobility necessary for very high speed circuits. In either case, the first step in the process is the production of a single crystal of near-100 per cent pure 'intrinsic' (i.e. 'undoped' or electrically neutral) material, grown from a seed crystal rotated slowly in a furnace. The manufactured crystal takes the form of a roughly cylindrical ingot measuring anything from one to eight inches in diameter. Efforts have been made over the years to increase the diameter of the ingots which, when sliced with a high-precision saw and then polished, form the wafers on which the integrated circuits are made. Mass production lines are gradually being converted to handle eight inch silicon wafers, which offer a 78 per cent increase in surface area, and therefore production throughput, over the six inch wafers which have been the industry standard in recent years. Increases in crystal diameter, which are technically very difficult to achieve in mass production, are sought in order to reduce unit costs of production but expensive new equipment has to be designed and built as each development is implemented. It should be noted, then, that even the technology of the relatively unknown and prosaic process of crystal growing represents a component of the drive down the integrated circuit production learning curve, and one which sees periodical surges in development.

Once the ingot has been sliced and the resulting wafers trimmed and polished, the wafer fabrication, or 'wafer fab', process itself begins. This process is in some ways analogous to an exotic form of screen printing in which the particle impurities to be introduced into the silicon to create the electronic circuits are the ink and the photomasks are the screens. When the circuit is designed, a computer generates the design for the 'mask-set', the set of often ten or more photomasks (optical stencils) which are used in sequence to build up the layers of interconnecting and insulated circuits which make up the final functioning device. Before they can be used, however, the wafer must be coated with a thin layer of photo-sensitive material called photoresist, which is applied evenly (usually by spinning) onto the polished silicon wafer. The first mask in the set is then brought into play in the first of the many photolithographic processes which the wafer will undergo.

The photoresist covered wafer is placed under an ultraviolet light source which is projected in a single shot through the mask. The pattern printed on the mask (in a similar earlier process) casts a shadow on the photoresist so that the areas which correspond to the desired circuit pattern react to the light and harden or soften (depending on the kind of resist being used). The soft parts of the resist are then washed off, leaving the surface of silicon wafer printed with the pattern of the first layer of a large number of circuits. The residual photoresist itself then forms the 'stencil' for the implantation of the first layer of impurities which will eventually direct the electrons around the circuit. Once this is done, in a diffusion furnace using very complex gas technology, the remaining photoresist is washed off and the whole process repeated, using the second mask in the set to print the second layer of the circuitry onto (very precisely) the same area of silicon, and so on until the circuit is complete.

Clearly, when the 'wires' on the circuit are less than one micron (one thousandth of a millimetre) in width, the degree of precision required in the equipment which lines up each mask over the previously 'printed' patterns which form the layers of the circuit is very high. Earlier generations of integrated circuits were made using a precision machine called a mask aligner which did exactly what its name implies. As the widths of the lines to be projected onto the silicon narrowed, however, optical problems were encountered as patterns on the masks become ever finer. In order to overcome these problems, and to ensure that the yield of good chips from each wafer was kept at satisfactory levels, the step-and-repeat machine, commonly referred to as the wafer stepper, was introduced.

Whereas the mask aligner takes a mask with perhaps 100 circuit patterns on it and projects these directly onto the silicon, the stepper uses a mask with, say, ten larger patterns and projects them in reduced form onto ten areas of the silicon in turn at intervals of a fraction of a second. It performs each step and then repeats it. The use of relatively large masks, whose images are optically shrunk onto the silicon, greatly reduces the likelihood of defects in, or contamination of, the masks resulting in defective patterns being printed on the device.

The replacement of the mask aligner by the stepper for the production first of the photomasks which represent the 'master' copies of the circuit patterns and then of integrated circuits themselves, enabled the industry to make the transition to true VLSI (very large-scale integration) circuits and was typical of the pattern of development in integrated circuit fabrication. The nature of the problems was fairly obvious – no paradigm shift was called for, just a high degree of ingenuity and some very sophisticated engineering. In the case of the stepper, this expertise was first delivered in commercial quantities by the two Japanese optics (and, increasingly, electronics) companies, Nikon and Canon, whose facility with the optics and precision engineering required is arguably second to none.

Japanese dominance in photolithography may be challenged by the introduction of a new kind of stepper developed in California, the so-called 'step-and-scan' machine, in which the mask and wafer are both moved past the light source and the lens. Development of this device, by Silicon Valley Group Lithography Systems, was funded by Sematech, a consortium set up by 14 US semiconductor makers in 1987 with the specific aim of recapturing ground lost to the Japanese in fabrication technology. It is also true that, although photolithography has often been the area in which innovation was required to allow a new generation of devices to be made, variations on stepper technology should be sufficient to perform the lithographic processes on devices of line-widths down to 0.35 microns. Until that point is reached, it is likely that it will be developments in the furnaces and vacuum chambers of the fabrication line which will be the key to producing complex devices. Logic circuits in particular require large numbers of interconnection layers between the device elements within and on top of the silicon and as many as eight layers of metal are applied, using thin film technology, to some devices for this purpose. American companies, such as Applied Materials, are acknowledged leaders in this field and it may be that leadership in the key fabrication technology is again in American hands, although Japanese fabrication lines are still generally believed to be the most efficient in the world.

Once the circuits on the wafer are electronically complete, the wafer is sawn up to separate the individual circuits in a process called dicing. The circuit is then made connectable with the outside world by wire bonding the contact pads around its edges to a metal lead frame, using gold wire. The whole is then encased in an insulating material, usually epoxy but sometimes ceramic, and the connecting pins are added to, or bent downwards from, the lead frame. This process is called packaging and gives us the black insect-like plastic rectangles which appear on most modern circuit boards. Before it can be shipped, however, it must be tested to ensure that no failure in one of the many highly fault-intolerant stages of its manufacture has resulted in an inoperable device. The chip is plugged into an integrated circuit tester which is essentially a specialist computer which is designed to test memory or logic circuits at high speed. As circuits have become more complex, it has become necessary to develop faster and faster (and more expensive) testers so that testing does not create a bottleneck at the end of the manufacturing process.

The progress of integrated circuit manufacture along the steep learning curve which it has traced so far – a curve which has, for example, cut the cost of integrated circuit memory in real terms to less than 4 per cent of what it was ten years ago – has been a product of incremental improvements in the above processes. From the 'front-end' crystal growing, through lithography and 'wafer fab', to the 'back-end' processes of packaging and testing, major enhancements have been introduced in response to the demand for higher and higher degrees of circuit integration. In some of these areas, such as lithography, the shift to narrower line-widths has called for the installation of new generations of significantly different equipment, such as steppers, in the fabrication lines. It can also be seen that generation changes in one area of integrated circuit fabrication technology influence technical requirements elsewhere and that this progress is bought at a very high cost in terms of capital spending.

Current equipment is capable of mass producing devices with line-widths of 0.8 microns. By 1996, 0.5 microns should be achievable and, by 2000, it is expected by some engineers that 0.3 micron devices will be in mass production. At this stage, it should be possible to manufacture 1 gigabit DRAMs and the theoretical 0.2 micron physical limit for the production of electronic devices in silicon will be challenged. Beyond this point, the lines become so close together that it may be impossible to prevent electrical interference between them, although some believe that it may be possible to produce commercial devices in silicon with line-widths as narrow as 0.1 microns. Before this stage is reached, however, step changes in lithographic equipment will be required. Integrated circuit lithography currently uses light in the ultra-violet (UV) part of the spectrum and UV lithography is sufficiently precise for the manufacture of, for example, 16 megabit DRAMs. When the next generation thereafter – the (inevitably) 64 megabit DRAM – appears, it is likely to be produced using a different radiation source because the wavelength of UV light is simply too long to project a clean enough pattern onto the photoresist to produce adequate production yields of working circuits. A number of candidates for this new radiation source have been mooted, including electron beams and ion beams and, for the futuristic 0.1 micron device, synchrotrons. When these transitions are made, much of the other equipment in the wafer fab line will again have to change, raising capital costs still further.

Many of the technologies necessary to bring about even these more dramatic generation shifts in fabrication are already incorporated into machines, tested and available, but the future trajectory of the circuit integration curve, which will have quite profound implications for the capabilities of future hardware, will be determined as much by commercial as by technological considerations. All integrated circuit manufacturers have to weigh the potential benefits of introducing a new and superior chip which will earn superior profit margins (until they are eroded by competition and the inexorable downward pressure on prices) against the enormous costs involved in tooling-up for a new generation of devices. If they can, for example, stretch the capabilities of their existing 4 megabit DRAM wafer fab line to cope with 16 megabit chips, even if production yields suffer to some extent, they may decide that an early move to the new product is worth while. If, on the other hand, the next generation of chips requires radically new equipment and the existing generation is still holding its price well (or very badly, because the market for end-user products has collapsed), they may decide that the shift is not commercially advisable for the time being. Profitability at the sharp end of the chip makers' business is about launching a new device, for a premium price, into a waiting market and getting production lines running at high yields as soon as possible and as far as possible ahead of competitors who will come into the market and drive prices down.

If the precise timing of the generation shifts in integrated circuits is subject to commercial considerations, the secular trend is clear and surprisingly regular. Past experience and a cursory survey of the range of next generation fabrication technology which is now available form the basis for some fairly confident predictions about the power of the integrated circuits which will be available in the early years of the next century. A senior marketing director in the Japanese semiconductor industry has predicted that, although the 1 gigabit DRAM will be technically feasible by the end of the century, it is most unlikely that it will be in mass production. It is in his view almost certain, however, that the 256 megabit DRAM will be available in large volume by then.

It is highly likely that the integrated circuit manufacturers will enjoy a period of sufficient buoyancy in demand by the mid-1990s that they will undertake a programme of capital investment which will enable them to use one of the available forms of next generation lithography, employing an energy source in the upper part of the electro-magnetic spectrum, in the production of ultra large-scale integration devices. If they do so, they will, by the turn of the century, be producing silicon devices whose internal structures will start to test the theoretical limits of electrical circuitry in such a medium, with line-widths approaching 0.2 microns. This will mean that, even if the historical pattern of integrated circuit generation shifts is broken, the lead times stretch out and the 1 gigabit DRAM fails to materialize, even as a technical possibility, two more generations of device will be produced before the currently perceived limits of the technology are reached by the year 2000. If this is the case, DRAM chips capable of storing 268,435,456 bits (colloquially, and only slightly inaccurately, referred to as 256 megabits and equal to approximately 33 megabytes) of data will be in mass production in the early years of the next century. Such a device could store over five million words of text (62 copies of this book) or, if used to record the signal on a standard 64,000 bits per second telephone line, more than an hour of telephone conversation.

The DRAM is used as an illustrative yardstick here because it is one of the best-known types of integrated circuit on the market and because its development has very conspicuously been powered by innovations in fabrication, but it is far from being the only type of chip which will be affected by this continuing trend. The DRAM is just one of a whole family of memory devices (including 'flash' memory, a type of chip now much fancied as a non-volatile mass-storage integrated circuit) whose power will expand at a similar rate and improvements in the speed and function of logic chips will also be facilitated.

Advances in fabrication technology alone will, almost as a matter of routine, make possible applications which look quite futuristic by today's standards and these ideas are often realized faster than even people in the industry expect. An authoritative prediction, made in 1991, that telephones would in the medium-term future incorporate motorless recording devices, for example, was realized in late 1992 using high density flash memory (see p. 142).

Smart American Chips

So, many of the predictions of wonderful gadgets to come are neither based on fantasy nor dependent upon unpredictable breakthroughs; they are based upon very realistic projections of well-understood developmental paths. But it would be a mistake to assume that the increases in power which integrated circuits will bring to the information processing business over the next few years will depend solely on developments in fabrication. While the Japanese companies work to consolidate their position in the manufacturing sector, the American companies will defend their manufacturing base and expand the added value which their industry provides by a continued emphasis on the most sophisticated and software-intensive devices.

Under the Japanese onslaught in fabrication, the Americans found themselves being beaten at the game which they had invented, and this has forced them to concentrate on those areas in which they can exploit their particular strengths. If the Japanese rule the roost in most memory and some standard logic chips, the Americans have a clear lead in microprocessors, microcontrollers and custom logic devices, and US firms are leading the charge along the other main path of semiconductor innovation – the design of integrated circuit logic. Integrated circuit logic devices range from the powerful microprocessors which form the central data processing units of personal computers (PCs) to the simple microcontrollers which direct operations in electronic watches, cameras, microwave ovens and photocopiers. They range from standard devices, which are as much a commodity as memory, through semi-custom devices which are largely standard but which are modified for (or sometimes by) the customer to suit a specific application, to full-custom chips which are designed specifically for the customer.

As is the case with memory, the device used in an application will usually be the smallest and cheapest which will perform the function. The 8 bit devices which ran the first rather slow and unsophisticated generation of PCs would be more than adequate to control any conceivable number of functions on a washing machine or microwave oven and many such appliances still incorporate 4 bit processors. The vast majority of logic devices, therefore, are comparatively simple chips with modest performance. Even simple control functions, however, tend to be specific to the application and the devices involved are therefore much more likely to be custom-made than are memory chips, which will indiscriminately store anything.

Custom memory chips – such as the so-called mask ROMs (a read-only memory, in which a program can be 'hard wired' into the circuit via the design of the uppermost mask in the photomask set) which are used, for example, in video games – do exist but memory devices on the whole leave the factory with no particular functional designation. Most logic circuits are different and the makers often need to have a much closer relationship with their customers who, in effect, become partners in the circuit's design. Once they have provided a satisfactory solution to one of their customer's problems, the custom logic chip makers have often established an advantageous 'inside track' in that customer's business because they understand the requirements better than a competitor who has never worked with that customer.

The logic game is not about production yields; indeed the chip vendor may subcontract the manufacture to an outsider, a so-called 'silicon foundry', which offers no design service at all. Rather, it is about ingenuity in design, a quick understanding of the customer's problem and the delivery of elegant solutions. It is an intellectually labour intensive business, although logic designers can call upon libraries of design modules which they can piece together to deliver a more particular function, and the customer's perception of the value added in the design process is often very high. For this reason, selling the more sophisticated integrated circuits can often be a much more profitable business than the trade in commodity circuits.

Although the Japanese-dominated memory chips account for most of the industry's production volume, logic devices account for more than half of the value, perhaps giving the Americans an opportunity to redress the balance. And some of the leading US firms have also redrawn the rules under which they are prepared to play the game. Whereas most logic chip makers design their products to fit the customer's application, some vendors are in the fortunate position of having customers designing products around their proprietary devices. The best examples of this phenomenon are to be found among the makers of microprocessors and, among these, the Intel Corporation is the classic case.

Intel held a 50 per cent share in the world microprocessor market in 1991 and such is the clout wielded by the company in the PC market that computer retailers and even users commonly describe their machines using the last three digits of Intel's five-digit product number. Thus, a PC system, perhaps made by IBM, Goldstar or Sanyo, which uses as its central processor Intel's 80386 microprocessor, will be referred to simply as 'a 386 machine'.

If step changes in memory result in great increases in data storage capacity, the shift from, say, a 16 bit to a 32 bit microprocessor results in a considerable increase in the speed or power with which a computer processes data. The speed of logic circuits generally increases in line with the degree of integration; as the circuitry shrinks, the device gets faster. The design of each successive generation of microprocessor, however, becomes more complex. The description 8 bit, 16 bit or 32 bit, when applied to a microprocessor or controller, refers to the size of the data 'word' (with the bits being analogous to letters) which the device can handle with each switching operation. If this is analogous to the cubic capacity of a car's engine, the 'clock speed', measured in megahertz, or millions of cycles per second, can perhaps be compared with its rpm. The two largely determine how fast the circuit will make any series of calculations and how quickly the computer will come up with the answers, move the text around, or whatever. The 80286 is a 16 bit chip, whereas the 80386 and 80486 are both 32 bit devices. As such, the last three digits of the device's model number also effectively define in the consumer's mind the capabilities of the machines which are built around them, with a 386 being generally known to be faster than a 286, the 486 being faster than either, and so on.

Until the advent of the 80386, Intel regularly sold licences for the use of its proprietary designs to other manufacturers. The idea behind this was known as 'second sourcing', which was a strategy aimed at assuaging customers' anxieties about becoming too dependent upon a single source of supply for vital components. If an Intel chip was available from a number of suppliers, the prospective customers were more likely to be prepared to make the commitment to the Intel design and design the chip into their products. In this way, although Intel would suffer opportunity costs in terms of revenues lost to second sources, it would receive the design royalties and the general popularization of its chip in relation to a competing product from, for example, Motorola, could in fact increase Intel's direct sales revenues. The object of the exercise was to make Intel's microprocessors the industry's standards and it was an exercise in which Intel was notably successful.

The 80286, which was second sourced by Advanced Micro Devices, was the last of Intel's microprocessors to be licensed to other manufacturers in this way. With the launch of the 80386 in 1988, Intel abandoned second sourcing because its position in the market was then sufficiently well-established to achieve scale economies in its own production that allowed it to compete, profitably, on price as well as on incremental innovation in device design. The company decided, in other words, to keep more of the benefits of the designs which it had created for itself. Not only did Intel monopolize the production of its proprietary chips, it also started to sell complete PCs, on an original equipment manufacturer (OEM) basis, to vendors who would market them under their own brands. In this, and in its sales of printed circuit boards which incorporate its proprietary products, Intel started to compete with some of its customers. All of this reflected the company's increasingly powerful position as a technological semi-monopolist, a position in the microcomputer world analogous to that held by IBM in mainframes.

Those whose products and processes become industry standards in information technology (IT) naturally tend to refer to one another when developing new products. The most popular operating system in PCs, Microsoft's *Windows*, was written to operate on machines based on microprocessors from Intel's 'X86' family. The result has been that large numbers of PC users, particularly in businesses which are large purchasers of standard multi-tasking software and whose IT managers often avoid risky or controversial purchasing decisions, now use applications programs which operate in the *Windows* environment on 386-based machines. The giants of the industry thus feed off one another's success.

There is no doubt that it has been the excellence of these products which has enabled their makers to become so powerful within the industry but technological semi-monopolies based on the achievement of industry standard status can, if unchecked, have anti-competitive effects and corrode technical progress. However, although Intel's position in the industry will no doubt remain a very powerful one, there is little chance that it will be unchallenged, or that lack of competition in the semiconductor logic business will lead to technical stagnation. The big challenge to Intel's near-hegemony in the microprocessor world will come from the same source as the threat to the hegemony of the PC in the business world. For some years now, powerful micro-workstations based on RISC (reduced instruction set computing) chips, have been increasingly used by the more demanding users of micro-computer systems and all the signs are that workstations and PCs are on a collision course. The prices of the basic entry-level workstations sold by companies like Sun Microsystems are now comparable with those of the most powerful offerings of the PC vendors and, as workstation volumes build and prices fall, and more sophisticated, user-friendly but processing power-hungry PC software is developed, PCs will become more powerful and the computing power on offer from workstations will start to seem more relevant to users of the hitherto less demanding applications. The attractions to the workstation vendors of capturing a slice of the huge PC market are obvious, as is the potential for volume-driven cost reductions if they succeed in doing so. RISC chips, then, will provide a competitive spur for Intel for the foreseeable future and will ensure that in microprocessors, as elsewhere, competition will continue to force the pace of development.

There are also good reasons to suppose that the pattern of functional specialization as between the two semiconductor superpowers, the USA and Japan, will continue to prevail. The Americans will not abandon efforts to catch Japan in the fabrication race; the likes of NEC and Hitachi will not give up the chase in the markets for software-intensive, design-rich devices. Intense international competition will, therefore, continue. But the increased *de facto* polarization of the industry into two camps, which have their own specialist infrastructures and intense internal competition, has probably created a situation in which the pace of development in these technologies is as fast as it could be.

In the run-up to the end of the century, the manufacture of commodity devices with line-widths approaching 0.2 microns will, under the relentless pressure of the Japanese fabricators, become a routine reality and these and an ever-widening range of more powerful, ingenious and specialized integrated circuit devices, mainly American in inspiration, will provide the basic feedstock of all information processing hardware.

The Search for Speed

Speed in the world of information technology is measured in a range of esoteric units. Hertz, MIPS, and FLOPS are part of the everyday parlance of information technology specialists, and units of time so minuscule that they defy the imagination are used as benchmarks. The picosecond, used to describe the switching time of some high-speed integrated circuits, is a unit of time which is fairly exotic even to members of that profession. The speed of light is impressive by anybody's standards – nothing can move faster – but even a photon would travel less than a millimetre in a picosecond.

Within the internal processes of an integrated circuit, the need for all this speed is due to the sheer complexity of the operations which the circuit must perform in a very short time. Even as simple a task as the formation of the letter 'A', for example, requires eight bits of data to be registered, as the standard binary code for that character is 00110001. The more elaborate the capabilities of the software, the more instructions the processors and memory circuits in the computer will have to handle. A simple program can run very fast on a modest processor but as soon as the demands which the software places on the chip reach a certain level, the processing time starts to stretch out and soon becomes unacceptable. And the users' demands for speed and for user-friendliness (which usually equates with software complexity and militates against speed) continue to grow.

It is ironic that processing power of which the scientists working on the Manhattan Project could only have dreamed is held in disdain by the schoolboys and word processor operators of the 1990s. Brief excerpts from a review of the Brother BCD5486 in August 1992's *PC Direct* magazine, chosen more or less at random, give a flavour of what the modern user requires:

... a machine which turns in a rapid performance. Hard disk read and write speeds are very impressive, with an average access time of 11.37ms, not to mention a data transfer rate of 1186Kb/s, and the SuperVGA display is also extremely fast.

This system is a sensible choice for anyone who needs a powerful, standalone DTP or Cad engine. With a large hard disk or two in the internal bays, there would be enough space for all your fonts and files.

... this is a seriously heavy piece of kit. The BCD5486 is built around a 33MHz 486 chip, supported by an additional cache and built into a box that has room for copious Ram, disk drives and expansion cards.

The applications mentioned in this review are both very demanding of computing power. Computer-aided design (CAD), until a few years ago, was a mainframe-based technology which was used only for major projects in major corporations; now small engineering shops, architects offices and fitted-kitchen suppliers routinely use PC-based CAD systems. Desk-top publishing (DTP) is these days commonly perceived as little more than sophisticated word processing (which, given the sophistication of the better word-processing packages, is all it is) and is used in a multitude of small businesses. So here we have an extremely powerful small computer system, priced at around $10,000, aimed at familiar, workaday applications and for use by ordinary people, not nuclear physicists. And one of its outstanding characteristics, as the review mentions repeatedly, is that it is very fast.

Speed in computer systems is a function of a variety of factors, some of which are concerned with the efficiency of the software itself. If the software instructs the computer to perform a task in an unnecessarily complicated way, it will obviously take more time to do so than it would if the processes were simplified. The internal architecture of the micro-processor central processing unit (CPU) and its switching speed are major determinants of the speed of the computer hardware itself and advances in CPU speeds have been dramatic. The original 4 bit micro-processors used in first generation PCs processed data at rates measured in thousands of instructions per second. The 32 bit machines of the early 1990s can manage 50 MIPS, or 50 million instructions per second, and engineers working for the industry leader, Intel, cheerfully predict that, by the year 2000, microprocessors packing 100 million transistors will be capable of two billion instructions per second, twice as fast as most supercomputers of the early 1990s.

However fast the processor, the distance which its signals have to travel, and the time which it has to wait for responses, as it sorts data from different sources, makes calculations and issues instructions to peripherals such as monitors, printers and disk drives, all have an influence on the speed of the total system. The dramatic slowing of computer systems which results from all this fetching and carrying of data between storage devices and logic chips is known in the trade as 'the I/O (input/output) bottleneck'. If the whole of a program can be stored in RAM (or some other integrated circuit 'firmware') rather than being stored on a hard or, worse still, a floppy disk, the bottleneck will be cleared and the program will operate much more quickly. Shorten the distances, speed the flow and get rid of such crude electro-mechanical devices and you can build a computer that is really fast. When you have done this, however, you will probably use your new-found power in rendering some mundane task easier or quicker. To do so is not to squander talents; this is what electronics is increasingly about.

We have already seen how developments in integrated circuit fabrication will enable us to get rid of most of the troublesome electro-mechanical memory devices in a few years' time and, when this happens, systems will get faster. But there are always some applications, often far removed from the humble PC, for which fast is never fast enough and the electronics industry will continue to seek to make circuits which will run faster, as the physical chemistry of their innards allows their frantic signals to run around at the speed of light or something close to it.

One major thrust of such efforts concerns the development of alternatives to silicon as an integrated circuit substrate material. The most promising material in this regard is gallium arsenide (GaAs), whose molecular structure in most conditions allows electrons to pass through it five to seven times as fast as through silicon. It is, however, a rather peculiar material. Arsenic atoms have a habit of evaporating and it is therefore very difficult to form a compound with a ratio of exactly 50:50 gallium to arsenic, and levels of impurity which have long since been banished in intrinsic silicon are still the rule in gallium arsenide crystals. Small electronic devices with very high switching speeds (2 or 3 picoseconds) have been made, using gallium arsenide and related materials produced using thin film technology, but the mass production of large-scale integrated circuits in these materials which, by comparison with silicon, are impure, soft and very difficult to work, is not possible with current technology. Even by the end of the century, it is expected that integrated circuits in gallium arsenide and similar materials will still be lagging six or seven generations behind their silicon counterparts.

Experiments continue with Josephson junctions – devices utilizing a powerful but difficult to exploit concept which makes use of super-conductivity at a microscopic level in electronic circuits – and other exotic technologies and materials but the odds are that the cultivation of speed-enhancing techniques in electronic circuits between now and the end of the century will bear most fruit in the well-established development path for silicon. For some specialist applications, how-ever, the phenomenal speed of gallium arsenide devices has already made them very useful and, when they are more commonly available, high-speed computing and communications will take another of those leaps forward.

As the physical limits of silicon are approached and the industry wrestles with the problems of increasing electron mobility in other materials and by other means, the possibilities of using light beams to replace electron flows in integrated circuits are also being investigated. Light, which travels at about 300,000 km per second in a vacuum, travels more slowly through other media. In an optical fibre, it travels at about three-quarters of its ultimate speed, but still considerably faster than electrons ever move in the conducting parts of semiconductors. While the idea of optical integrated circuits seems bizarre, some of the technologies which could be used to create them are already in use in everyday electronic equipment. The light-emitting diodes (LEDs) used in the mass of little indicator lights which are fitted to television sets and other domestic electrical equipment and the laser pick-ups used in CD players are both opto-electronic devices.

The basic elements required in the construction of an optical integrated circuit (i.e. the parts analogous to the gates and lines in an electronic integrated circuit) are semiconductor lasers or light-emitting diodes, light-receptor diodes and some form of optical wave guide. The way in which optical integrated circuits will probably be de-veloped is similar to the way in which electronic integrated circuits evolved. Initially, it is likely that hybrid circuits, which include the opto-electronic components such as the gallium arsenide and indium phosphate LEDs and photo-receptors, will be superimposed onto a substrate in which the semiconductor or quartz glass wave guide has already been laid. This is because it will take time to resolve the fabrication problems caused by the widely differing processes required for manufacturing and handling the various components and materials. Once the problems have been resolved, however, it is expected that monolithic optical integrated circuits, in which the various components are formed sequentially on a substrate like those in an electronic integrated circuit, will start to appear. The pace of current research suggests that the first modest optical integrated circuits of this kind will start to appear in the early part of the next decade. This will open the door to another jump in computer processing speeds – perhaps late in the first decade of the new century.

It seems very likely, then, that the silicon revolution, which got started at Bell Labs in 1948 and gained such tremendous momentum with the evolution of the integrated circuit, will be entering its final phase in the last years of this century. New technologies which take advantage of the strange opto-electronic properties of exotic materials such as gallium arsenide and indium phosphate and which depend on the ability to lay minuscule wave guides for light beams will be waiting in the wings and the design and fabrication of the very fastest integrated circuits will enter a new phase.

Most of the incremental increases in computing speed which will have been achieved in the meantime, however, will have been as a result of the stretching of silicon-based fabrication technologies and enhancements in the internal logic of semiconductor devices. The removal of many of the weak electro-mechanical links in the computing chain, again a function of the advancement of integrated circuit technology, will also be a crucial factor in the speed of systems.

It would be difficult to overstate the importance of the role of the integrated circuit in the development of information processing hardware. It is central to information machines of all kinds and its development will continue to be critical to the enhancement of their capabilities. We cannot guess what types of information equipment will be in use in the early years of the next century unless we have some idea as to how integrated circuits will develop in the intervening years. Fortunately, the technological and competitive dynamics of the semiconductor industry have become very clear in recent years and the indications are that, although progress will continue to produce some spectacular innovations in applications, the development of the components will be along fairly predictable lines. The path which this development will take over the next few years suggests that the mainstream hardware of 2005 will be much faster than today's machines and that it will still be based on souped-up silicon devices. Thereafter, the front-line will probably be occupied by the optical exotica which we see in embryonic form today.

Corning versus Cape Canaveral

Ever since mankind started to communicate and process information, efforts have been made, in most of the related disciplines, to speed the flow. The images of Pheidippides, the original message-bearing marathon runner, of Paul Revere, of the naval frigate sailing with dispatches (indeed, 'with dispatch'), of the post-chaise, the Pony Express and the motor cycle courier are all synonymous with the transmission of information with more or less reckless haste.

Signal fires, smoke signals, jungle drums, flags, mirrors, and semaphore arms all represent past attempts to circumvent the problems of the physical conveyance of the written word, whose slowness often had dire consequences, but it was not until the advent of the electric telegraph in 1837 that any reliable alternative to one or other form of the mail was found. Initial trials of the telegraph suggested that the problem had been banished for ever, because electrical transmission, for a Morse code operator sending over a relatively short, low-capacity land line, was, to all intents and purposes, instantaneous. The pioneers of oceanic telegraph cables, however, were soon to discover that, although electricity can travel at speeds close to that of light, it very often does not. So concerned were they with the physical and mechanical specification of the thousands of miles of cable which were laid by Brunel's Great Eastern, that they failed to realize that the chemical purity of the copper core really mattered and that impurities in the core interfered with the cable's electrical performance.

This problem was easily soluble and the transmission delays which resulted from the limitations on the speed at which electrons could travel along the pure copper wire, an excellent conductor which was subsequently laid in huge amounts around the world, were of no consequence to the telegraph operator, nor have they ever seriously inconvenienced users of the telegraph's direct descendent, the telephone. The arrival of solid state electronics, however, and the new materials used in electronic devices, were soon to place new problems with transmission media on the technical agenda, as situations were created in which a signal which travelled at a significant fraction of the speed of light was no longer fast enough.

Probably nobody would have ever worried too much about the speed at which electrons travel through conductors had it not been for the invention of the electronic computer and its associated paraphernalia. In the pre-computer era, human beings were the originators and recipients of all messages and the telephone, which allowed them to do so instantaneously, looked like a technology upon which it would be difficult to improve. In many ways that was true and remains so but the data transmission requirements of computers, both internally and externally, have created problems of a higher order of magnitude.

Speed in the microscopic world of the integrated circuit is measured in the picoseconds or nanoseconds of switching or access times; in the macroscopic world of telecommunications, it is measured in bits per second or Baud. At the level of the electronic or optical particle, the two are essentially aspects of the same thing but the subtle difference in the way in which data transmission speeds are described reflects the differing pre-occupations of the semiconductor and telecommunications engineers. Semiconductor engineers are concerned with developing fast computers, whereas the objective of the communications engineer has always been to create a transmission medium which will convey as much tariff-paying traffic as possible. Insofar as the speed with which a signal passes through a transmission medium is a major determinant of how many signals can be sent through it, the telecommunications engineer is justified in seeing speed and capacity as being more or less the same thing.

The potential demand for telecommunications transmission capacity today seems virtually limitless because more people are now routinely transmitting more, and more complex, data to more places in an ever greater variety of ways. An accounting entry sent to a bank's computer, the pictures and sounds of a television programme, a telephone call or a computer program can all be reduced to streams of analog or digitally encoded data and all become potential subjects of telecommunications flows. The world communications network which copes with these flows is a complex hybrid system which contains very modern equipment alongside the relics of virtually every type of electrical transmission device employed since the mid-nineteenth century. The growth in demand for communications services and the availability of technology which can provide them at greatly reduced costs will, over the next few years, interact in a way which will ensure that much of the uneconomic, obsolete capacity in the system will be replaced.

All transmission systems involve the generation and sensing of electromagnetic wave patterns, either through some form of cable, or through the atmosphere or space. Different media are suitable for different situations, depending on the nature of the traffic and the location of the user. The various media also have their own particular advantages and disadvantages. Of the many high speed, high volume transmission media currently in use, there are perhaps two whose increasingly related development tracks will bring about the most significant changes in the technological infrastructure over the next decade or so: satellites and optical fibre.

The idea of the communications satellite was first suggested by the science fiction writer Arthur C. Clarke in *Wireless World* in October 1945 and became a practical possibility after the launch of Sputnik I in 1957. The best known type of telecommunications satellite is the equatorial geostationary type, which orbits at an altitude of 35,786 km, an altitude which gives it an orbit time of 23 hours 56 minutes and 4 seconds, exactly the time which the earth takes to complete one rotation. (The shortfall of 3 minutes and 56 seconds relative to the familiar 24-hour day is due to the deflection effect caused by the Earth's orbit around the sun.) Less well known is the geosynchronous type, which describes a similar orbit but at an angle to the equator and which therefore seems, when viewed from the ground, to move north and south along a constant line of longitude. Equatorial geostationary satellites work well for countries which occupy relatively low latitudes but countries like Russia, where most of the land is above 55 degrees latitude, and which extends for 170 degrees east to west, have places which, as a result of their geography, cannot 'see' a geostationary satellite and instead use a number of low-earth orbit (LEO) satellites with polar rather than equatorial orbits.

Satellites have certain advantages which will ensure their continuing place in the communications armoury, even when faced with competition from greatly improved terrestrial systems. The long 'reach' which they have as a result of their high altitudes means that the signals which they relay can be received simultaneously over a very wide area. Because the satellite is a broadcast medium which can carry a variety of transponders, multiple simultaneous inputs and outputs are possible. Satellites have near-infinite flexibility of signal routeing (relative to cables) within the area of their 'footprints'; any contracting satellite users can aim their transmitter or receiver dishes at the appropriate part of the sky and immediately make use of the medium. They are safe from earthbound disasters, such as fires and earthquakes and even the effects of insulation-eating rats, insects and birds and cable-snagging fishing trawlers, which can be enormously disruptive of terrestrial and undersea cable systems. In 1990, by a statistically improbable chance, five long-distance communications cables in different parts of the world were severed simultaneously.

Satellites have their own problems. Their signals weaken when passing through atmospheric water vapour and they are therefore, to some extent, affected by the weather, as anybody who has watched satellite television during a thunderstorm will know. Satellite signals are also prone to solar radiation interference and the vehicles themselves are not entirely safe from the ravages of the elements. Old satellites retrieved by space shuttles have been found to be suffering from quite severe damage from bombardment by the multitude of particles of solid matter which fly around in apparently empty space.

Currently, satellite communications work from ground station to satellite to ground station, and the transmission lag which results from the quarter of a second or so which it takes for the signal to travel the round trip of at least 71,572 km to the high orbit geostationary vehicles can cause real problems with some kinds of equipment and can make it difficult to talk on international telephone lines. In future, satellite-to-satellite communication will also be possible and this will shorten the chain of communication in some cases. Motorola has proposed the so-called 'Iridium' system, named for the 77 electrons orbiting the iridum nucleus, originally conceived as a network of 77 low orbit satellites linked together to create a global system for mobile communications, combining the advantages of satellite-to-satellite links and the reduced transmission distances resulting from the low orbits. This system, with a reduced number of satellites, is expected to be in place in 1996.

The developmental history of optical fibre has been concerned with the battle to minimize signal loss resulting from impurities in the material used. Thick window-grade glass distorts light very badly and, when it is made any thicker than about 200 mm, it effectively absorbs or reflects back most of the light which shines into it, because it contains ions of impurities such as iron and nickel. If the ultimate intention is to transmit a signal through glass which is several thousand kilometres in thickness, glass of a very high purity is required and it is in the manufacture of such a material that one of the major critical paths in the development of optical communications is to be found.

When Corning produced the first low-loss optical fibre in 1970, they achieved a 20 dB per kilometre rate of loss, which meant that the signal emerging from the end of a kilometre length of the fibre had one hundredth of the strength which it had when it was fed into the other end. Since then the pace of development has been very impressive and fibres with losses of only 0.2 dB/km are now used in long-distance communications links which are capable of carrying 1.6 gigabits per second, or 23,040 standard 64 kilobit voice channels. The purity of this material is such that the loss rates are now approaching the theoretical limit for quartz glass, which is reckoned to be 0.15 dB/km.

This is impressive enough, but long-distance transmissions using such fibre still require signal boosters to be inserted at regular intervals, as is the case with traditional coaxial electrical transmission cables. In the case of optical fibres, these intervals are currently around 50 kilometres. Development is proceeding, however, with alternatives to quartz glass, such as zirconium fluoride, which have much lower loss rates, with theoretical limits as low as 0.001 dB/km which, if achieved, would make it possible to lay a boosterless optical fibre link across the Pacific Ocean. This kind of material could be in mass production by 2005, although systemic incompatibility with existing quartz glass capacity could delay its widespread use.

The wavelength of the light in the fibre is crucial to the loss rate over distance and is itself a function of the internal structure of the fibre. Optical fibre today is generally made by inserting an ingot of high-purity quartz glass into a tube of glass which has a lower refractive index and stretching the two out over a huge distance to produce a fine fibre with a differentiated core and cladding, This is called multimode fibre. The light waves in the fibre bounce off the cladding and travel down the fibre in a wave pattern which is determined by the charac-teristics of the fibre and the frequency of the input signal. The longer the wavelength which can be achieved, the lower will be the rate of loss to scattering and absorption in the fibre. The early Corning fibre had a wavelength of 0.63 microns; fibre in common use today has a wave-length of 1.3 microns and 1.55 micron fibre is predicted by the end of the decade.

By using improved lasers, which generate coherent light in a very narrow spectrum, and using single mode fibre and frequency multiplex-ing, it is confidently predicted that it will soon be possible to increase the transmission capacity of a single optical fibre so that each hair-breadth is capable of handling up to 1 terabit – that is, one trillion, or

10^{12} bits, per second, the equivalent of 16 million telephone voice channels. Such fibres have already been produced in laboratory quantities and, although everyday availability of this kind of transmission capacity still looks somewhat futuristic, optical fibre's technical capacity has been increasing tenfold every four years or so and seems likely to do so for the rest of the century, to give rates of perhaps 100 gigabits per second by the year 2000. If such a rate of progress were to continue, 1 terabit per second would be a routine technical, if not commercial, reality by our horizon year of 2005.

In handling such prodigious flows of data, new technologies for handling the mundane problems of signal switching, filtering and dividing and joining fibres will be necessary. The development of such techniques is expected to follow the exponential path necessary to more or less (but perhaps not quite) keep up with the developments in the capabilities of the fibre itself. It is currently possible, for example, to splice 16 fibres into one or one into 16; by the end of the decade one into 256 should be possible. Other developments in optical signal handling techniques are expected to enable engineers to eliminate many of the opto-electronic devices which are currently incorporated into optical communications circuits, leading the way to more fully optical systems.

Whatever the precise development path of optical communications technology, it is clear that by the turn of the century, optical fibre will have the potential to provide colossal transmission capacity in any application which can be connected to some form of cable. All data trunk routes will be of optical fibre and any other applications which require an easy-to-install high capacity data link will also increasingly use the material. As a data conduit between pieces of equipment which are more or less fixed in position, optical fibre seems set to sweep aside all competing technologies. Its potential power, it seems, is only just beginning to be tapped and it is highly likely that, within the next decade, shortages of capacity in long range transmission lines will have been banished for ever. According to Professor Peter Cochrane of British Telecom:

> The release of full fibre bandwidth will bring about the realisation of the transmission engineer's dream: near infinite bandwidth, near zero path loss, near zero path distortion, near zero material usage, near zero power consumption, near zero cost (quoted in *Intermedia*, November–December 1992).

Such a statement sounds absolute and final but, although there can be little or no doubt that optical fibre links will create this kind of capacity, it is perhaps less clear what it will be used for and how fibre and satellite will compete and complement one another. Bruce Crockett, President of Comsat Corporation, addresses the issue thus:

> We must ask ourselves, 'What does the customer want?' And the answer is that the customer doesn't care if he or she gets information via a mobile or fixed capability, or fibre optic or satellite, for that matter ... The convergence of telecommunication, computer, broadcasting and information technologies is creating demands for open global networks capable of supporting a variety of voice, data and video services (remarks made to Telecom '91, October 1991, quoted in *Satellite Communications*, December 1991).

This is undoubtedly true and it is the satellite industry, which is conscious of being on the defensive in the face of the fibre onslaught, which is taking the initiative in finding how profitable synergies can be achieved. NASA's advanced communications technology satellite (ACTS) programme is intended to address many of the problems, such as rain fade, which routinely impede satellite communications, and to increase the bandwidth which a satellite can provide to a user. In so doing, the project is intended to facilitate the full network connectivity to which Mr Crockett refers.

The trump cards which the satellite industry holds are very small aperture terminals (VSATs) and increasingly intelligent satellites. However easy it may become to lay optical fibre (by comparison with the cumbersome coaxial cable), small fixed or mobile satellite stations will continue to have advantages where the user is either mobile or isolated from a centre of population. The VSAT first emerged in the late 1970s and is designed to be used either in isolated locations or in situations where large communications capacity is required on a temporary basis. The technology is now in its third generation, offers great operational flexibility and has been the fastest growing segment of the satellite business. In the 25 years since the launch of Early Bird, satellite transponder capacity has increased about 2,000 times but their ability to cope with large data flows is still modest by comparison with that of optical fibre.

Once satellites are capable of providing bandwidth even distantly comparable with that delivered by fibre, however, it will be possible for

VSAT users to link up, through satellites and terrestrial switching hubs, to mainstream fibre optics networks, thus supplementing the global fibre network in places where it cannot be extended for economic or logistical reasons. The intelligent satellite is a logical response to the highly variable requirements of VSATs. On-board processing capability in the satellite will aim and activate antennae and allocate transponder capacity in response to the needs of the VSATs on the ground and the networks with which they connect.

Satellites and their VSATs, then, have the capability of bringing a degree of flexibility to the global communications network which it would lack if it were dependent upon cable systems alone, but some expert observers suggest that the intrinsic characteristics of satellites and optical fibre ought logically to be utilized in a manner which is at odds with the way in which, at this stage, the market seems likely to be carved up between them. George Gilder, a senior fellow of the Hudson Institute, suggests that:

> The 'phone will become wireless, as mobile as a watch and as personal as a wallet; computer video will run over fiber-optic cables in a switched digital system as convenient as the telephone is today (quoted in *Satellite Communications*, December 1991, p. 16).

In other words, the nature of the personalized mobile telephone of the future suggests that it should be a medium of the airways, whereas the spectrum-guzzling high quality video transmissions which currently battle for space in the broadcasting universe could more sensibly be transmitted through those intimidating fibre networks – a complete inversion of the conventional wisdom.

Certainly there exist satellite systems – in the form of Inmarsat, with more than 10,000 users world-wide, and the newer Geostar and Qualcomm services, which provide information links – which could, without major reconfiguration, form the basis of world-wide mobile communications networks. Any satellite system which can provide data on the positions of mobile customers, be they in ships, aircraft or trucks, is capable of communicating with those customers in other ways. Such services could easily include message switching, putting the satellite industry into contention in the rapidly growing mobile communications business. Such a service could be provided by satellite technology or a combination of satellite and fibre and, if all telephone communications eventually become personal, cordless and mobile, as many believe they will, the stakes in the battle between the celestial and terrestrial messengers could be very large indeed.

It is interesting to reflect that the telecommunications monopolies grew up providing point-to-point communication using cables while the radio and television companies were given franchises to broadcast material of general interest over the airwaves because it was clear at the time that the technologies at their disposal were the most suitable for their respective purposes. By the beginning of the twenty-first century, the technological distinctions will be completely blurred. and technological and functional convergence will mean that the battles for these huge businesses will be determined by other factors. Here again, the developmental paths of the relevant technologies are tolerably predictable; the commercial outcome is anything but.

The Optical Bodleian

A technology a thousand years old still dominates the mass storage of information but it is likely that its dominance will, in significant ways, come under threat within the time horizon of this book.

The printed word has such a long history that the management of the accumulated wealth of information, thought and knowledge fossilized on paper has become an industry of some size. Government, administration and scholarship are equally dependent upon the information stored on countless sheets of paper, whether they be personnel records, business accounts or centuries-old books and newspapers stored in library stacks. Whole professions (filing clerks, archivists and librarians) have grown up solely for the purpose of ordering the storage of this material and assisting users in locating it.

In technological terms, there has not, until very recently, been any viable alternative to this approach, and paper has, in fact, always been an excellent information storage medium. The huge increase in the output of all parts of the information sector in recent years has, however, started to shift the balance of power in information storage away from paper and towards electronic media. Such has been the dominance of paper that it is still often the case that the only effective permanent record of information produced through an electronic medium is in print. This book is being written using a computer and its entire text and graphics will be stored on a magnetic disk, but nobody other than the author and editor is ever likely to read it on a computer screen. Book publishing is unlikely to become totally electronicized in the foreseeable future but there is a small and growing minority of people which is becoming accustomed to doing some of its searching for information electronically and the day when reference libraries start to be less congested with human traffic is perhaps not far off.

The early devices for the storage of computer-generated data offered no competition at all to the printed word. The punch-cards and tapes used could be read, to a limited extent, by experts but it was not until the advent of the word processor and the PC that access to electronically recorded data (other than sound recorded on magnetic tape) was of any interest to ordinary users of information. The development of electronic storage media and the proliferation of equipment through which it can be accessed and manipulated, however, has resulted in a gradual erosion of popular resistance to the use of such data. The book, magazine or 300 dots-per-inch laser printer output is still preferable to the fuzzy and ephemeral display on the screen but the idea of electronic reading is less strange to us than it used to be.

The impressive developments in integrated circuit memory described above will have a considerable effect on the way in which computers are used and modest amounts of data (say, 1 or 2 gigabytes) will be stored in a few years' time but, when somebody decides that the time has come to take a back-up copy of a major library or national archive resource, it is unlikely that they will decide to load it into an integrated circuit memory board. For really massive data storage of this kind, or even for the storage of the amounts of archival and semi-archival data which are accumulated in the network file servers of large organizations, integrated circuit memory is unlikely to be the storage medium of choice for the foreseeable future.

Early computers used magnetic tape for mass storage. Tape drives still exist for some applications (although they are much more sophisticated than those which whirled around on computers in 1960s movies) but disk storage of one kind or another has become the familiar norm. Flexible, or floppy disks are used in applications where portability matters more than speed of access but the late 1980s and early 1990s have been the age of the hard disk. Hard, or Winchester, disks (named after the IBM plant where they were invented) are the habitual mass memory companions of the main RAM memory in PCs. A typical PC today might have 2 megabytes of RAM for use where really rapid access to data is important but will also tote, say, 80 megabytes of hard disk capacity for the convenient storage of large numbers of files. Disk drives of this type can now be crammed into the corners of notebook computers and have become a familiar feature of office and even domestic life. Much larger, industrial-strength versions, of course, are the mainstay memories of large computer systems.

The life history of hard disk drives is the now familiar one of exponential improvements along a more or less linear developmental path but a brief examination of how they work is enough to induce incredulity that they ever function at all. So close to the surface of the disk does the magnetic head which reads and writes the magnetic data spots 'fly' that it has been compared to a scale model of a Boeing 747 flying at supersonic speed at an altitude of 2 centimetres. It is a tribute to the precision with which the disk platters are made that the catastrophic disk 'crashes' which reduce computer users to jelly are as unusual as they are. Developments in platter and head design have created, in the humble Winchester, a heroic and surprisingly reliable technology and its many supporters believe that it still has significant development potential, perhaps using a technology in which the magnetic 'domain' of the disk is manipulated in the perpendicular dimension and its storage capacity is thus greatly expanded. Magnetic disks also still offer the fastest data access times of any non-integrated circuit medium and it is likely that several more generations of smaller, faster and more capacious Winchester disks will appear before the technology finally rides off into the sunset of obsolescence. For the purposes of storing really huge volumes of data, however, electricity is probably giving way to light as the energy source of the cutting edge.

Optical disk data storage has become a commonplace phenomenon in the form of the audio compact disk and such is its storage capacity that larger but still quite handy versions of the disk can hold hour-long video programmes in full colour. There is also a steadily growing 'bibliography' of data versions of the compact disk (CD ROMs) which hold masses of small computer programs, or large archival sources, such as atlases and encyclopedias, which can be summoned up onto the computer screen using a cheap disk reader. The difference between these disks and the magnetic hard disk, of course, is that, whereas the hard disk user can save and retrieve data at will, the data in the CD ROM or its audio or video cousins is recorded onto the disk by the manufacturer. The Holy Grail of the optical disk makers is a disk which is fully recordable and erasable and has very fast data access times, while maintaining its huge storage capacity. Such a disk could be all things to all men; it could displace not only the ubiquitous Winchester disk but also audio and video tape recorders.

Mass production of the audio CD was established in the early 1980s, by which time the manufacturers, led by Philips and Sony, had achieved satisfactory production yields in the tricky process of pressing the microscopic pits used to encode the data into the plastic disk. The presence or absence of these physical holes in the disk surface is sensed by the photo-receptor in the semiconductor laser pick-up and the resulting signal is translated by the machine's circuitry into high quality sound (or video, or data, or whatever). It is the ability of the laser pick-up to sense the presence or absence of very small holes at a very high speed which makes the whole thing work and gives the disk its large storage capacity. The pits on the conventional optical disk surface, however, cannot be filled in and re-excavated by any existing kind of disk reader/recorder and so the data on the disk is a once-and-for-all affair.

Provided, however, that the surface of the disk can be marked in some way so that the laser pick-up can differentiate between the presence and absence of something, it matters little what that something is and the physical pressing of a pit is not the only way of achieving this. This realization led to numerous research projects, using different methods of writing, and erasing, optically recognizable spots on disk surfaces. Three different approaches have been taken. One, used in the current generation of WORM (Write Once Read Many (times)) disk, employs a pulsed laser beam to burn physical holes in the disk surface, a method which produces a viable recordable disk but not one on which data can be erased and re-recorded. Another, the phase-change technique, uses the laser beam to heat up spots on the surface of a disk whose surface was coated with a material whose reflective characteristics can be altered and then reversed by the application of heat.

The third, the magneto-optical method, takes advantage of two strange physical phenomena. The polarity of the magnetic fields of some materials can be altered by external intervention when they are heated to a certain critical temperature, called the Curie temperature, and can be re-reversed when the material is re-heated. This means that it is possible to create very small magnetic fields on a disk surface using a laser beam as a finely focused and controlled heat source. Repetition of the process erases the magnetic 'spots'. As the direction of travel of light is slightly altered by the presence of a magnetic field, by a phenomenon known as the Kerr effect, a reflecting laser pick-up beam can be induced by such a magnetic spot to alter course slightly on its way back to the sensor and to be read as (by inference) positive or negative in its orientation. The absence of the returning beam can then be interpreted by the circuitry as the presence of a spot and the encoded data can be read as if it was a physical pit on the surface. Thus are alterations to the curvature of space-time brought into the mundane world of data storage.

The magneto-optical disk has emerged as the leading technology in the re-recordable disk market but, as has often been the case in the past, the market seems to be waiting for some undefined improvement in performance, price or useability before it is willing to embrace optical mass data storage systems whole-heartedly. It is quite common for the commercial gestation period of an important product to run to a decade or longer, as the product is refined for the mass market and potential users gradually get used to the idea that the product is available and might be useful. Rudimentary optical filing systems became commercially available in the mid-1980s and should, if precedents tell us anything, achieve major market acceptance in the 1990s, although any confusion over standards and compatibility, those old bugbears of the electronics industry, could result in significant setbacks.

The development of the technology itself could, ironically, result in delays in market acceptance as any potential major enhancement which is known of in advance can cause potential users to delay purchases. Each of the competing technologies also has advantages which might become decisively important when particular developmental milestones are reached and which may change the direction of the industry's thinking. The speed advantage of the phase-change disk over its magneto-optical cousin, for example, might become critical once some of its own shortcomings, particularly worries about media durability, have been overcome. But, however technological development, industry politics, economics and consumer psychology may interact to speed or slow mass implementation, optical mass data storage looks like something which, during the 1990s, should achieve the status of what Arthur C. Clarke has called 'a technology whose time has come'. In this context, the creation of a quickly accessible storage medium with massive capacity, should not be viewed as an event occurring in isolation. Enhancements in the speed of computers and in the software used to arrange and access very large amounts of data are likely soon to render such huge storage capacity useful in new ways.

Estimates of optical disk capacities in the next decade are couched in terms of terabytes of data. By the summer of 1992, Bell Labs in

New Jersey had claimed to be able to fit more than half a terabyte of data onto one side of a 12 inch optical disk. A terabyte is a trillion (one with twelve zeros) bytes, or eight trillion bits of data. Similar storage densities, accompanied by very high access and data transfer rates (100 nanoseconds and 1 terabyte per second respectively) are claimed for a new non-disk holographic storage device called holo-store which is still at the prototype stage but which might emerge as a surprise winner within the remaining years of the century. One way or another, it seems almost certain that rapidly accessible terabytes of data will be on call by the turn of the century.

Relating the terabyte disk or hologram to a more familiar collection of data, we can compare these new storage media with a famous example of the still-dominant paper and ink medium. The Bodleian Library, the principal library of Oxford University and a national reference library which has been accumulating material steadily since its origins in 1320, contains 5,567,000 volumes. A back-of-envelope calculation suggests that this might represent, at, say, 125,000 words per volume, about 700 billion words, or, say, four-and-a-half trillion characters. (The average word in this book is 6.45 characters long.) If the whole library could be transferred onto disk at 1 byte per character, the entire Bodleian might be crammed into half a dozen of those early twenty-first century optical disks or holograms.

The advance of optical character recognition (OCR) should render this feat possible with little difficulty and so, provided somebody is prepared to bear the tedium of scanning the entire collection, which the back of our envelope suggests that a dozen people should be able to manage in ten years or so, there is a prospect that the most of the scholarship which has ever been committed to print in the English language could be brought into the electronic domain and stored in a small filing cabinet before the first decade of the new century is out.

The above description might appear, at first glance, to be a simple indulgence in statistical gee-whizzery but the potential implications of such technology, when seen in the context of the other technologies which will be available by that time, are stunning. If copies of the Bodleian, the Library of Congress and Japan's National Diet Library can be mass produced and distributed to libraries everywhere, connected to large professional data networks, or even sold to households like encyclopedias, the whole process of scholarship and research could be revolutionized. It currently takes an average of two hours for readers in the Bodleian to receive a book ordered from the New Library Stack.

When they receive it, they may discover that it does not contain the information which they are seeking and hand it straight back. By 2005 or 2010, as retrieval and indexing systems capable of coping with such huge volumes become commonplace, it should technically be possible for readers to scan not only the catalogues, but the actual text of whole libraries, to identify books (transmogrified into computer files) which contain relevant information and retrieve all or part of the required material within seconds.

The potential for the application of this technology to research and scholarship is exciting but this is not the only area in which something as mundane as mass data storage could have a huge impact. The ability to create massive and easily accessed statistical databases could, for example, have profound implications for the ways in which countries are governed and corporations managed. If the world's great libraries, public archives and statistical databases can be packaged up and sold at affordable prices to anybody anywhere, the implications for countries still hard at work developing their infostructures could be dramatic. The copyright and intellectual property implications, however, would be likely to cause a good deal of discussion between lawyers and legislators and, as usual, it will not be the development path of technology itself which will determine how these capabilities are utilized but rather the preparedness of people, organizations and institutions to adapt to new possibilities.

Towards a New Intelligence?

The technologies described above are the key enabling technologies of the information industry. Their developmental paths are linear and even their timetabling is reasonably predictable. While no area of technology is wholly free from political and commercial constraints, these hardware technologies are evolving in an environment in which the objectives are clear and even the emerging patterns of inter-corporate and international specialization are being at least tacitly accepted. The development process is therefore not, on the whole, politically impeded. On the contrary, competition between the large US and Japanese corporations shows every sign that it will give rise to the kind of exponential developments in information technology described above as inevitably as the space race, which the launch of Sputnik I inaugurated in 1957, put an American on the moon in 1969.

Most of the developmental milestones in the basic enabling technologies are concerned with the understanding of the physical world and the ability to manipulate its substances and forces. Competing solutions to a single problem often exist and it is not unknown for the industry to change its collective mind with regard to which to adopt, with wasteful consequences, but such confusion is usually resolved with reference to objectively measurable criteria. The best machine, in other words, usually wins and, in the world of hardware, it is usually relatively easy to spot the winners.

The basic hardware of computers, communications and data storage provide ever-improving capacity for the manipulation, transmission and storage of data but the ways in which people want to use this capacity create a need for a whole range of 'soft' technologies, procedures and standards whose performance is much less measurable against objective criteria. As the soft technologies and standards are crucial to the successful operation of information systems and as the costs of development, and the costs of failure, in this area can be so high, the soft area is much more susceptible to institutional and political vagaries and political pressures.

The determination of industry standards sounds like a very dreary pursuit but there is very little in information technology which can advance far without them and, because the advocates of any candidate have invariably invested huge intellectual, emotional and, usually, financial capital in them, they arouse great passions. They are generally arrived at in one of two ways. Either a leading operator in the market introduces a product whose dominance makes it a *de facto* standard or the industry leaders get together to agree on procedures, protocols and standards by which they will all abide. There are often prolonged periods during which either multiple standards apply or there is no clear understanding as to what will emerge as the standard. This results in delays, false starts and detours down blind alleys.

The future development path of soft technologies is thus rendered less predictable than that of hardware. The more 'humanistic' the development path within the infostructure, it seems, the more nebulous it becomes, with 'hard' technologies at one end of the predictability spectrum and the business and political aspects at the other. But if we are to draw a scenario for the infostructure of the world in 2005, it is necessary to predict the trajectory of the soft as well as the hard technologies because they will have a profound influence on the manner in which the exponential developments in hardware will be translated into economic and social realities.

How then is the bounty of MIPS and baud and terabytes created by the hard technologies to be expended in pursuit of the broader interests of humanity? What is technically possible and how do we agree upon which of the options are desirable? Which of the already elected options are technologically constrained at present but will be untethered by the predictable hardware developments of the next decade? What, in other words, are we going to do with all this power?

Past experience suggests that one thing which we will do is to play with it. Advanced technologies devised for serious purposes have a long history of being hijacked by the playful side of human nature and have seldom suffered as a result. The existence of leisure-oriented markets for electronics, for example, has created considerable economies of scale in the manufacture of components which are also used for serious applications and an enhanced understanding of how and why we play may well enable us to provide learning tools which will help us to cope with the increasingly complex information environment in which we live. Some might argue that pure fun should be the most uncontroversial of the types of utility (to use the economists' boring word) which information technology can provide; it is, after all, very purely an end product. Others will express anxieties about the youth of the nation wasting its time on the latest vacuous fad, the moral and intellectual fibre of society being destroyed and so on. We can predict that new toys will be a product or a by-product of the new technologies and past experience suggests that their effects will not be all bad. They will perhaps enable people to see the world in new ways and they will certainly create some big businesses.

The main thrust of development in information technology, however, will continue to be what it has always been. It will be concerned with understanding and control and, if the information revolution is to live up to its name, the technology must be applied in ways which will significantly enhance our understanding of our environment and enable us to control it to positive ends. There is nothing new in that; any scientific or technological innovation which has ever been hailed as revolutionary has offered the same. But the ways in which this cause will be advanced over the next decade or so have already been well signposted and it may be that, by developing machines whose purpose is to handle and present information, never forgetting or losing any of it, and to offer advice on the basis of the logic which we have taught them, we will for the first time start to understand our own intellectual and social strengths and to bump rather painfully up against our ultimate limitations.

The application of technology to the world's traffic in information is likely, over the next few years, to result in the emergence of new kinds of intelligence, in both senses of the word. Certainly there will be opportunities to gather information in new ways and on a new scale and to harness the power of the thinking of others as never before. It also seems likely that some forms of machine intelligence, in some ways analogous to, but in important and useful ways different from, human intelligence will start to have an impact on daily life.

The Wider World of Networks

Compartmentalization of information and knowledge occurs naturally in any group of two or more people, whether it be a family, a small business, a multinational corporation or a government department. It is a necessary corollary of the division of labour and specialization which has contributed so much to the effectiveness of social and economic organization. There always exist large stores of information which are not only inaccessible to any individuals but to which they also would have no need or desire to have access and yet more to which they would not be allowed access to even if they were interested. Most of the world's stores of information are thus accessible only to their few specialist custodians and, because decompartmentalization often requires considerable effort and because compartmentalization has highly desirable functional aspects anyway, it is the norm to which the libraries and other public information sources are the rather cumbersome exceptions. The continued existence of this condition, however, is the source of major difficulties to most organizations, particularly large ones and those which purport to be information-driven, because information which could usefully and legitimately be used is irretrievably buried, wastefully re-purchased, or reconstructed at great cost and immeasurable opportunities are lost. All of this means that information is habitually used very inefficiently.

The problems which organizations suffer as a result of compartment-alization apply to society in general but their seriousness is particularly evident in large information businesses such as multinational financial institutions. These institutions are crucial components of the control sector; they intermediate in the market mechanism and so important are their activities to the health of economies that they are closely controlled by governments everywhere. A typical example of such an organization might employ 50,000 or more people in perhaps 20 countries, would certainly be represented in the world's three major financial markets – New York, London and Tokyo – and would have elaborate information systems linking these and other offices. Even such a sophisticated organization, however, is still typically very compartmentalized and such information flows as take place tend to do so along regular functional paths. Attempts to acquire information along other lines are often frustrated by a lack of flexible information networks and the habits and forms of the old, compartmentalized infostructure obstruct legitimate and desirable flows. Members of such companies often simply do not know what kinds of information the organization possesses, who holds it and whether or not they are allowed access to it. And, if such problems exist within a single organization, whose members are supposed to co-operate in pursuit of common goals, they become much more complex as the search for information crosses organizational boundaries. These are the problems which modern electronic data networks are ultimately intended to solve.

The potential of any technology which gives access to huge shared stores of information and arrangements for co-operative data processing and which will enable users to transcend the limitations of their own computers is clearly enormous. This is already happening in limited ways, such as in local-area networks and public databases, but, before networks can put meaningful dents into the tyranny of compartmentalization, it is necessary to resolve a number of practical problems.

One of the most salient characteristics of information networks is that they have predominantly been established by users for their own purposes or for the provision of services to their customers and have not been provided by third parties such as telephone companies. In such circumstances, it has been natural that a wide range of proprietary hardware platforms and software tools should be used and the potential for a proliferation of non-standard communications protocols has been considerable. This does not matter if communication between networks is not required but if the real potential of networking is to be realized, some way of enabling information to pass smoothly and efficiently between different systems has to be established. With this in mind, the International Standards Organization (ISO) in 1977 announced an initiative which, it was hoped, would ameliorate the problem in the short term and prevent a descent into longer term chaos. The initial result of this effort was the publication, in 1983, of the guidelines for the Open Systems Interconnection, or OSI.

The OSI is a set of ground rules which prescribe what form communications between computers should take at each of seven levels or layers: the physical, data link, network, transport, session, presentation and application layers. The rules governing the physical layer, for example, prescribe the mechanical and electrical aspects of physical connections between devices – what kinds of cables and connectors should be used, what voltages should be applied, etc. This and the data link layer represent the hardware layers, while the rest are concerned with software issues, in ascending order of complexity as they move closer to what the user actually does and sees. The specification of the lowest four layers is complete but practice with regard to the remaining three is not completely defined and it is difficult to see how it ever could be, as new problems and solutions are constantly appearing and the ISO is aiming at an increasingly fast moving target.

Critics of the approach adopted by the ISO believe that it is impractical and that any attempt to force compliance with any but the simplest standards would have catastrophic effects on the efficiency of networking systems. This is because networking technologies are still comparatively undeveloped and it is the competition between purveyors of networking systems which is forcing the pace of enhancement of the technology. Market forces have created many *de facto* standards at higher levels and, although their designers all seek to achieve efficient and user-transparent interconnectivity, they do not generally believe that this will be achieved by adherence to a single set of standards, at least not for the foreseeable future. Some corporate and government customers have taken the side of the ISO by refusing to buy equipment which does not comply with OSI standards but such compliance is never more than partial – partial adherence to partially defined standards – and, although formal standards and the *de facto* standards of the market-place may converge in some way as the technologies involved mature, interconnectivity is likely to be pursued by other means in the meantime. In effect, this will mean that the equipment which links small networks (local-area networks or LANs) together to form larger ones (wide-area networks or WANs) will need to be capable of handling data from different systems, using different protocols, and will itself need to evolve as those systems and protocols change. Over time, this should result in an increased degree of *de facto* compatibility and improvements in systems performance.

Another early attempt to create a unified standard in data communications was the Integrated Services Digital Network. The ISDN was first conceived in the early 1960s and specifically defined in 1972. Like OSI, it developed over time and has changed in response to changing circumstances. Unlike OSI, however, it is a specific system which is intended to be implemented in detail. The Council of the European Community in December 1986 made specific policy statements and recommendations with regard to the implementation of the ISDN throughout the Community, describing it as a natural evolution of the telephone system and aiming for a penetration rate equivalent to 5 per cent of 1983 subscriber main lines and accessibility by 80 per cent of the population by 1993.

In the early 1980s the ISDN seemed to many to be a solution which the telephone companies were offering in response to a problem which did not yet really exist; by the early 1990s the market had understood the problem but, given the technological progress which had taken place in the meantime, was not convinced that ISDN was the solution. The problem with which it was confronted was one which the ISO tried to avoid in the framing of OSI, namely, that it was very specific and that it specified standards which many deemed to be inadequate to meet the burgeoning demands of users and which newer technology was proving to be well able to satisfy. The advocates of the ISDN responded to this by proposing an evolutionary approach to the system which would provide for enhanced capabilities over time, but the initiative seems to have remained with the builders of functionally specific networks and many now argue that the ISDN has been overtaken by events.

History may judge both the ISDN and OSI to have been ideas which were formulated at too early a stage in the development of the technology and which were therefore bound to fail. However, the functional vision upon which they were based is pertinent in any case. It is clear that the networks of the future will be digital and that they will carry services in an integrated fashion but their technical standards may continue to differ for a long time yet and users may have to choose between a wide range of systems, a choice which they may consider to be an imposition or an opportunity.

Some believe that most networking services will be provided by the telephone companies, through a multifunctional communications conduit accessed literally or metaphorically through a single socket in the wall but, however they evolve – and a universe of information networks could evolve in any of a number of ways – they will be ISDNs of one kind or another. Any network worth its salt will be capable of carrying multimedia data and will have to offer a large bandwidth and considerable flexibility to its users. The main thrust may come through global systems provided by PTTs (the Postal Telegraph and Telephone administrations of national governments), through a host of functionally specific proprietary systems whose owners agree to agree where it matters and to differ where it does not, or through some combination of the two.

Whichever pattern emerges, the advent of network technologies which enable powerful computers to be linked together using rapid and sophisticated communications links has already brought about a fundamental change in philosophy with regard to data processing. Networks previously consisted either of a powerful host computer and a series of 'dumb' terminals or of distributed processing systems in which the terminals were intelligent and the host was comparatively dumb but provided basic services to the terminal users. Co-operative processing offers a much more flexible approach to computer use, as well as to information access, in that functional power is distributed through the network in whichever way best suits the demands of the user community and the network can easily be reconfigured to accommodate changing requirements. As such, it brings data processing much closer to the ideal of the network of computers which, from the viewpoint of the users, effectively functions as one large computer (a 'virtual machine') to which each has a customized form of access, according to his needs.

Such an approach creates a system structure analogous to a mode of operation which users of information technology could themselves adopt in the future. The co-operative pursuit of information and knowledge is a principle to which scholars, researchers and most delegates to conferences implicitly subscribe but, with traditional technology, it is a very cumbersome business and the study process is, as a result, largely solitary, compartmentalized and disjointed. If people can learn to use the information networks of the future as easily and naturally as they use newspapers and public libraries now, the growth of a universe of powerful, interconnected networks will represent nothing less than a transformation of the supporting infrastructure for most intellectual and managerial processes. The signs are that the technologies, methods and standards necessary to enable such a transformation to occur will be well in place by the turn of the century.

The Friendly Machine

There has probably never been a machine invented which did not become more user-friendly as it evolved. From the humble axe to the automobile, the original inventors were in search of a new functionality and that functionality took precedence over everything else. Only later, as people ceased to marvel at the function and grew impatient with the callused fingers which they suffered from using hand axes or the hernias which they got crank-starting their Model T Fords, did ease of use become an important factor in the design process. This seems to be an invariable law governing the nature of the evolution of machines and it is therefore significant that the expression 'user-friendly', which has quickly become well-established in the lexicon, is a creation of the computer era.

Few who looked at early computers envisaged that they would ever be the ubiquitous tools of society which they have become. So esoteric were their uses that the concept of the PC, to a scientist of the 1940s, would have seemed as improbable as the emergence of a consumer market for wind tunnels or diffusion furnaces and user-friendliness was consequently not an important consideration in computer design. Nor did the available technology lend itself to the provision of user-friend-liness in computing for many years to come; even the early PCs were unfriendly creatures by comparison with today's models. But it has long been realized that user-friendliness is possibly more important in computers than in any other machine ever invented. This is because the gap between the potential of the computer and the ability of the average human being to utilize it is so great. If people have to learn even a comparatively high level and friendly language such as *Basic* in order to have access to computer power, they will elect to live without it. If the machine presents itself in a way which is less likely to induce feelings of inadequacy or panic, its range of potential customers and its real functionality is likely to be much greater and, if interaction with a computer can become a pleasant experience, so much the better.

The representative interface set-up between a general purpose computer and its user in the early 1990s is a cathode ray tube (CRT) display and a more or less standard 'qwerty' keyboard with around 100 keys.

There are numerous variations on this theme, with different keyboards, 'mouse'-type pointing devices and liquid crystal or electro-luminescent displays but the effect is much the same and such set-ups represent the public perception of what computers are. In spite of the efforts which the computer and software industries have made to render the computer's functional cogitations 'transparent to the user' and the steps required for its operation more intuitively obvious, this is still a forbidding image to many people who cannot and will not type and who shy away from anything with more than half a dozen keys, knobs or switches.

This kind of technophobia inhibits the use of computers even in simple dedicated functions, such as the programmable controls of video recorders, and manufacturers of these machines have made considerable efforts to simplify their operation, using bar-code readers and other sophisticated devices. The second unwritten law of machine design, it seems, is that if you want to make it simpler, you have to make it more complex; the machine has to be smart so that the person can be dumb. The constant search for user-friendliness, therefore, means that one way in which increased computing power will be utilized is in the provision of ever more sophisticated user interface functions for computers of all kinds. Some clues as to how this development will proceed can be seen in the research projects which are being conducted in the area and some of the embryonic products which have already appeared.

Anyone who remembers the mellifluous tones of 'Hal', the spacecraft computer in Stanley Kubrick's film *2001 – a Space Odyssey* will be aware of the author's (the ubiquitous Arthur C. Clarke) implicit prediction that computers capable of complex conversation in natural language will exist at the end of this century. Current technology would need to be developed at quite an impressive pace if this prediction were to be met in quite such a convincing form and even a nearish miss seems somewhat unlikely, but speech recognition and synthesis are certainly areas which are likely to see significant progress within our time horizon of 2005 and, indeed, by 2001.

Quite complex voice synthesis is already commonplace. Telephone answering machines which announce 'end of final message' in reasonably human tones and cars which remind their drivers of the potential hazards of 'door open' are familiar but this kind of trick is, in reality, comparatively simple. All that is done in speech synthesis is to take a known data pattern and to translate it into an equally well-defined series of sounds, although really clever systems can make the intonation convincingly human.

The recognition of natural language is quite another problem and one which is very demanding of computer power. This is because spoken language is much more complex than written (or keyboarded) language. Received British English pronunciation has 44 phonemes but the phonetic values vary markedly between individuals and the 12 recognized pure vowel phonemes (not to mention the diphthongs and triphthongs), for example, vary significantly in regional accents, making the number of vowel sounds to be recognized much greater than this. The first 'a' in 'camera' will be pronounced quite differently by a schoolgirl in Southport, an operatic tenor in Sydney and a housewife in Saskatoon and, while the human listener will understand the sound from context, even if it is delivered in an unfamiliar fashion, the computer can only seek to differentiate, from a microphone input, the sounds themselves. The capability of a computer to recognize words can be enhanced if some much more complex heuristic logic is available to it but all of this requires complex programming and guzzles computing power.

Voice recognition for simple functions exists today but it is a far cry from the elegant capabilities of Hal. Existing equipment typically copes with very limited vocabularies uttered by a wide range of voices or rather broader vocabularies spoken by a single voice whose characteristics are recognized and sampled for comparison purposes. AT&T, for example, recorded the voices of thousands of passers-by enunciating the five phrases which its computer system was required to recognize when some of its operator functions were automated. Machines cope tolerably well with voice inputs on this basis and their capabilities can further be enhanced by providing them with probability data relating to the occurrence of certain combinations of words in sequence or in context. Even a computer so equipped would, however, be likely to miss Warden Spooner's famous joke, 'You have hissed all my mystery lessons and must leave by the next town drain', by guessing 'town drain' to be less plausible than the 'down train' from which it derived and simply mis-hearing it.

Voice recognition is an unfamiliar technology today because its capabilities are currently so limited that technically possible applications tend to be trivial. Voice activated power switches and channel selectors for television sets have been displayed in the technology showrooms of some major manufacturers for several years but have not been commercialized because a control microphone offers no advantages over the familiar push-button remote control unit. The strides which have been made in recent years, however, are likely to result in some rather more meaningful applications by the end of the decade. Extrapolating the trend, reliable voice input database enquiry systems and perhaps some form of voice input word processor seem reasonable bets by 2001 but, even then, the prospect of discussing politics with Hal will probably still be a long way off.

If asking computers to listen to things is likely to continue to present difficulties, asking them to read things will be much easier. Optical character recognition (OCR) systems are already in widespread use and are becoming more accurate, easier to use and much cheaper. They already cope with routine sorting and counting work in many commercial settings and, more importantly, are able to capture printed words and numbers which have never existed in electronic form and, by bringing them into the computer domain, render them electronically manipulable. If the CD ROM version of the Library of Congress is to exist in 2005, OCR systems will represent a key enabling technology and, if current performance is anything to go by, they will not be the critical missing link.

Recognition of the printed word is a somewhat less demanding task for a computer than is the deciphering of handwriting. The reluctance of many potential computer users to touch keyboards, however, has led the industry to work on systems which enable inputs to be made using an electronic 'pen' – actually a stylus which can be used to hand-write on a scratch pad. Using a system similar to the now common 'mouse' pointing devices, the so-called pen computing equipment recognizes handwriting (within reason) in any language for which it is programmed, more esoteric forms such as musical notation and a series of prescribed 'gestures' which instruct the computer to save, backspace, escape etc. Existing systems cope well with form-based computer applications and some expect their continued development to result in the replacement of the familiar qwerty keyboard in everything but heavy-duty text input functions in a very few years.

Pen computing, OCR, touch-screens, icons and other such helpful additions to conventional computer systems will undoubtedly continue to appear in the same accretive fashion in which electric self-starters, power steering and rear window de-misters were added to automobiles, as technology is applied to the cause of user-friendliness. In addition, aids such as the *Equalizer* voice synthesis program made famous by Stephen Hawking, will utilize the same technologies to give new freedoms to some disabled people but the kind of speech-based user-friendliness exemplified by Hal still belongs in the realms of science fiction.

One new medium has, however, appeared which has already attracted considerable attention and which seems likely to advance the user-friendliness cause rapidly, if in a somewhat unexpected direction. 'virtual reality' or VR, is already the subject of intense activity in a number of places around the world, has attracted considerable media attention and has had some spectacular claims made for it. It is not a single technology, although it is already perceived by some as having become a distinct technological discipline, but represents the assembly of a number of technologies to create an application which some say will change the way in which we view the world.

Virtual reality is concerned with complex simulation and owes its potential power to the realization that comparatively modest computers now have sufficient data processing power that, through suitable peripherals, they can simulate more or less anything. The concept of electronics-based simulation is well known in particular contexts. Pilots and tank crews have for many years been trained to cope with highly dangerous situations using simulators. The simulator, for example, obviates the unacceptable dangers of starting engine fires or inducing stalls in real aircraft in order to train pilots to deal with those problems when they arise in reality. They are also cheaper to operate for training purposes than real aircraft. But simulation has long since made the transition from flight simulators into the real world of aviation. Many modern aircraft are controlled using computers and electronic links to servo motors which control the elevators and other control surfaces, in place of the old systems of cables, levers and pulleys. Early examples of such fly-by-wire systems, however, brought complaints from pilots that the controls completely lacked 'feel' and that it was therefore less easy to fly the aircraft in some circumstances. Later systems therefore created artificial feedback so that the pilot could feel a simulated version of the pressure of the air flowing over the control surfaces. In this sense, most pilots today routinely experience a kind of virtual reality. It feels real and, indeed, it reflects a very relevant reality close by but it is not real.

A form of low-cost virtual reality technology is being developed in Japan by Namco (creators of the famous *Pac Man* video game and of the car-racing machines found in games arcades everywhere) for use in driving schools. The body of a real car is connected to the activators, sensors and electronics and surrounded by a curved screen with simulated three-dimensional road scenes and the novice drivers, like airline pilots in a flight simulator, can be exposed to virtual reality road hazards without danger to life and limb and their reactions analysed using a playback function.

When this concept is extended, using the wrap-around 3-D goggles, sensor pads, robot arms, treadmills and other paraphernalia which surround virtual reality today, the possibilities expand dramatically. Howard Rheingold, author of the book *Virtual Reality* (1991), describes his experience of a serious scientific application of the technique, a chemical modelling simulation, as follows:

> When I tried to push the models together by exerting force on the ARM [Argonne remote manipulator], the force I felt in reaction was an analog of the way the physical molecules would behave if pushed together in physical space. The grip enabled me to use arm and hand movements to manipulate the models in relation to one another. The more I used the grip to rotate the models that floated in midair, the more three-dimensional they seemed. My job was to use the ARM grip to maneuvre the 3-D puzzle pieces together close enough, in precise spatial relationship, to bond together – a successful dock (p. 27).

Perhaps the most significant feature of virtual reality (and here it may be helpful to strip it of its slightly 'showbiz' label and refer to it simply as advanced computer simulation) is that it is thus capable of simulating not only physical reality but also abstract reality. As such, it may in future help us to address some of the abstract intellectual problems – the solution of which commonly enlist the help of computers – in completely new ways. In so doing, it may, for some applications, provide a user-friendly interface which enables us to side-step even the encumbrance of our natural language. Perhaps we do not need to talk to Hal.

The Thinking Machine

It is generally the case that the implications of new technologies which are to have a significant impact upon the ways in which people conduct their lives are not really understood until they start to be utilized and to exert pressure for change. The more intellectually or socially challenging the technology, the more tardily are its implications accepted. It is hardly surprising, therefore, that the concept of artificial or machine intelligence, which threatens the normal human perception of man's place in the world quite fundamentally, is regarded with extreme scepticism and that people are quick to point out, for example, that there is more to intelligence than an ability to make calculations with lightning speed. The debate surrounding artificial intelligence is an extremely complex and emotive one, in which comparisons between the actual and potential abilities of computers and the human brain loom large.

Comparatively little is known about the architecture of the human brain or about why it possesses such stupendous capabilities. Silicon circuits are more than a match for it as conductors of signals (brain waves move at a sedate 200 kilometres per hour or so) and yet in most ways it out-performs any electronic computer by a very wide margin. Such superior performance is a function of architecture and serves to underscore the ultimate inadequacies of the classic Von Neumann architecture upon which virtually all modern computers are based. In the Von Neumann computer, the memory and logical processing circuits are separate; in the brain, and in the embryonic neural network computers which have been constructed, the circuitry which holds the memory also does the thinking. The classical computer can do nothing which it is not specifically programmed to do; the neural network computer is capable of learning. The difference between the first crude neural network computers and the brain whose architecture they seek to emulate is one of capacity. The human brain contains some hundred trillion neurons capable of interconnecting in a quadrillion ways, a scale which could not be replicated synthetically in the foreseeable future. Existing electronic neural systems contain only 1,000 or so processors, although this number can be expected to increase several hundredfold before the end of the 1990s, by which time such systems will probably be used in voice and pattern recognition in robots and other machines. Simple as electronic neural networks may yet be, they are capable of learning and have already quietly crossed the line which demarcates the proto-intelligence of the familiar electronic computer from the natural intelligence of biological brains.

Although the construction of a brain-like computer is no longer so remote a possibility that it exists only in science fiction, the ways in which machine and human intelligence will interact in the next few years will be rather less dramatic. The computer pioneer Alan Turing devised a simple test which, in his opinion, would settle the question as to whether a machine is intelligent or not. The test involves putting an adjudicator into a room with two terminals, one connected to a computer, the other to a human being. If, when interrogating the two, the judge is unable to distinguish which is which, the machine, according to Turing, is proved to be intelligent. An artfully prepared computer, Joseph Weizenbaum's ELIZA, could be argued to have passed this test as long ago as the 1970s but its success owed more to the ability of its programmers to create an illusion of comprehension than to the kind of intelligence which would be necessary to pass the test in the spirit in which Turing intended it.

It is highly unlikely that any machine this century will pass a no-holds-barred Turing test, although it may well be that a few computers which depend upon analogy and associative reasoning and learn from experience, as human beings do, will exist by the end of it. It could be argued, however, that such a focus on anthropomorphic behaviour in machines is largely irrelevant to the tasks in hand. Impressive, and very useful, machine intelligence of a kind already exists and is likely to be applied to real-world situations increasingly often from now on. It is unlikely that people will have to get used to sharing the world with anthropomorphic computers by 2001, but they may by then be accustomed to the idea that not only can a combination of man and machine create knowledge but that the machines may be able to do the job by themselves in due course.

Expert systems, computer systems which are designed to replicate, and provide consistent analytical judgements on the basis of, the knowledge of human experts in specific fields, have been around, in one form or another, since the 1950s. In some fields, computers have surprised experts by making correct judgements significantly more often than the human beings on whose knowledge and analytical processes they are modelled. It is highly likely that the next generation of chess computers, by increasing the speed of their analysis a thousandfold will by the mid-1990s turn the tables on the human grandmasters, who have maintained an edge over the most powerful existing machines. Although such an achievement will be very conspicuous, it will be more significant as a landmark in machine intelligence than as a perhaps rather dispiriting end-game for human chess players. This is because it will represent not a simple triumph of computer logic over human creativity but a powerful combination of the two – a triumph of human teamwork and man–machine co-operation.

The application of expert systems to more workaday tasks, such as medical diagnosis, nuclear reactor control, bus timetabling, mineral exploration and the planning of retail store locations – all applications in which such systems are already used – will be less conspicuous but more significant than their ascendancy in chess. And their power and significance will be greatly enhanced by the access which the growth of computer networks will give them to huge amounts of data, data which the 'idiot savant' computer can analyse with ruthless logic and blinding speed. Networked computers will increasingly become nodes in a new kind of collective intelligence which has the potential to exist on a global scale, a colossal extension of human intelligence which will not yet depend on the evolution of the 'non-Von' neural computers which promise eventually to lift it onto a higher plane.

The popularity of artificial intelligence (AI) as a concept has fluctuated wildly, largely reflecting the way in which the prospects for anthropomorphic computers have advanced and receded, and it has been a somewhat unfashionable idea in recent years. But the steady progress of AI techniques, combined with the tremendous increases in the power and capacity of hardware and the explosive growth of computer networks, is creating a scenario in which a greatly increased role for machine intelligence by 2005 looks a near certainty. The capability for abstract thought raised man above the other primates as a successful species, speech compounded the advantage and the great inventions of writing and type created competitive advantages for those societies in which they first emerged. The development of a global man–machine intelligence complex in the last years of this century may be creating the pre-conditions for a similar leap early in the next.

The Information Technology of 2005

The technological environment which prevails at any point in time can be described in various ways. There is a natural tendency, when the topic is being discussed, to focus on the latest available technologies and those which are expected to appear in future and have for some reason captured the imagination of the media and the public. Old technology, no matter how complex, is not even thought of as being technology. When references are made to technology industry they are not generally concerned with railways or water filtration. It is invariably the case, however, that the bulk of the technology which creates the civilized human environment is always that which has been gradually accreted over the years and the new technology seldom makes the world look markedly different in a short space of time. There have been times and places where all-pervading technology-driven change happened very quickly. Parts of Victorian England and the USA around the turn of the century perhaps furnish examples of such exceptional circumstances, but technology generally changes life-styles by a process of stalagmite accretion.

In this sense, much of the impact which the emergence of the key enabling technologies mentioned in this book will ever have upon certain aspects of the environment has already been felt and it is only when a deliberate effort is made to recall what life was like without word processors, pocket calculators, electronic fuel injection and the like that the cumulative effect of such change is appreciated. Even the *ex post facto* view of the impact of technology is thus obscured by this creeping familiarity and the more pervasive and varied the effects, the more difficult they are to evaluate. In any attempt to predict the impact of technology on the information environment in 2005 it is therefore much easier to predict the stage of development which the various key enabling technologies will have reached by then than it is to envisage the precise ways in which they will be applied and how people will feel about the results.

The number of key, critical path technologies is quite small. A good deal of space in this book has been devoted to developments in semiconductors, optical fibre and satellite communications and mass data storage because their development is so fundamental to the scale and performance of the systems which will be built upon them. The ways in which they relate to one another, and to other important but less crucial technologies, often create a kind of clustering which generates applications whose performance is enhanced geometrically as a product of the rates of change in all of them. Such multiplier effects suddenly render possible products which were previously not just difficult but impossible to make. This means that new products, based on known developing technologies, will from time to time appear in the public domain with surprising suddenness. But, however unpredictable the range of technology applications may be, it can be predicted with some confidence that, by 2005:

- Silicon integrated circuits approaching the theoretical design rule limits of 0.2 microns will be in mass production, providing, for example, dynamic RAMs of at least 256 megabits capacity and a whole family of similarly capacious memory circuits and powerful logic devices. High electron mobility VLSI devices using materials like gallium arsenide will be commonplace, although much less massive than their silicon counterparts. All this will make huge computing power in very small packages and at very low cost available for even routine functions.

- A hybrid network of optical fibre and improved satellites will provide enormous data transmission capacity to a much larger area of the world. Attitudes to distance and the frequency and mode of communication will be subject to considerable change as a result.
- The capacity of optical memory devices will be so massive that considerations of cost in mass data storage will virtually disappear and the data will be so quickly accessible that methods of and attitudes towards the acquisition of information will start to undergo radical change.
- The power of the new computer circuitry will be used to make computers of all kinds much more accessible to the general public. User interfaces such as voice input for word processing and advanced simulation or virtual reality displays for many scientific and business analytical functions, as well as for entertainment, will be commonplace.
- Expert systems will be providing decision support for professional people in a much wider range of applications than is today commonly contemplated.

The convergence of these predictable technological developments at a point around the end of the century has the potential to bring about changes which might justify classification as a true information revolution and might even presage a revolution in intelligence. Technology, however, does not exist in a vacuum and the nature and pace of change in the ways in which people understand and manage their environment will be subject to a complex interaction of political, economic, social and educational factors. In the make-up of the infostructure of 2005, technology is the most, not the least, predictable element.

4

THE FUTURE OF THE INFORMATION SUPERPOWERS

While Bermuda nudged the USA out of the top position in our Information Access Index league table and the score for Switzerland topped that for Japan, there can be no doubt as to the identity of the world's two information superpowers. The USA and Japan provide very information-rich environments for their citizens, not only in the basic terms measured by the Index but also in ways which are so much the preserve of the most developed nations that many countries would not figure at all and could provide no statistics. In infostructural terms the two countries are at the top of an exclusive senior league. They are also, in their rather different ways, at the forefront of all aspects of information technology and provide much of the most modern information equipment for each other and for the rest of the world.

Such is the prominence of the USA in the global information sector that it could be argued to be the only information superpower in the world. So prominent are Hollywood in the movie business, Madison Avenue in advertising, and Silicon Valley in semiconductors that America seems, at first sight, to be part of an information culture which operates on a higher level than any other. And yet, two major Hollywood studios are now subsidiaries of Japanese consumer electronics groups, Japan dominates certain parts of the semiconductor market and has the largest newspapers and second largest advertising industry in the world. Linguistic and cultural barriers make Japan's role in the information sector less prominent than that of America, which has the advantage of operating primarily in English, but when American companies in the sector are asked to name their most important competitors (and, sometimes, their most important allies), the names are usually Japanese.

The USA and Japan compete with one another at the highest level across the breadth of the information sector, broadly defined, and this competition has, from time to time, become acrimonious. Books with titles such as *Japan as Number One*, *Comeback*, *Trading Places* and *The Japan that Can Say 'No'* catalogue this competition and this conflict, which is an important and interesting topic in itself. The pages which follow, however, are intended primarily to describe the kinds of information environment which these two countries represent and the ways in which some of their citizens perceive the information society of the future.

America's Information Frontier

Muhammad Ali once claimed that he was the most famous man in the world and it would have been difficult, at the time, to deny the truth of such an assertion. Certainly he would have been recognized in the street almost anywhere where there were streets and in most places where there were not. As heavyweight boxing champion of the world, he was naturally the subject of the kind of mass attention and adulation which is invariably given to those who exhibit superlative talent in the most revered of human skills: running, fighting and, in the case of some exalted groups such as chess masters or particle physicists, thinking.

Many Americans, including all recent Presidents, have occupied similarly prominent positions in the global consciousness and, even before the USA emerged from the Cold War as the sole surviving superpower, the world's most famous people in most spheres of endeavour were numbered among its citizens. As the richest, most technologically advanced and militarily and politically powerful nation on earth, and one in which professional and technical specialization in the pursuit of excellence has been developed to the highest degree, it is perhaps natural that America should produce more prominent people than any other. The fame which these people achieve, however, is also partly a product of a media machine which sets all the standards in the projection of mass culture. Americans produce and consume images like no other nation and have a huge trade surplus in them. If our Information Access Index were to be replaced by an Information Production Index, which measured what was produced for the consumption of all those readers, listeners and viewers world-wide, the

USA would be in a league of its own. If Americans did not invent the mass media, they certainly re-invented them and exhibit an abiding passion in continuing to do so which sets them apart from other nations. Soap operas, sound-bites, photo opportunities, tele-evangelism and couch potatoes are all American inventions and reflect a level of media consciousness which is without parallel elsewhere.

The pervasive influence of the American media, modified as it may be in the course of transmission, means that most people outside of the country and everybody within it, have fairly coherent images in their minds of what America is. This has been very important in uniting a nation of a quarter of a billion people, which spreads across the southern half of a major continent and which consistently defines itself in terms of its breadth and diversity. It has no doubt contributed to a situation in which there have been no attempts by any state or other entity to secede from the Union since the Civil War. As the National Telecommunications and Information Administration says in its 1988 publication *Telecom 2000*:

> The United States is becoming even more culturally and economically pluralistic. Moreover, ours remains a highly mobile society, a phenomenon which will continue to affect family, community and other relationships. It is thus important that there continue to be effective and, optimally, improved means by which all citizens, irrespective of geographic residence, social, economic, or educational attainment can share in common national experiences (p.78).

The ethnic diversity which has grown on top of the strong, white, Anglo-Saxon substrate which still represents the basis of much of American culture is manifested not only in the mass media but also in the publications of the establishment. It is hard for the student examining official statistics describing the fabric of the USA to ignore the preoccupation which the statisticians seem to have with ethnic origins. Everything from infant mortality to high school drop-out rates and television viewing statistics is categorized not only by state but also by racial group. We are told, for example, that black women over the age of 55 are the most avid television viewers and that 46.9 per cent of children of Hispanic origin in grades 1–8 used computers at school in 1989. The reason for much of this attention to ethnicity has been a concern for equality of opportunity; and opportunity is itself often defined, as might be expected in an advanced society such as the USA, in terms of access to education, to information and to knowledge.

Official statistics and the results of opinion polls regarding education in the USA suggest a slight long-term decline in standards during the 1960s and 1970s which started to level off in the latter part of the 1980s. Scores achieved in the national standard Scholastic Aptitude Tests (SATs) of mathematical and 'verbal' (i.e. general English language) skills taken by 17- and 18-year-olds declined from peak levels of 501 and 479 respectively in 1956 to 474 and 422 in 1991.

Student enrolments increased sharply over the period and the large nominal increases in educational funding were more than offset by this and by the rapid inflation of the 1970s. Overall educational expenditure per student in the USA actually decreased 19.7 per cent in real terms between 1970 and 1988, falling in the public sector by 20.3 per cent and in higher education by 43 per cent.

The SAT achievement figures exhibit predictable positive correlations between parental income and educational attainment and the scores achieved by children from ethnic minority groups were also lower than those for white students. The disparities between the average total (i.e. mathematics plus verbal) SAT scores of students from different ethnic backgrounds, however, narrowed markedly between the mid-1970s and the late 1980s. The gap between white and black students' scores narrowed from 258 (944 to 686) in 1976 to 200 (937 to 737) in 1989, while Mexican Americans narrowed their shortfall relative to white students by 30 points to 125 and the already slim gap between white and Asian Americans narrowed further, to just three points in 1989.

Literacy and other educational standards in the USA are regularly monitored by the National Assessment of Educational Progress, which classifies literacy at four levels (basic, intermediate, adept and advanced). The overall picture in literacy, as described by the NAEP figures, is rather more encouraging than the trend in verbal SAT scores might suggest, with improvements being seen in the scores of all ethnic groups at most levels, the only exception being a decline in the percentage of white 17-year-olds with reading proficiencies at or above 'advanced' level between the years of 1971 and 1988. In 1988, 42 per cent of all American 17-year-olds were reading at or above 'adept' level, a level at which the reader 'locates, understands, summarizes and explains relatively complicated information'. It was still the case, however, that only one-quarter of black and Hispanic 17-year-olds had achieved this level of proficiency.

Although equality of access to the output of the information/intellectual sector is a matter of concern, the benefits which America has derived from multicultural inputs to the sector are manifold and clear. Names like Von Neumann and Grove became famous as a result of the contribution made by European *émigrés* (in these cases by Hungarians) to American science and technology, while a multitude of Tandons, Yus, Dhams and Chens form the latest wave of Asian immigrant talent to fuel the intellect-driven technology industries of the country. America has benefited from 'brain-drains' from everywhere because it can still project itself as a land of opportunity and still provides high living standards and real rewards for talent.

America is already an information society in many senses, and in some ways it is almost compelled to be. That such a huge and diverse country has been at the forefront of change for the last century *and* has maintained stability and integrity to such a high degree is a tribute to the extent to which the nation's information systems have supported the maintenance of control and have projected a strong and coherent image of the national culture and polity. A firm belief that knowledge and technology can fuel perpetual economic growth and social enrichment is central to American culture, and Yankee ingenuity (with a little help from newcomers) has continued to fuel the American Dream.

The position which the physical frontier once held in the American psyche has been usurped by the information frontier and much of the leading edge work which is now being done in information technology is carried on in America. The signs are that, in this sphere at any rate, the USA will continue to draw strength from its diversity.

Media De-massification or Proliferation?

The pattern of newspaper publication and distribution in the USA reflects not only the difficulties of distributing newspapers over large geographical areas but also the inevitably parochial nature of much of the news which impinges on daily life. Most American newspapers are local papers and only half-a-dozen or so, including the *New York Times* and *Wall Street Journal* have truly national circulation. This fragmentation of the general news market means that the USA produces far more newspaper and periodical titles than any other country, including Japan (and the former Soviet Union), where circulations and readership levels are higher. In recent years, however, increasing costs and competition from local radio and television have undermined the viability of many of the independent local papers and mergers and acquisitions have transformed the proprietary shape of the industry. Large newspaper chains such as Gannett, Thomson, Dow-Jones and Knight-Ridder now own about three-quarters of America's newspapers and account for about 90 per cent of the circulation.

The policy of acquisition proved to be very profitable for these companies for several years, as they achieved economies of scale in a business which was still open to such treatment but, as the pressures of competition from other media grew and the scope for further cost-cutting was exhausted, they were forced to look for other avenues of growth. Gannett launched *USA Today*, a national circulation daily which made losses from the time of its launch and is expected by some analysts never to be more than marginally profitable, while Knight-Ridder took the rather more successful view that the path to salvation was through electronic news services, sticking with news but moving away from newspapers. The new press groupings, with editorial and planning resources superior to those of the independents which they acquired, made the content and presentation of newspapers more responsive to the changing requirements of their readers, and editorial policy in most American newspapers now reflects far more sophisticated demographic analysis of the readership. Innovations in design, such as the introduction of colour presses, have also been made in recent years. The general consensus, however, seems to be that the newspaper industry in the USA is moribund and that the rationalization process which resulted from the proprietary restructuring merely delayed its inevitable contraction.

Newspapers have become steadily less important as a primary source of general news to the American public over the last three decades, and substantially less than half of the respondents to media questionnaires now cite newspapers in this capacity. Television is now the preferred source of news for most, not only for its timeliness but also for its perceived reliability and it is only with regard to some very local issues that local newspapers retain primacy as news providers. The total circulation of daily newspapers in the USA in 1946 was around 50 million copies, a number which grew gradually and peaked at 63 million copies in 1973. Circulation has since dwindled and, given the 77 per cent increase in population since the War, the gradual increase in sales has masked a marked long-term decline in America's newspaper reading habit. Even at the peak of absolute circulation in 1973, per capita circulation rates were down 12 per cent by comparison with 1946.

Television viewing, however, has become increasingly entrenched in the American way of life. Between 1950 and 1985, the viewing hours of the average household increased steadily from 4 hours 43 minutes to

7 hours and 7 minutes before levelling off in the latter part of the 1980s. By the end of the 1980s, the average American was watching 4 hours 15 minutes of television per day, while women, blacks, the elderly and those with lower incomes watched more, often considerably more, than the average. In 1990, 98 per cent of households had a colour television set, 65 per cent had more than one, 56 per cent were connected to cable television, 66 per cent had a video recorder and 59 per cent of households had access to 20 or more television channels. All of this adds up to a television culture of gigantic proportions and, in spite of the apparent super-saturation of the market, efforts are continually being made to expand it in new directions, with new types of programming and innovations such as interactive television.

Some see this proliferation of television media and programming, and the appearance of ever more specialized print publications, as reflecting a clear trend towards specialist media fragmentation in response to increasingly diverse consumer taste. In a country such as the USA, where the diversity of ethnic and regional cultures is so great, there is at least a *prima facie* case for the idea that this proliferation results from dissatisfaction with the very consciously massified and homogeneous media of the past. As the cultural melting pot mentality of the early part of the twentieth century has been replaced by a resurgence of ethnic and regional pride and an urge to assert diversity, many segments of American society have used the media to project their subcultures and their world view. This has only become possible with the advent of highly flexible communications media and an increase in the number of communications channels of all kinds, but the coincidence of increased media availability and editorial and programming diversity does not necessarily reflect a strong causal relationship between what consumers want and what is being provided.

In his book, *The Third Wave*, Alvin Toffler (1980) made what are perhaps the best known predictions of the future emergence of 'narrowcasting' and media 'de-massification'. The gist of his argument is that mass circulation newspapers and network television are under attack from local, small-circulation regional papers, mini-magazines and video media such as cable television because new technology allows the nascent demands of diverse and very finely segmented audiences to be satisfied, and that more of the same is to be expected in future.

Certainly, life-styles in the USA have changed and the demands of the population at large in terms of editorial content in the media have diversified as a result. The mass media, however, have not only been a conduit for expressions of social and cultural change but have themselves changed over the years in order that they should not become out of tune with their audiences and are sufficiently varied in their content that they cater quite well for a broad range of interests.

It is difficult to assess the extent to which the proliferation of mass communications media and of the programming which they provide is serving a market which is increasingly finely segmented in terms of the types of material which it requires and to what extent it is merely providing a selection of broadly similar programmes which consumers can choose between. Americans are great believers in choice and seem to be prepared to pay a price for the provision of many options, whether or not they exercise their choice of those options. Choice, in other words, might be regarded as a commodity in itself.

Although there are statistically significant differences in the viewer ratings of individual programmes or interest expressed in particular types of newspaper article, according to the age, sex or ethnicity of viewer or reader groups, the overall differences are surprisingly small. An in-depth study of television viewer motivation conducted by a market research organization in 1979 (see Neumann, 1991, p. 121) found that most people watch television for rather similar reasons (mainly relaxation and entertainment) irrespective of their age, sex, education, income or ethnic group and that their viewing choices, and their preferred overall mix of programming, are very uniform. Another study (see Neumann, 1991, p. 125), in which respondents from a wide range of demographic groups were asked to describe their ideal newspapers, in terms of editorial mix, also produced remarkably uniform results.

There is ample evidence of the emergence of what might be regarded as a kind of narrowcasting in the US television market, in the form of cable networks which cater to large Hispanic minorities in particular localities, mainly in California and Florida, with Spanish-language programming. This is particularly attractive to new arrivals or for older people whose facility in English is limited and, in cultural terms, it reflects the growing ethnic diversity of American society. It is by now the conventional wisdom that, as the Hispanic, Asian and other sections of the community which are not of European origin become better established, the national cultural changes which their arrival has brought about will be manifested in the replacement of America's traditional 'melting pot' with a multi-cultural 'salad bowl'. The salad bowl society will inevitably create large ethnic market segments which cable and other pay-TV operators will be able to exploit profitably. There will, for example, be around five million Hispanic households in the USA in 1995, but the existence of ethnic market segments of this kind does not provide compelling evidence in support of the broader argument for narrowcasting as a major trend in mass communication everywhere because it is clear that the driving force behind these ethnic markets is language and not highly specialized programme content. In more ethnically homogeneous countries, there is little evidence of the kind of media de-massification which the proponents of narrowcasting predict.

Certainly Toffler's prediction that cable television would 'spread with hurricane force' during the 1980s proved to be correct, as the number of households connected increased from less than 15 million in 1979 to more than 50 million by 1990 and 63 million by mid-1992, but there is little evidence to suggest that this spread was part of the broader process of media de-massification which he described. More persuasive, perhaps, is the analysis commonly offered by media theorists who suggest that any new communications medium typically goes through three stages as it matures. The first users of a new medium, according to this theory, are elite groups, who are the most likely to be informed of its existence and able to afford to take advantage of it. This initial limited market penetration is followed by a period of popularization and then a third phase of specialization. The specialization phase tends to begin when audiences for the old medium have fallen well below peak levels and its operators seek to fight back against market-usurping new media by utilizing its particular characteristics for specialist purposes. Television, for example, may have driven radio and audio out of the living room and into the bathroom, car and Walkman, and newspapers have sought to survive the television onslaught by concentrating on the things, like share-price listings and material aimed at commuters, which they do particularly well.

It is anyway far from clear that the apparent fragmentation of the mass audience which was observed in the 1970s and early 1980s was anything more than a redistribution of market shares between old and new communications media resulting from the arrival of technologies which provided attractive functionality. The growth in penetration of video recorders into American homes in the early 1980s, for example, exceeded even that of cable television and, while VCRs themselves have significant potential as a narrowcasting medium, there is no reason to believe that this was why they became so popular so quickly. The increased availability of affordable video software, either for purchase or rental, has changed the pattern of video usage in recent years, lending some support to the narrowcasting theorists, but the most popular use of VCRs in the early years was for 'time-shift' recording of programmes so that they could be viewed at more convenient times. The initial VCR boom, then, was not a response to increased diversity in popular culture or a deep-seated desire of consumers to replace the standard fare of the mass media with more esoteric programming. Rather, like the television remote controller, whose diffusion in American households followed a similar trajectory to that of the VCR, it was popular because it offered convenience at a rather more utilitarian level.

The debate about media de-massification in the USA will doubtless continue but, although the television networks and large circulation newspapers have seen their audiences eroded by new media which augment viewer and reader choice, the signs are that this is more a reflection of proliferation than of fragmentation. Communications media in America compete for the attentions of a society which is already obsessed with choice, seemingly for its own sake, in all aspects of life. It has also demonstrated a singular, near-obsessive interest not only in information but in passive entertainment. It remains to be seen to what extent it is choice itself which has been the commodity for sale in this media boom and how far the desire for a genuine segmentation of the market will provide economic justification for the mass of alternatives on offer.

The Stuff of Dreams

The USA has maintained a leading role in the technology of semiconductors, computers, telecommunications equipment and the hardware of the consumer electronics industry. In all of these areas, Japanese companies challenge American supremacy and, in some areas, have clearly overturned it. In software, however, and in the creation of new markets in the overlapping areas of information and entertainment, America's leadership is virtually unchallenged. In the broad communications market, others tend to follow America's lead and it is accepted, at least tacitly, throughout the world that this is the case. It is hardly surprising, therefore, that most of the well-known visionaries of the communication sector and its academic hinterland are Americans.

American authors, lobbyists and propagandists produce a steady stream of images of the information society of the future and their output forms a basis for discussion and planning in an area in which there are no role models to follow. These treatises are the most tangible embodiment of the concept of the post-industrial information society to be found anywhere and are characterized, for the most part, by absolutism and a kind of breathless enthusiasm. Their visions are absolutist: limitless demand for information in limitless forms demanded anytime and anywhere and used with great creativity. They foresee a society of infonauts and knowledge navigators, implicitly the mainstream of society, and predict a rapid transformation of American life. These works are, however, more prescriptive and propagandist than analytically predictive. As is usually the case with propaganda, even that of the most positive and useful kind, the case tends to be overstated, its attractions exaggerated and potential difficulties ignored. The futurists tend to be fixated with technology and to conjure up pictures of what might soon be technologically possible, putting into abeyance considerations of economic or social viability. The value of their work is that it focuses debate and it is in many ways helpful that they emphasize opportunities rather than problems because, in so doing, they assist in the formation of a collective vision, however fuzzy, of what might be achieved. Their evasion of problematical issues lays them open to criticism for being utopian but they serve a useful function as trial balloonists.

It is the corporate sector, however, which is expected to play the leading role in translating these dreams into realities through a process of competitive innovation, which is an intrinsically chaotic mechanism wherever the product is, to a greater or lesser extent, a solution in search of a problem. The landscape of American technological entrepreneurship is littered with the wreckage of companies which bet their futures on the success of products which either failed to find a market at all or which were overwhelmed by competitors who were more skilled in matching the innovative concept to the real market. The process is one of collective trial and error, in which the winners often make their fortunes and the losers lose their shirts.

By reading the publications of the academics and futurists, observing the stream of new product launches and talking with the managers of technology companies it is usually possible to piece together a picture of the conventional wisdom of the American information sector with regard to what the public will want – or will at least be prepared to buy – over the next few years. It is clear, for example, that some form of nation-wide switched broadband communications network is expected to come into existence over the next decade or two but it is less clear

what, with the exception of conventional video entertainment programming, will be transmitted over it. Some speak of interactive video
services which would allow, for example, basketball fans to select their
preferred camera angles while watching a game: others go as far as to
suggest that fans may be offered the chance to watch the game projected
holographically in a kind of televisual cube. The more prosaic projections talk just of a 'video dial tone' system whereby consumers could
access movies on demand. Many observers suggest that, in one way or
another, through the operation of some kind of electromagnetic Parkin-
son's Law, applications will soon be found to absorb the bandwidth
made available by optical fibre networks. But it is only moving video,
usually for entertainment purposes, which can currently be envisaged
as requiring anything like the bandwidth which such networks will
provide.

Interactive video of one kind and another is a recurring theme in both
the publications of the futurists and the utterances of industry strategists.
Many believe that conventional classified advertising will be replaced
by huge interactive public databases, often utilizing high resolution
video images which enable customers to peruse the goods before
purchase, and that most day-to-day purchases will be made remotely.
Much of the pain of house-hunting could be eliminated, argue the
interactive video advocates, if prospective purchasers could compile
short-lists using computer data and video previews of property anywhere in the country.

Mobility is another watchword in the American information sector
of the 1990s. Largely at the behest of America's huge computer-using
population, computers have evolved from the luggable to the truly
portable, to the lap-top, to the notebook and to the palm-top. This trend,
together with the parallel developments in mobile communications was
bound eventually to spawn a new generation of mobile computing
systems. By our horizon year of 2005, it is confidently predicted that
notebook or palm-top terminals which can be linked over the airwaves
using cellular technology will be available for use by any people who
have cause to detach themselves from the hard-wired networks in their
offices.

But it is seldom clear what effect these seminal products will have
on the ways in which people live and work, except in the very narrowest
sense. What impact such innovations will have on advertising agencies,
local newspapers, retailers, real estate brokers, banks and transport
services is not hinted at. The archetypal American perception of the

innovation process is that technology teases out new markets and that regulators are towed along behind. The efficiency of the market demands that anything which can be done must be done, that people will be persuaded to buy it and that regulators will eventually be persuaded to let them.

America's Information Society of 2005

Americans have a deep-seated aversion to central planning and direction of their affairs and have in the past only resorted to the use of government agencies in the management of major projects when faced with major real or perceived external threats. The attack on Pearl Harbor resulted in the government-sponsored Pacific War and, although the motivation behind it seems curious in retrospect, the massive government-run space programme was occasioned by the launch of Sputnik I. Foreign commercial threats have from time to time caused the US government to abandon its ideological attachment to free trade and to impose punitive tariffs on foreign goods but the business of building a vibrant, competitive American economy has traditionally been left to private enterprise.

The all-embracing and systemic nature of the nation-wide large capacity digital communications network which, it is generally agreed, the USA will need if it is to maintain its position at the top of the world info-business league (or any other business league, for that matter) has, however, given rise to a vigorous debate about the need for central co-ordination of telecommunications policy. Advocates of a co-ordinated approach have pointed to the progress which has been made in European countries and, more pertinently, in Japan, as the postal, telegraph and telephone administrations (PTTs) and government departments have started to implement ambitious national schemes, many of which will not be completed until well into the next century. This they have contrasted with the comparatively chaotic and short-termist approach taken in the USA.

In 1991 Senator Albert Gore Jr. proposed the adoption of a High Performance Computing Act, under which government funding would be made available for research into the use of high speed computers and the kinds of national data networks which might link them. This initiative stopped far short of proposing a centrally managed approach to this strategic issue and merely advocated the provision of modest government funding to stimulate a more co-ordinated approach in the private sector.

Few doubt that it will be necessary to build a comprehensive optical fibre trunk network across the country and that much of the existing copper network will need to be replaced if the requirements of future data and multi-media communications traffic are to be met, but there is disagreement about how far down the branches this network will need to extend. There are also debates about technical standards and frequently expressed reservations about the wisdom of asking existing telephone subscribers to foot the massive bill for the installation of such a system. In countries where publicly owned and/or operated telecommunications monopolies exist, such scruples are seldom exhibited and it is a comparatively simple matter to achieve sufficient official consensus for work to be started. In America such decision taking is likely to continue to be a much more complex and fluid process.

Specific projected scenarios for the American infostructure of the early twenty-first century are found more in the writings of the think-tanks and futurologists than in the strategic planning documents of government agencies. Whatever collective consciousness exists with regard to the topic is constantly subject to modification in light of hard technological developments or even enlightened speculation. If the prevailing culture dictates that the infostructure of 2005 is to be determined by the interaction of market forces and entrepreneurial initiative, it follows that the nation will define its goals more through collective hunches than through detailed central planning. It is a much more dialectical process than is seen in most other countries and has been largely successful in the past.

Such a free-spirited approach, however, tends towards chaos unless some form of external discipline is imposed and it is quite clear that the most acceptable form of discipline in American society is a competitive one. For this reason, the identification of a competitor which is threatening American dominance of a market which they consider to be their own, or even hurting collective corporate pride in some area, serves as a useful focus for the nation's consciousness and can even result in a form of tacit collective action. The Japanese, with their much more cut-and-dried attitudes to strategic planning and their well-publicized strategic targets, fill this role very well and it is for this reason that debates about the co-ordination of work of national importance are so often peppered with apocalyptic references to what will happen if Japan is allowed to assume a leading position. It is therefore implicitly assumed that if the Japanese have specific objectives for the infostructure then America must go at least one better. Indeed, beating Japan is one of the most frequently-cited explicit objectives of entrepreneurs and administrators in the information sector.

While corporate America has strategic objectives which accord only with whatever longer term competitive scenario its planners and management consultants envisage, it is the responsibility of some government departments to make projections of the broader economic scenarios which are likely to result from the interplay of observable commercial trends and attitudes. One such body is the Bureau of Labor Statistics (BLS), which makes long-term projections of the shape and size of the labour force by age, sex, industry, occupational category, ethnicity etc. The most recent set of such projections conveniently forecasts labour market statistics for our horizon year of 2005. A brief summary of the Bureau's exhaustive projections serves to illustrate at least one official view of the shape of the manufacturing and service economies in the USA in that year.

The BLS makes three sets of projections, based on varying GDP growth assumptions – respectively 1.4 per cent, 2.2 per cent and 2.8 per cent for low, moderate and high-growth scenarios. The moderate growth scenario implies a continued rise in the ratio of tertiary to secondary employment from a 1990 level of 2.72 (excluding government) to 3.5 in 2005. Manufacturing output, in constant terms, is projected to increase by 39 per cent over the period, with a labour force increasing by only 1 per cent. Service sector output, on the other hand, is expected to increase by 43 per cent with labour force growth of 30 per cent. The implied productivity growth in the manufacturing sector broadly extrapolates the trend seen between 1975 and 1990, when manufacturing output increased by 50 per cent with labour force growth of 11 per cent, while the service sector (excluding government) is projected to do rather better than it did over the earlier period, when value added increased only 63 per cent while employment grew by 68 per cent.

The tertiary/secondary ratio of course only very indirectly reflects the trends in the information sector but the BLS projections of the fastest growing and fastest declining industries and occupations in employment terms give a clearer picture of what is envisaged. The fastest growing industries between 1990 and 2005, according to the Bureau, will be those which fall into the broad categories of care and information/ control. Not one of the top 20 projected employment growth industries is in manufacturing and only one of the projected fastest declining employers is not in manufacturing, namely 'communications except broadcasting'. This reflects the planned automation of telephone exchanges and directory enquiry functions and is the sole exception in what is otherwise an extremely clear picture of manufacturing decline and service sector growth.

The care and information emphasis in the growth sectors is illustrated clearly enough by the two industries projected to grow fastest – residential care and computer and data processing services – employment in both of which is projected to grow at around 4.5 per cent compound throughout the forecast period.

The shrinkage in the two fastest declining employment sectors (footwear and ordnance) probably reflects extraneous factors (foreign competition and the 'peace dividend') which are of little relevance to the changing vision of American life, but the other fastest declining occupations are more revealing. For instance, automation is expected to result in massive declines in the numbers of assembly workers, telephone operators and statistical clerks.

The high-growth occupations include home health aides (+91.7 per cent), paralegals (+85.2 per cent), systems analysts (+78.9 per cent) and psychologists (+63.6 per cent) and the picture is generally one of a continued move away from the manual and menial to the cerebral and meaningful, the whole being supported by a straight-line extrapolation of productivity growth in manufacturing. However, when viewed in terms of rather broader occupational categories, as opposed to narrowly specified occupations, the projected pattern of change in occupational structure is a rather muted extrapolation of the 1975–90 trend and it is striking how the high growth rates which were seen in the heart of the control sector in the earlier period are expected to slow in future. Most notably, executive, administrative and managerial occupations, which grew 83.1 per cent between 1975 and 1990, are expected to grow by only 27.4 per cent from 1990 to 2005.

A more caring, more informed and more efficient society is envisaged, then, with the material wherewithal supplied by an ever more productive goods-producing sector with virtually no additional people working in it. Certainly this is what the post-industrial information society in its ideal form is supposed to be about and it is an image which recurs frequently in official and institutional publications.

The NTIA, which published the *Telecom 2000* report cited above, is a division of the US Department of Commerce. The report, which runs to nearly 700 pages, reasserts the non-interventionist doctrine and, perhaps in this spirit, generally shies away from making specific longer term projections about the shape and role of the infostructure. Rather, it describes recent trends in related areas in some detail and identifies issues which an improved infostructure will help to address.

In cataloguing the role which information technology will continue to play in the commercial world, the report is more reflective and descriptive than predictive and prescriptive. It does, however, shed some light on the reasons for the expected stagnation in manufacturing employment within the USA. As US wage costs cannot be expected to decline, American companies are expected increasingly to conduct their more labour-intensive operations in countries where personnel costs are low and to depend on high-grade and high-cost American manpower only in critical design and control functions. This is a fundamental assumption, as is the idea that location decisions in manufacturing will increasingly be driven by considerations of the local availability of a high quality infostructure and an appropriately skilled labour force.

Although the tone of the report is robustly non-interventionist throughout, under a section entitled 'Ensuring the quality of individual, community and national life', the importance of telecommunications in fulfilling some 'fundamental national responsibilities' is alluded to. Defence, law enforcement and air traffic control are deemed to be suitable subjects for federal communications policy, while law enforcement and traffic control are areas in which state and local governments are expected to use communications and information technology to a greater extent in future. What form this might take, however, is not described.

The provision of communication and information services to rural areas is a recurrent theme in the report. The provision of educational and health care services to remote areas, the reduction of urban congestion and the tapping of intellectual skills which reside far from where they are required are reasons cited for this emphasis, and the report goes as far as to suggest that federal and state policy might be used to encourage the development of the rural infostructure where market forces might be deemed to fail to deliver the goods. The implicit contradictions, here and elsewhere, of the non-interventionist approach are freely admitted:

> While pressures to reduce the size and growth of government should continue, it seems probable, paradoxically, that underlying demand for

education, health care, employee training, and other public services will expand over the decade (p. 99).

Telecommunications and information technology are, however, expected to assist in the bridging of this widening gap by making finite skills and intellectual resources go further. In the delivery of education and training, the use of interactive, electronically handled material compiled by expert teachers and, possibly, augmented by some form of artificial intelligence, is expected to ameliorate the shortage of appropriately skilled teachers and to provide educational opportunity beyond the scope of conventional classroom teaching.

Similarly, in health care:

> The consumer should be able to access databases on health, from preventive care to first diagnosis and treatment for specific maladies . . .

and

> With the ability to conduct a videoconference with data exchange between two or more locations, doctors and patients will be able to obtain almost instant consultation and second opinions. Surgeons would participate in surgery via high-resolution video links (p. 108).

Stretching existing resources in these ways would enable government to remain small and to become involved only when a modest amount of intervention could bring major benefits by helping people to help themselves. The emphasis in American official policy, it seems, is always on access and opportunity and seldom on central planning, provision or co-ordination, even in many areas which are fundamental to the well-being of the nation and which are subject to extensive state intervention and regulation in most other countries.

Americans, then, envisage enhanced choice, mobility, care, control and opportunity as the main fruits of the information revolution in their country. These benefits will flow from the operation of a now familiar technological–commercial dynamic and all parties seem to be determined that they will be delivered in accordance with traditional market forces and not on the basis of any blueprint emanating from a government agency.

Japan – Recipe for an Information Society

An eminent Japanese conductor was, a few years ago, invited to conduct a famous European orchestra and, after his return to Japan, he was asked for his impressions of the experience. His rather apologetic reply was that, having being accustomed to conducting Japanese orchestras, which present the man on the podium with a uniform vista of black hair and olive complexions, he had been surprised and slightly distracted to look up from his music to see such a range of human shapes, sizes and colorations. His strongest impressions, he admitted with a smile, had been visual and not musical.

It is often said of the Japanese, by the Japanese, that their homogeneity is their most outstanding cultural feature and that, in this, perhaps lies their greatest strength. Although the descendants of the original indigenous inhabitants of the archipelago are now only to be found in very small numbers in the northern island of Hokkaido and the vast majority are the descendants of migrants from continental Asia, all the moving around happened so long ago that it is not pertinent to contemporary Japanese culture. The Japanese have been ethnically unmixed for many centuries, and during the two centuries of the Tokugawa shogunate actively excluded all foreign influences. Although the quiet pride with which the Japanese often regard their cultural homogeneity is regarded by many observers, Japanese included, as being 'politically incorrect', there can be no doubt that this relative homogeneity has given rise to an extraordinary degree of social and political cohesion for a very long time.

Although there was a brief period during which Christians were brutally persecuted in Kyushu, religion has never been a major cause of division in Japanese society. The majority of the population casually professes Buddhism, a large minority espouse Shintoism and some follow both. The two principal religions coexist to a remarkable degree and some of the most famous Buddhist temples even have Shinto shrines within their precincts. Shintoism was state-sponsored during the period of ultra-nationalism before the war and has retained something of a right-wing extremist stigma. As a result, a recent Japanese Prime Minister caused a minor political controversy by making a private visit to Tokyo's Yasukuni Shrine, the Shinto memorial to the war dead. At a more day-to-day level, the zealots of some of the Nichiren Buddhist sects can disrupt sidewalk traffic by their public proselytizing and local shrine festivals can cause traffic jams but this is usually the extent of religious disruption to the calm of what is, on the whole, a robustly secular society.

Nor are their any real internal language barriers in Japan. A farmer from Ehime Prefecture can render himself virtually incomprehensible to a slick Tokyoite, if he chooses to do so, by speaking his own local brand of Japanese, and some young Tokyoites could retaliate with the peculiar argot of the self-styled *Shinjinrui* ('new humans'), but both will speak, read and write *hyojungo*, the Ministry of Education approved standard Japanese, perfectly well if it suits them, as will their fellow countrymen from Kumamoto to Sapporo and beyond.

In spite of the fearsome complexity of the written language, Japan claims one of the highest literacy rates in the world. The vast majority of primary school children will have mastered the two 50-character *kana* syllabries and the 880 basic *kanji* (Chinese characters) by the time they enter junior high school and will generally have racked up the balance of the 1,945 *toyo kanji*, or general-use Chinese characters recognized by the Ministry of Education, by the time they emerge from compulsory education at the age of 16. The adult literacy rate, as defined by completion of this formal education process, rather than objective independent testing, is 99.7 per cent, and it is generally believed that, given the rigour with which school testing is conducted, this approximates to actual literacy levels.

Literacy levels are perhaps bound to be high in a country in which education is a national obsession. Competition within the education system, pushed by the obsessive *kyoiku mama* (education mother) at one end and pulled by the rigorous educational requirements of major corporations at the other, is murderous. Competition for entry into the more prestigious schools and colleges starts before kindergarten and there is a whole commercial and social infrastructure which surrounds the education system. In the immediate post-war decades *juku*, or cram-schools, were commonly used by children who were having difficulty in keeping up with the relentless pace imposed by the national curriculum. Now they are a nation-wide industry, catering to under-achievers, normal achievers and over-achievers alike.

Nationally, 95 percent of children complete three years in senior high school and fully 35 percent go on to either four years at public or private university or two years at junior college. Among males in the metropolitan area, these figures are much higher. The results of the system, as measured by international comparative tests, are impressive, with Japanese students scoring notably highly in mathematics and science subjects, but the real results are seen in the workplace. The ferocious competition seen in the education system is slightly dampened by the seniority system as the student moves into a corporate or government organization but this generally results not in organizational torpor but in a highly proficient management structure in which ability and high educational standards are relatively evenly spread through all strata.

Competition in Japanese society is intense and yet the differentials in living standards which it produces are smaller than those seen in comparable societies. The persistence of a promotion system which gives great emphasis to age and length of service combines with near-confiscatory tax rates for high earners to create a society in which differentials in living standards which might otherwise result from differentials in ability are largely levelled out. The result is a society in which the majority consider themselves to be middle class and in which the everyday problems of life are confronted by most people in a very similar fashion.

Japan is a narrow, mountainous country of 378,000 sq. km, only 15 per cent of which is cultivable or normally habitable. This means that the 120 million Japanese are concentrated in the major coastal plains and in mountain basin cities such as Nagano, and that urban population densities are consequently very high. Within this pattern of high urbanization, the concentration of approximately 30 millions in the Keihin megalopolis, which consists of Tokyo, Kawasaki, Yokohama and their contiguous satellite cities, represents the largest urban concentration on the planet.

The Japanese population contains as many personality types as can be seen among the citizens of any other nation and yet there must be very few nations on earth which lend themselves so easily to overall categorization as the Japanese do. They are, for the most part, urban, wealthy (GNP per capita was $28,346 in 1991), well educated, healthy (they have the highest life expectancy in the world), competitive middle-class people. They live close together, they all speak the same language and, although they engage in a very wide range of industrial and commercial activities, they, perhaps to a higher degree than is true of most nations, share a world view. If there is any nation culturally and intellectually equipped to become an information society, it is Japan.

Media Saturation

If newspaper circulation figures mean anything, the cities of Japan represent some of the largest concentrations of newspaper readers in the world. With an overall figure of 572 copies per thousand people every day, Japanese newspaper readership is exceeded only by that in Hong Kong (574) and the Soviet union (670 according to the last figures available).

With the demise of *Pravda*, Japanese titles also take all the top slots in the world circulation league. The top-selling *Yomiuri Shimbun*, which sold a massive 14.47 million copies per day in 1991, sells 35 per cent more copies in metropolitan Tokyo alone than the UK's largest seller, the tabloid *Sun*, sells nation-wide. The second-ranked *Asahi Shimbun*, also a quality broadsheet, tops 13 million copies and these and several other national dailies dwarf the circulation of America's largest daily, the *Wall Street Journal*. Japan's equivalent business newspaper, *Nihon Keizai Shimbun*, is twice the size of the *Journal* and, with its evening edition, sells more copies than the Beijing *People's Daily*.

The size of these newspapers is partly a reflection of a high degree of concentration in the industry. Although the Ministry of International Trade and Industry (MITI) lists around 1,400 newspaper companies in Japan, the 115 or so members of the Japan Newspaper Association account for virtually all of the circulation figures, with the big three – *Asahi*, *Mainichi* and *Yomiuri* – dominating the national daily scene. With nation-wide circulation and a number of printing and distribution centres around the country, the national dailies are available in a reasonably timely fashion in any part of Japan, although the logistical difficulties of distribution mean that evening editions are not available in some areas. In such cases, the editions which are dispatched to those regions include evening edition stories in the following morning's editions. All the national dailies have a large number of editions.

Huge as they are, the big three face surprisingly strong competition from 70 or so regional newspapers, many of which have large local circulations and high diffusion rates, often reaching over 80 per cent of households in their territory. The majority of these titles are long established (30 of them were set up in the nineteenth century) and draw their readership from the prefecture. Circulation figures in excess of 200,000 are common in this group and some of the larger ones run to 500,000 or more. To put this in perspective, the middleweight *Niigata Nippo* has a circulation similar to that to that of the London *Times*. The regional papers compete with the national dailies largely on the basis of their local news coverage, but they all have access to national and international news via the Kyodo News Agency and some have their own overseas correspondents. Their coverage of wider issues therefore suffers neither in content nor in timeliness by comparison with the national dailies and their local printing and distribution facilities often give the regionals the edge.

Perhaps the most surprising thing about the Japanese newspaper reading habit is the sheer volume of serious broadsheet material which is consumed. Many households in Japan will take not only one of the big three national dailies but also a regional daily and often, in business families, *Nihon Keizai Shimbun* as well. Much of this reading is done directly for professional reasons and, in addition to the serious popular press, there is a body of semi-specialist and specialist publications which enjoy large circulations. Japan's dwindling agricultural community still manages to read 470,000 copies of the daily *Nihon Nogyo Shimbun*, while the two leading semi-specialist papers serving the engineering and manufacturing sector between them clock up sales of around a million copies a day. *Dempa Shimbun*, a daily broadsheet serving the electrical and electronics industry, achieves a circulation of 285,000 and even produces a weekly English-language synopsis issue. The Japan Specialist Newspaper Association has over 100 affiliated papers, whose circulations run from a few thousands to 200–300,000 copies, which comprehensively fill in the specialist end of the market.

This may sound like a Red Square parade of publishing might, but the industry's generals, atop Lenin's mausoleum, are far from happy. The obverse of large circulation is market saturation and, although the newspapers often succeed in winning circulation from one another, sometimes on a large scale, there are no prospects whatsoever for growth in the total market and advertising revenue, although still trending gently upwards, is under pressure from competing media. In attempting to win circulation from one another and to defend their industry's share of advertising revenues, the newspapers have increased the number of pages, started printing some pages in colour and modernized their presses. The costs of pushing hard into an inelastic market have resulted in very thin profit margins for the industry at large.

Advertising revenues for other media have grown far faster over the past 20 years than for newspapers, whose share of the total has fallen from 34 per cent in 1971 to 24 per cent in 1990. Advertising revenue for newspapers exceeded subscription revenue for the first time in 1962 and grew sharply during the two decades of almost uninterrupted rapid economic growth which followed, reaching a point at which they often exceeded 60 per cent of total revenue. By the late 1980s, however, there were many cases where, under competitive pressure from other media, advertising income had fallen to or below the level of subscription revenues.

The newspapers play an important role across the whole country and the whole range of Japanese society. Their role as political watchdog has been conspicuous in their treatment of the various political scandals in recent years, notably in the 'Recruit' affair, in which a junior reporter from *Asahi* uncovered a bribery scandal which rocked the political establishment. Although the relationship which senior political editors have with politicians continues to be very close, the ultimate impartiality of the press was well demonstrated over the course of the various scandals.

In addition to this kind of political coverage, which is the bread and butter of the press in any free society, the Japanese press offers information and serious comment on an immense range of issues of general and specialist interest. In spite of competition from as wide a range of alternative media as can be found anywhere, the newspapers still command a huge and discerning readership. They are generally perceived to have maintained their credibility very well in relation to the broadcast media, and to have moved with the times in their editorial policy and their production technology, and yet a siege mentality prevails amongst the industry's managers. From such a lofty position, it seems, there is nowhere to go but down.

Commercial broadcasters have enjoyed strong growth in advertising revenues over the past decade and, even in the general economic gloom of 1991, saw their income from this source grow by 5 per cent. Revenue growth is, however, no longer fuelled by growth in audiences, as the broadcasters face problems of saturation in radio and television coverage of the nation similar to those being experienced by the newspapers.

The national broadcasting corporation, NHK, transmits one FM and two AM radio channels, as well as a short-wave international service, and two terrestrial and two satellite television channels. These services cover the whole country, with only slight regional variations in programme content. There are 32 commercial radio companies, 67 television companies and 36 which offer both services. While NHK, in principle, broadcasts to the nation, the commercial channels are intended to have a more regional flavour and this creates a network of coverage which is analogous to that provided by the big three dailies and the regional newspapers. The spectrum allocation activities of the Ministry of Posts and Telecommunications are prefectural in their focus and are based on a policy of equal provision of broadcast services to all parts of the country. The broadcast network which reflects this policy is essentially complete, and listeners and viewers all over the country are provided with four AM and two FM radio channels, seven terrestrial and two satellite television channels.

In programme content, NHK maintains a somewhat serious image, with flagship news coverage and a judicious mix of high-, middle- and lowbrow general programming on television's channel 1 and heavyweight educational and cultural content on channel 3. NHK's one FM channel is the principal source of classical music broadcasts, while several hours of its peak weekday evening airtime is devoted to educational broadcasts aimed at high school students, a surprising use of FM bandwidth which reflects an official policy that students should not be distracted from their studies by popular music. The commercial television and radio channels offer general programming with a somewhat larger light entertainment content and a continuous supply of pop music.

The market for television receivers in Japan was saturated by about 1972 and effectively every household in Japan now has one or more colour sets. During its growth period, from the mid-1950s until the late 1960s, television viewing cannibalized radio listening hours. Radio listening revived quite sharply in the latter part of the 1970s, coinciding with the diffusion of FM broadcasts, peaked in 1980 and then declined, apparently falling quite sharply during the second half of the decade. A recent survey of the national lifestyle shows that the average Japanese devotes 20 minutes per weekday to reading newspapers (a figure which has been extremely stable over the last 20 years), listens to the radio for 26 minutes (as in 1970 but down from 39 minutes at the peak in 1980) and spends three hours in front of the television. The secular trend in television viewing, however, seems to be slightly downwards, as people are spending more time in leisure activities outside the home. Taro and Hanako Suzuki (the Japanese equivalent of John and Jane Smith) spent 10 per cent less time watching television in 1990 than they did in 1980.

In any developed nation there is a clear community of interest between the commercial broadcasters and the advertising agencies but there is, on the whole, little that they can do to influence overall audience figures in their mature markets. If superior programming fails to keep the customers glued to their sets, the impact of advertising in the broadcast media is prone to erosion. The Japanese media complex, however, is unusual in that, in addition to the broadcasters and their advertising customers, it contains a third major force which is missing in most countries, namely, the media hardware manufacturers.

The Japanese manufacturers of audio and video hardware have traditionally used their large domestic customer base as a springboard into exports and, like the broadcasters, are constantly searching for new ways to sell into the super-saturated domestic market. This is manifested in a constant stream of new consumer electronic products in the audio-visual sphere, some of which are sufficiently appealing that they can have a significant beneficial impact on audience or usage figures for the medium concerned. Some of these, such as CD players and digital tape recorders, can be developed and marketed without co-operation between broadcasters and manufacturers but products such as satellite television, high definition television, pulse code modulation (PCM) radio and videotex services require close collaboration.

Japan is a consumer society with a high level of media consciousness and it is therefore comparatively easy for any new consumer electronics product which genuinely adds value to achieve the marketing critical mass necessary to establish it as a viable proposition in the broader world market. Any enhancement of the technical aspects of the broad-cast medium, such as the introduction of FM stereo broadcasting, bilingual multiplexing of television sound channels, or colour television itself, increases audience figures, for a time at least, and is beneficial to manufacturers, broadcasters and advertisers alike. The effects of such enhancements on usage are, however, largely unpredictable. Surveys conducted during the period in which colour television was being introduced showed that, even in the first five years after its introduction, colour was increasing viewing figures by less than 5 per cent.

The hardware statistics can, nonetheless, be quite impressive. Direct satellite broadcasts commenced in 1988 and, by the March 1992, 5.43 million Japanese households had satellite receivers and it is estimated that a successful launch of PCM radio services, which will provide CD-quality music broadcasts on a subscription basis, could result in over half a million receivers being installed in five years' time and three times that by the end of the century. Huge sums of money are spent in Japan on audio-visual equipment which is surprisingly little used. The life-style survey statistics show average video viewing at only 4 minutes per day in 1990, suggesting that usage of the video tape recorders installed in virtually every Japanese home is highly concentrated. Anecdotal evidence and casual observation suggests that the main users of video in Japan are children.

In 1990, the average citizen of Japan spent 3 hours and 26 minutes consuming the products of the broadcast media, 12 minutes using other audio-visual media and 35 minutes in leisure reading, to give a total of 4 hours and 13 minutes of media consumption. This, for most people, represents almost all of their free time and, in the apparent absence of the kind of media obsession which characterizes the American market, and whatever changes may be brought about in its composition, the market for the mass media in Japan shows every sign of total saturation.

Japanese Visions of an Information Society

The question of the impact which the rise of information technology was likely to have on society at large received a good deal of attention in business, government and the media in Japan in the early 1980s. The Industrial Structure Committee (*Sangyo Kozo Shingikai*) of the Ministry of International Trade and Industry (MITI) in June 1981 referred to the *johoka* ('informatization') which would take place in the 1980s and thereafter as the 'Second Information Revolution'. The Second Revolution, according to MITI, was to be distinguished from the First by the breadth of its scope. This revolution was not to be restricted to the computerization of big business; it would reach into all aspects of economic and social life.

Hot on the heels of this declaration came the publication by the Nippon Telegraph and Telephone Corporation (NTT) of detailed plans for implementation of its Information Network System, a plan for the data communications infrastructure of Japan based on a fully digitized network. By the late 1980s, most of the major ministries and governmental bodies had followed this lead and had published their policy documents relating to the informatization of the nation. The Ministry of Posts and Telecommunications (MPT), in 1983, offered its 'Teletopia' scheme for national development, with a regional flavour, MITI was soon talking about the 'New Media Community' and the Ministry of Construction was advocating the building of the 'Intelligent City'. Not to be outdone, and carrying on the utopian imagery beloved of the Japanese in the early 1980s, the Ministry of Agriculture and Forestry offered a vision of an information-based 'Greentopia'.

The MPT view of Japan as an information society was predicated on the early installation of the infrastructure of optical fibre data highways, INS, interactive CATV, satellite broadcasting, the 'Captain' videotex system, and value added network services in the major cities and their subsequent dissemination to the regions. The services which were to be offered in the model cities and regions on the back of this infrastructure were aimed at resolving problems in family, commercial and public life. The Regional Data Communications Study Group (*Chiiki Joho Tsushin Kenkyukai*, 1984) describes the social functions addressed by the MPT's 1983 Teletopia model as follows:

Social function	Relevant 'Teletopia' service types
1 Improved living conditions	A, B, I, K
2 Improved health and welfare	A, B, K
3 Response to varied study and education needs	A, C
4 Disaster warning and accident prevention	A, G
5 Promotion of regional industry	D, E, F, I, K
6 Development of data communications business	C, E, H
7 Modernization of agriculture	F
8 Promotion of energy and resources conservation	E, G, H, J
9 Reinforcement of local communities	A
10 Alleviation of isolation	A, B, D, F, K
11 Enhancement of local health authorities	B
12 Promotion of regional internationalization	J

and the services with which it proposes to address the problems as:

'Teletopia' service types	Proposed services
A Community/town type	Various home services based on interactive CATV and videotex
B Health/welfare type	Regional health information system and home examination/diagnosis service
C Academic type	Technical and reference systems
D Traditional/regional industries type	Information systems for small businesses
E Advanced industries type	Technical reference systems
F Advanced agriculture type	Agricultural information and management systems
G Urban Problems type	Disaster, police and environmental management systems
H Commerce and distribution type	Distribution network systems, POS etc.

I Tourism and recreation type	Tourist information and reservation, and recreation management systems
J International type	International teleconferencing and automatic interpreting systems
K Outlying island type	Outlying island medical information systems etc.

The outpouring of official statements on the subject of informatization in the early years of the 1980s undoubtedly reflected a fashionable preoccupation of the time but this early statement of official policy on the subject also illustrates the down-to-earth approach typically taken by the Japanese authorities in this connection. The emphasis is, for the most part, placed on problems to be solved, rather than on capabilities on offer. The availability of new technology may have been the stimulus of this activity but the authorities were clearly mindful that the technology must not be allowed to become a solution in search of a problem. The views of the various ministries inevitably reflected their own preoccupations but it is probably true to say that, by the end of the decade, this specialist focus, and the interdepartmental debate which inevitably resulted, had resulted in a well-considered view of what the information revolution was and was not going to mean for official policy in Japan.

However, whatever the role of government ministries in spreading the gospel of the information society might be, the task of implementing the installation of the infrastructure fell, and arguably still falls, mainly to NTT. It is unsurprising, therefore, that it is the views of NTT with regard to the Second Information Revolution in Japan which are the best documented and the most widely aired. Here again, the starting point is the longer term strategic problems which confront Japanese society. As the Corporation's chairman, Haruo Yamaguchi (1990), says in his book:

If the cultural theme of the twenty-first century is to be a suitable balance between our outer (that is, material) and inner (that is, emotional and spiritual) lives, and if the decisive factor here is the existence of a rich environment, then Japan must deal with problems in four main areas: the information environment; the cultural environment; the economic environment; and the natural environment. These four problem areas may be understood as: the provision of expanded information networks necessary to support the remedies for the other three problem areas; the attainment of a richer cultural life; the reversal of the population decline in rural towns; and the protection of the natural environment (pp. 22–3).

NTT expects the existing demographic and cultural trends to continue and to create a significantly different environment for information businesses in the early part of the next century from that which prevails now. More specifically, the issues which underlie the chairman's statement are summarized by an NTT planning committee (NTT Mirai Yosoku Kenkyukai, 1991) as follows:

- Japan's population will not only be ageing, but it will be ageing more rapidly than that of any other nation. By 2020 it is estimated that 23.4 per cent of the population will be over the age of 65, compared with 21.9 per cent for Sweden, the second most aged nation.
- There will be a trend towards individuality and towards an emphasis on spiritual, rather than purely material, fulfilment.
- Industry will become 'softer', with services, education, medicine, leisure etc. accounting for 31.5 per cent of GNP in 2000, by comparison with 25.4 per cent in 1985.
- With Japanese corporations increasingly active abroad and foreign firms increasingly active in Japan, national borders will become less relevant.
- There will be increased environmental and social problems, particularly associated with population concentrations in big cities.

The development of services which have been identified by planners as answering public needs but which have yet to undergo public scrutiny is inevitably a long process. Future services in the communications and information sphere have for many years been the subject of debate within the organizations which will eventually be providing them but, experimental projects apart, few of them have achieved any prominence in Japan so far.

NTT has, however, made it very clear what it expects will be the characteristics of the advanced communications systems which it will provide in the early part of the next century. The company's 'service vision' is encapsulated in their marketing catch-phrase 'V I & P' – 'Visual, Intelligent and Personal'.

The development of high performance two-way videophones and other devices for the transmission of video signals is an abiding preoccupation of the Japanese telecommunications industry. Artists' impressions of the Japanese office or home of the future, as commissioned by organizations in the communications/media complex, usually feature a large, wall-hung, flat screen television monitor which is used for the reception of television and video signals of all kinds. Telecommunications and teleconferencing services, it is envisaged, will be linked into this kind of system, as well as to stand-alone videophones in both working and domestic environments.

'Visual' services form a major plank of the Corporation's future strategy, but the real demand for such services, and the willingness of the public to pay for them, is given little prominence in the literature on the subject. The attractions of being able to compliment grandma on her tan when she calls from Waikiki or to show the baby's rash to the doctor without having to call him out are easy to imagine but some proposed applications of videophone technology perhaps suggest that it is to some extent a solution in search of a problem:

> One possible application of such visual communications is the use of 'telemonitors,' which are now being tested. These instantly transmit the sights and sounds of the head office to satellite offices, thus reducing the feeling of isolation that accompanies working in far-away places (Yamaguchi, 1990, p. 110).

The 'intelligent' aspect of the V I & P policy refers to the provision of value added services on communications networks. Some of the functions proposed, such as 'electronic secretary' (schedule management, electronic mail, filing support, electronic telephone answering) and database services already exist in one form or another; others, such as automatic translation and interpreting services are as yet nowhere near being technically possible. In essence, the 'intelligent' part of the catch-phrase is marketing shorthand for networking services of one kind and another.

The ideas for 'personal' telecommunications centre on the concept of making communications person-oriented rather than, as at present, machine-oriented. The idea is that the telecommunications system should be modified to meet the needs of the customer and not the other way around. Having to a large extent conquered distance, runs the official logic, communication must now conquer time and place. This means that communications must be made available where, when and in the manner in which the customer wants them. Mailbox and message storage and forwarding systems will help to break the constraints which the existing inflexible system imposes on its users.

The problems of privacy, given that communications systems hitherto have always operated at the initiative of the message sender, rather than the receiver, will grow as more communications media, with greater invasive potential, are developed. It is believed that the application of a sophisticated version of the existing mobile telephone technology and personal ID numbers for subscribers could enable the service operators to route calls to the individuals, wherever they may be, rather than to a specific telephone. The ID number of the caller could also be displayed on the telephone receiver so that recipients of calls can choose whether or not they want to answer them.

Developments in telephone hardware will mean that very small pocket-size telephones with multiple functions will appear. These telephones, to which personal numbers can be assigned, will work underground and in other places where mobile telephones of the present generation will not. Motorless recording devices will also be incorporated in them.

If it is to provide a technical infrastructure for the delivery of such services, the management of NTT reasons that it is necessary to construct a nation-wide standard digital network and, in an attempt to avert the technical confusion which so often results from debates over standards, the company espoused ISDN standards at an early stage. When the project was started in the early 1980s, the task facing the corporation, if it were to convert the existing networks to ISDN, involved the replacement of 54 million subscriber telephone lines, 4 million local intermediate switching lines, 1.6 million long-distance intermediate switching lines and 10,000 switching stations. Under the medium-term plan, according to which the whole country will be covered, so as not to de-emphasize rural areas, the construction of the network will be completed in three phases:

1   All remaining crossbar switching equipment will be replaced with digital gear by 1995.
2   ISDN, and the related services, will be extended across the country by 1999.
3   Broadband ISDN (B-ISDN) will be introduced by 2015.

The management of NTT believes that, if a transmission network capable of providing the bandwidth necessary to deliver the information services of the twenty-first century to the population is to be constructed, it will be necessary to install optical fibre links to homes in the major cities by 2005. Although, as will be seen later, some serious doubts surround the viability of this scheme, it can be said to be more than just a statement of intent and, for the time being at any rate, should be regarded as an action plan.

Japan 2005–2010

Projections for the various sectors of the information market up to 2005, drawn together by NTT and the Mitsubishi Research Institute, suggest that a major shift in the balance of that market will occur over the next decade, as shown in table 1.

The information sector in total is estimated to grow at a compound rate of 9 per cent and to increase fivefold in value by 2005. Within this, network businesses and software are expected to show the highest growth rates, increasing by 16 per cent and 14 per cent per annum

Table 1 Projections for the information market

Sector	1986	1990	1995	2000	2005
Audio-visual production	0.6	0.8	1.1	2.0	2.0
VAN, databases etc.	0.7	1.3	2.6	6.0	12.0
Electrical communication	5.7	7.3	9.8	15.0	22.0
Broadcasting	1.6	2.3	2.7	3.0	4.0
Newspapers, mail etc.	4.9	5.9	7.3	9.0	11.0
Software	1.1	1.8	3.6	7.0	14.0
Computers and hardware	9.2	13.6	21.1	33.0	52.0
Related construction	0.9	1.3	1.9	3.0	4.0
Totals	24.7	34.3	50.2	78.0	121.0

all figures ¥ trillion
Source: NTT Mirai Yosoku Kenkyukai, 1991, p. 182

respectively. Data processing and communications hardware is expected to grow at a compound rate of around 8.4 per cent, expanding its share of the sector from 37 per cent currently to 43 per cent in 2005. The electronic (i.e. non-print) sector of the information business is projected to increase from 71 per cent to 86 per cent over the same period. Overall growth in audio-visual production, a category which includes audio and video software manufacture, is projected to be less than 7 per cent, although software for new audio and video media, such as optical disks and high-definition television, are expected to grow by around 12 per cent.

These forecasts illustrate how gradual, in terms of industrial structure, the Japanese expect the shift towards the information society to be. There is nothing in these figures which suggests that there will be a radical shift in the mix of Japan's economy towards 'soft' information services before the year 2005. In fact, given the very high base from which it starts and the healthy growth rate which is still forecast for it, the hardware sector is expected to increase as a proportion of the broad information sector, even though its growth rate will be lower than that for software and network services.

Labour productivity in the Japanese electronics industry is already very high and there are no signs of plans for any colossal programme of capital spending which would increase it to such an extent that the numbers of people employed in the hardware businesses in the information sector will decline. On the face of it, employment in hardware manufacture is likely to grow more, in absolute terms, than it will in the 'soft' sectors. It seems highly likely that the 'soft' electronic businesses will be making inroads into the strategic position held by the traditional 'soft' sectors – the press and broadcasting – and that the hardware makers may 'soften' the mix of their business, possibly by acquisition or by the creation of subsidiaries.

Tadahiro Sekimoto, the president of NEC, has forecast rapid growth in what he calls *dai-ni-ten-go-ji sangyo*, a phrase which cannot smoothly be translated into English (meaning, literally, something like 'two-and-a-half industry') and which refers to manufacturing activities with a very large intellectual or 'soft' input – a kind of half-way house between secondary and tertiary industry. There are no signs at all, however, that Japanese electronics companies plan to de-emphasize their hardware manufacturing.

The 1990 report of the 2010 Committee of the Keizai Shingikai (the Economic Deliberation Council) makes projections of employment in three broad categories: the physical production, 'network', and knowledge services sectors, to the year 2010. Recalculation of its figures, bringing the groupings back into the simple secondary and tertiary categories, suggests that the ratio of tertiary to secondary employment in Japan will grow only to 1.89 by 2010, a very gradual increase indeed, and one which would leave it well below that current in the USA and even further behind the ratio of 3.5 projected for the USA in 2005 by the Bureau of Labor Statistics.

Examination of the Council's figures in more detail shows a further drastic projected decline in primary production (i.e. production in agriculture, fishing and mining), so that it accounts for only 1.1 per cent of GDP and 3.9 per cent of the workforce in 2010, as opposed to 2.9 per cent and 7.7 per cent in 1991. It will be for the primary sector workforce that those entering the new information sectors will be substituted. The secondary sector is projected to increase its share of GDP from 29.5 per cent to 29.9 per cent by 2010 on an only marginally reduced 22 per cent of the working population, while the cutting-edge knowledge-based sector, which includes management, health and educational services, is expected to increase its share of GDP from 25.3 per cent to 27.3 per cent with a workforce which grows from 29.5 per cent to 36 per cent of the total employed. The growing information sector, it seems, is expected to be supported by increased productivity in manufacturing and is not expected to pay its own way in terms of maintaining GDP per capita, a pattern similar to that which has been seen elsewhere – the UK in the 1980s being one example.

Insofar as these projections are clearly being made with a view to the demographic and social trends which are expected to continue into the next century, the acceptance of some potential dilution of the formally monetary GDP per capita in exchange for an improved quality of social and intellectual life is implicit and perhaps inevitable. As one of the wealthiest nations in the world, it is also perhaps something which the Japanese have decided they can afford. It is noteworthy, particularly in view of the speed with which the Japanese population is ageing, that the Keizai Shingikai figures for health and medical services, within the knowledge-based sector, show a growth from 3.3 per cent of GDP in 1989 to 3.9 per cent in 2010, with employment in the sector growing from 3.9 per cent to 5.5 per cent of the working population, a similar pattern to that projected for the USA.

All of this tallies quite closely with the scenario, drawn by NTT's chairman, of 'a suitable balance between our outer (that is, material) and inner (that is, emotional and spiritual) lives' and perhaps highlights the question as to what might be deemed to be a *suitable* balance. The scenarios for the first part of twenty-first century drawn by government agencies and large corporations in Japan bespeak a high degree of pragmatism and not inconsiderable analysis of observable trends. The Japanese people are highly educated, wealthy and ageing. They are increasingly inclined to enjoy the fruits of their labours, rather than to re-invest most of their wealth in industries which are regarded by their overseas trading partners as being too competitive already. They will therefore take steps to improve their intellectual and social environment and to provide for care and support in their increasingly healthy old age. 'Soft', information-based industries will be encouraged to grow accordingly. But nobody is likely to forget what has created the nation's enviable wealth and the information sector will continue to be called upon to support a vigorous high-technology manufacturing sector. Japan's competitive advantage here has been carved out over the whole of the post-war period and will not be relinquished lightly.

If their future goes according to the current plans, the Japanese will realize their existing potential to become one of the world's leading information societies and, in so doing, they will in many ways create the kind of 'infotopia' of which many of their planners dream. Their non-material living standards will probably rise and it may be that Japan will, on the surface at least, become a less demanding place to live in. But the ethnic homogeneity and rather insular culture of the Japanese belie a very worldly-wise nation which can only become more so as it develops its infostructure further and, although its citizens may in future spend more time on personal affairs, Japan will continue to be one of the great manufacturing workshops of the world and a formidable competitor. That, it seems, will be what the Japanese people regard to be an information society with a *suitable balance*.

The Superpower Nexus

The relationship between the USA and Japan has a long and turbulent history. Ever since the arrival of Commodore Matthew Perry's squadron off Uraga on 8 July 1853 started a chain of events which brought Japan out of the self-imposed isolation of the Tokugawa period, the two nations have exerted strong political and economic influences on one another. Since the early 1980s, the focus of this mutual influence has been commercial and, increasingly, technological. The sometimes bitter disputes between the two nations over such issues as automobile exports and subsidies to rice farmers are well documented but the area in which Japan's competitiveness perhaps disturbs Americans most is information technology. As far as semiconductors, computers and related industries are concerned, the two countries have, in effect, been locked in a battle for the technological high ground.

The use of the 'high ground' analogy in this connection, and in the context of the development of the infostructure, is appropriate because it encapsulates the element of fear which exists in the process of intellectual and technological competition. The strategic high ground has been occupied since ancient times by people with reason to fear that somebody might creep up on them unobserved or bombard them with missiles from above, with uncomfortable consequences in either instance. The fear of losing the intellectual or technological high ground today is no less intense because military, political, economic and social security has become so dependent upon knowledge and the control which it brings.

During the Cold War, the flow of information technology, and other advanced technology from the non-communist to the communist world was strictly controlled by a multilateral body known as the Co-ordinating Committee, or Cocom. The USA was the leading light in this organization and it is believed by some that it was used to further the interests of US high-technology industry in ways which were injurious to the interests of other members. Fear can therefore be said to have surrounded Cocom on all sides. It was itself a product of fear and the potential or actual abuse of its influence was feared by some of its members as well as by those whose access to technology it was designed to inhibit.

It has been claimed, moreover, that the USA, by playing on the (justifiable) fears of technological uncompetitiveness in the Soviet Union with its Strategic Defence Initiative ('Star Wars') plans, precipitated a collapse of national self-confidence and, eventually, of the Union itself. The SDI is regarded by many as having been nothing more than an elaborate bluff but it seems that the fear which it generated was very powerful, possibly instrumentally so.

At a less apocalyptic level, we have already seen how fear of Japanese dominance of some areas of information technology has become a significant element in competitive motivation in the USA.

It is legitimate to ask, however, to what extent the competitive dynamic in the information sector is propelled by primitive fears and to what extent by a friendly and constructive rivalry. The question is relevant because the progress towards the intelligent state at a global level is likely to be hampered by excessive secrecy, failures to benefit from inter-corporate and international co-operation and wasteful and damaging competition.

The USA and Japan have striking differences and similarities. America is sub-continental in geographical scale, populous and ethnically diverse and has a geographically and culturally dispersed population, while Japan is a small, densely populated archipelago and has a naturally high degree of ethnic and cultural homogeneity. The mass media in the USA have traditionally played an important role in the promotion of national unity, a function hardly necessary in Japan. The markets for the mass media in Japan show signs of saturation and a degree of continuity which is in marked contrast with the continuing process of proliferation and change in the USA.

The successive waves of immigration which have given rise to the ethnic diversity of American society have thereby also contributed to the hybrid vigour which seems to be at the root of American creativity. The continuity and unity of purpose which characterizes Japanese society has bred a kind of fastidious developmentalism which has powered Japanese dominance in many areas of high-technology manufacturing. America's rapidly changing market-driven educational system struggles to cope with the demands of an increasingly diverse culture in which there is constant concern over apparently declining standards and even the relevance of standards for performance evaluation is constantly being questioned. Gruelling competition in pursuit of education along well-established lines in a clearly defined hierarchy is the rule in Japan, where anxieties are often expressed, not over competence or performance against objective standards, but over a system which appears to stifle creative thought.

In the USA, the information sector, and indeed the economy as a whole, has a strong bias in favour of services; in Japan, manufacturing is still the mainspring of both the sector and the broader economy. Official projections on both sides of the Pacific reflect expectations that these biases will continue to exist, although both economies are expected to show an increased orientation towards services in future.

It is probably not much easier, in reality, to predict the shape of the infostructure in Japan in 2005 and beyond than it is in America, although Japan's official pronouncements on the subject are both more predictive and more prescriptive than anything coming out of government departments in the USA. The Japanese government constantly exercises a kind of loose administrative guidance over industry and seeks to provide a framework for strategic consensus-forming. It is also more willing to get involved in national infrastructure projects than is the US administration, which adheres to aggressively *laissez faire* principles. But Japanese industry is well able to look after itself and is, in reality, as likely to be influenced by what is happening outside Japan as it is to be guided by the government. The major external influences which impinge upon the information sector are usually American in origin because the two countries are increasingly technologically and commercially interdependent. The unpredictability of developments in America introduces unpredictable elements into the Japanese scene.

It is interesting to reflect how, different as they are, the world's two information superpowers act as near-perfect foils for one another. The stereotype has Americans innovating and the Japanese developing and providing manufacturing wherewithal. Japanese hardware runs American software, Hollywood movies appear on Japanese television sets and Japanese memory chips cluster around American microprocessors on printed circuit boards.

Superpower relations, however, tend to have knock-on effects elsewhere and this is as true of US–Japan conflict and co-operation in the information sector as it was of the US–Soviet confrontation in world politics. The two nations have similar visions of their socio-economic futures and both perceive the development of an advanced infostructure to be crucial to their ability to compete. They are very conscious of one another and their intense competitive and dialectical relationship in the information sphere has resulted in the creation of a model for the infostructures of the developed world.

The two nations between them dominate all aspects of information technology and, to the extent that their predictions of the availability of enabling technology coincide, a commonality of view naturally arises with regard to one important aspect of the future infostructure. The demographic characteristics of the two nations differ in some respects but are similar in the ways which perhaps have the greatest effect on policy. Both populations are ageing and becoming more affluent and have reached similar conclusions about how they will use an enhanced infostructure to address pressing socio-economic problems. Big as it is, America suffers from severe traffic congestion which might be alleviated by the use of information technology and, small as it is, Japan has some isolated communities which could benefit from the new kinds of communications services designed to alleviate some of the problems of rural America.

Japanese pronouncements on the future information society perhaps lack the visionary flamboyance of those from American futurologists but there can be little doubt that the vision, in general terms, is shared. That is not to say, however, that the vision is identical or that two nations can or will move towards the common objective in the same way, as they start from different points of departure and are differently equipped for the journey. They will contribute to the progress towards the global information society in their own particular ways and will also deal with the impediments which will confront them, and all the other developed nations, along the road in ways which reflect their particular strengths and weaknesses.

Because America and Japan are in the vanguard as the developed world moves towards an information society, they are likely to encounter the problems sooner and perhaps in more intense a form than those who follow. The motivations for change are clear but it may be that the first truly successful information societies will be built not where the opportunities are most readily realized but where the accompanying and resulting problems are best dealt with.

5
THE TROUBLED DREAM
OF THE
POST-INDUSTRIAL STATE

The developed world generates its own role models, created in popular culture and projected via the mass media, which reflect and crystallize the life-style aspirations of people at large and these aspirations are in turn reflected in the behaviour of commercial and governmental institutions. Vague as these aspirations often are, they seem to be converging in most western societies to create mass cultures with quite a high degree of commonality. When the ideal life-style model, which is essentially American in its origins, is translated into social and economic policy in the USA and elsewhere, however, the implied direction becomes less clear, the policy alternatives proliferate, and the debate surrounding them intensifies. It is difficult to predict the shape of society in the future when your only role models are yourselves and, in such circumstances, future societies can only be imagined. And a good deal of imagination has indeed been applied to such questions. One notion which has been born of the collective imagination of the futurologists and planners is that of the 'post-industrial information society'.

This is one of the few conceptual templates which, since its rise to popularity in the early 1970s, has become well enough defined that it can be used when examining the pattern of development in the information-rich nations of the world, and yet it has recently been under assault and appears in some ways to be at odds with the observable trends. Although the term was coined to describe a society in which manufacturing industry no longer dominated the lives of the majority of the people, a situation which has for some time obtained in most industrialized countries, it also contained ideas of a kind of post-materialism based on affluence – an affluence which most citizens of the developed world would be unlikely to recognize in their current circumstances. Certainly it seems strange to characterize as post-industrial any society in which not only does the production of physical goods continue to grow every year but also in which increased physical production is still one of the most pressing and all-pervading priorities.

It may well be the case that the citizens of the developed world on the whole aspire to escape from servitude in the machine shop, the strip mill or the bakery and instead sit in airy offices dealing with abstractions – information in one form or other – and, indeed, many have managed just such an escape. The term 'post-industrial society' is often used interchangeably with 'information society'. Advocates of the 'electronic cottage' further suggest that factory-style organization in offices is not necessary or appropriate for brain workers and that in future many will be able to work more efficiently, more comfortably and more economically at home. Some have already made this transition and their mode of operation perhaps epitomizes one aspect of the classical view of the information society. And yet, this way of life is available only to a minority and even some of its most enthusiastic advocates recognize that it is not appropriate even for all brain workers. Factories, offices, suburban homes and the perils of travelling between them will be with us for the foreseeable future and, if we are indeed living in an information society, it does not, at this stage, seem to differ markedly from the smokestack world which preceded it. By that judgement, contemporary society is neither yet post-industrial nor an information society. This is not to say, however, that these terms have no descriptive value; and potentially important changes which are resonant with the idea of a post-industrial information society are occurring. It is therefore important to identify what, in practice, an information society is or might turn out to be.

There is a strong *a priori* case for saying that, if the information society is about anything, it is not about information as an end product or as a commodity in its own right. It is true that 'news junkies', quiz contestants and some scholars may pursue information for its own sake, seeking to satisfy a voyeuristic desire for real-life drama or pursuing useless erudition, but the demand for information is, on the whole, a derived demand insofar as the possession or transmission of information is usually intended to influence a pattern of action. The relationship between information and action may be direct and instantaneous, as in the reaction of a pilot (human or automatic) to the signal of a stall warning device, or indirect and delayed, as in the cumulative effect of a mass of varied information on voting patterns, but the commerce in information is usually intended to facilitate decision taking of one kind or another.

When using the term 'information *society*' in the context of decision taking, it is tempting to use the word to refer not to a whole nation but rather to a section of the community, as in 'high society' or 'café society'. Its use in this latter sense implies that the trade in and use of information continues to be dominated by one segment of society – the controllers, managers, administrators and accountants. The choice of meaning will perhaps depend upon the observer's view of the distribution of the power to control. If information has become more available, and more usefully available, to increased numbers of people and the locus of control has thus been greatly widened, then the changes of recent years will have created something which might be called an information society in the broader sense. If, on the other hand, the advances in technology have only strengthened the hand of the managers and, by increasing the volume and complexity of information to be handled, swelled their ranks, then the term information society should be used to refer to this group alone. The former view of the situation, with its democratic-populist overtones, seems the more attractive; the latter is perhaps the more plausible.

If the premise that information as an economic commodity is primarily intended to support decision taking is accepted, it is a short step to the position taken by some communications studies specialists and information economists that the information society is primarily concerned with control. James Beniger, in his much-cited book *The Control Revolution*, identifies the origins of the information society in the required response to the greatly increased complexity and geographical dispersion of American industry resulting from the railroad boom in the late nineteenth century and suggests that the development of control methodology (book-keeping, etc.) was more important than was the advent of mechanical, electrical and electronic devices which facilitated it. Beniger makes a powerful point and one which, if taken together with the idea that the information society might refer only or mainly to a controlling class in society, has potentially sinister political connotations. The idea of the information revolution as being principally concerned with control, however, has validity across a wide spectrum of applications, from the transnational to the microscopic, and perhaps says more about the true nature of the boom in information technology than any other concept used in describing the phenomenon. It also lays open to question any assertion that modern information technology merely augments an existing control structure.

At the sharp edge of its applications, information technology does much more than just enhance control and efficiency in an existing function. It can render possible things which were previously impossible. Anti-lock brakes on cars and automatic landing systems for aircraft are examples of the previously impossible in the electro-mechanical sphere and, while examples of feats which were previously systematically impossible in the organizational sphere are less easy to cite, modern information systems commonly allow simple management decisions to be taken with absolute confidence in situations where the necessary information would previously not have been available. Sophisticated electronic control systems allow right decisions to be taken instead of wrong ones, allow decisions to be taken where a lack of information would otherwise have made decision taking too dangerous and, in a much broader sphere, replace human art and experience with logical processes based on certainties.

Control has always been big business and a random listing of phrases containing the word illustrates its enormous scope. Inventory control, skid control, air traffic control, crowd control, temperature control, political control, financial control, police control and process control could be offered as starters in what could be a very long list of control words but such a listing is more than a word game. All of these phrases describe processes which have very similar elements. In all cases, data are collected and processed according to some prescribed pattern and actions are formulated in response.

The technology, routines and organizational structures involved in these different forms of control differ so widely that the common elements may seem obscure but all have been profoundly affected by developments in modern information technology and it is the increased scope which technology has brought to all these types of control which constitutes the very stuff of what is sometimes referred to as the information revolution.

The dark side of control of all kinds is that it can be excessive, inconsistent or inept. Control is more easily defined and specified in the physical world than in management or politics and it is therefore easier to identify where value has been added in direct applications of technology to physical control than in management decision support.

Energy-saving process controllers are installed, save energy and add measurable value. Excessive or erratic control in physical devices can be designed out because it exists within a well-defined systemic whole. Where a catastrophic control failure occurs in an X-ray machine or a fly-by-wire system it is the result of either a hardware problem or a software problem; operator error is comparatively easy to isolate in the diagnostic process. It is seldom, however, possible confidently to assess whether the application of a new technique or technology to management or planning is functioning optimally. If a traffic control system, treasury forecasting system or a computer trading system fails to achieve the desired result, diagnosis of the problem is intrinsically more complex because of the great range of extraneous variables and human intermediation which impinge on the systems.

The use of micro-electronics in physical control has seen explosive growth, but the products have been commoditized and the greatly enhanced control which we have over various aspects of our physical environment is now largely taken for granted. The mass of nitty-gritty electronic controllers of one kind and another appear in the statistics for the manufacturing sector and are incorporated in end products or the machines used to make end products. They are simply very useful information-driven physical tools.

The proliferation of managerial and administrative applications of advanced technology, on the other hand, raises complex issues and leaves many questions outstanding. Geoffrey Mulgan (1991) refers to what he calls 'the control economy: the set of techniques, institutions and people concerned with co-ordination, decision-making and command' (p. 17). His 'control economy' looks rather similar to our tongue-in-cheek, narrow definition of the information society and his analysis raises some important related issues, particularly with regard to the appropriate size of the control sector within the broader economy. The costs of control are tolerably measurable, but the benefits are often disturbingly unmeasurable and the efficiency of the system can usually only be guessed at.

In a reasonably unfettered market economy, the mechanism of competition lends a hand by bankrupting the least efficient operators and enriching the most efficient but, in the shorter term at least, the forces of the market can only highlight *relative* inefficiency. If the control sector as a whole is systematically inefficient and the differences between the participants slight, the natural selection process of the market could take a very long time to have any significant impact. And there must be reason to doubt the systematic efficiency of large parts of the control sectors of most developed nations, as they struggle to cope with the increased complexity of their tasks. The advent of electronic support equipment in these areas offers no panacea. Indeed, inappropriate use of the powerful electronic tools which the people of the control economy now have at their disposal can pile complexity on complexity and result in a spiral into entropy.

The classical view of the post-industrial information society envisions the releasing of an ever larger part of the population from physical production as a result of automation and greatly improved productivity. Those displaced go into services, into technical work connected with the productive sector and into the more narrowly defined control economy; but it is clear that this process can only go so far. Theories have been offered with regard to the limits on the growth of the control sector within the whole economy, but the point at which diminishing returns set in is difficult to spot in the real world and there is no case which can with any confidence be identified in which a market economy has become so control-saturated that the process has been thrown into reverse.

The control economy is difficult to isolate in official statistics because all forms of economic activity, in the primary, secondary and tertiary sectors, contain control elements, and the progress of automation has increased their relative weight virtually everywhere. It is in the tertiary sector, however, that the activities which make up what might be described as the third-party control sector of the economy are concentrated, and the pattern of growth which has been seen in the tertiary sectors of the advanced economies in recent years perhaps offers some clues as to the way in which the control economy is expanding.

In most countries in the developed world, the absolute numbers employed in the tertiary sector have grown steadily over the past 20–30 years and the portion of the total workforce which they account for has also increased. Employment in the primary sector typically has declined or has stabilized at a low level. The secondary sector has in most cases stabilized in absolute numbers, while declining relatively. Notable exceptions to this pattern are Japan, where the secondary workforce has grown almost as fast as the tertiary, and the UK, where employment in the secondary sector, conversely, has declined by 40 per cent in the last 20 years. Figure 1 indicates the ratio of tertiary to secondary sector employment in eight developed countries and the pattern of change over

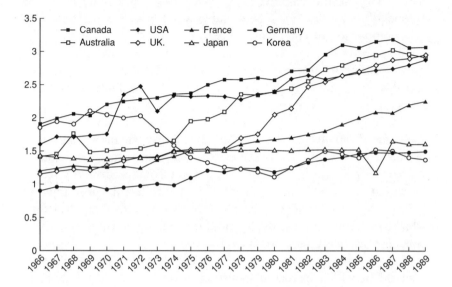

Figure 1 Ratio of tertiary to secondary employment (times)

the past quarter-century. It is interesting to note how the 'Anglo' nations – Canada, the USA, Australia and the UK – have converged to virtually identical tertiary/secondary ratios in the make-up of their labour forces, while those members of this selected group which have enjoyed long-term balance of payments surpluses also cluster together, but at a much lower level. While the tertiary sectors in Canada, the US, Australia and the UK typically employ around three times as many people as do the secondary sectors, the figures for Germany, Japan and Korea are only one to one-and-a-half times.

The high ratios seen in Canada and Australia can perhaps be explained by the importance of primary production and relative unimportance of manufacturers in the export trade of those countries and, for our purposes here, the UK, once a major manufacturing nation, seems to offer the most interesting example of the secondary-to-tertiary shift. In 1958, British workers in the secondary sector marginally outnumbered those in the tertiary. The crossover occurred in 1959 and, from the early 1960s, the trends in the two sectors started to diverge at an accelerating rate. The really rapid divergence, however, coincided with the years of the Thatcher government. In 1979 the tertiary sector employed just over twice the number in the secondary sector: by 1989, the multiple was approaching three to one.

A comparison of employment breakdown by sector with growth in GDP by sector through the 1980s, however, suggests that productivity growth during the period came mainly from the declining secondary sector, not the growing tertiary (see figure 2). Insofar as changes in productivity are a reciprocal of the changes in employment levels, the pattern in the secondary sector perhaps represents nothing more than a shedding of labour which has been rendered redundant as a result of technical innovation but which it was previously more difficult to offload for political and legal reasons. The dismal productivity record in the tertiary sector, on the other hand, may reflect the absorption of labour into new business areas which have yet to hit their stride and which will generate great wealth in future, although this might seem to be an unreasonably sanguine interpretation.

What we may be seeing here is a manifestation of the classical scenario in which increased industrial efficiency liberates labour to more amenable tertiary occupations and yet continues to provide the real wealth to support them. The figures do not, at any rate, suggest that the tertiary sector is generating sufficient growth to support the rising living standards which many in the sector have undoubtedly enjoyed

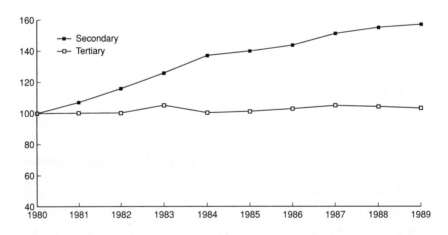

Figure 2 UK secondary and tertiary sector productivity growth (1980=100) (computed from national income statistics in the Central Statistical Office Blue Book)

over this period. The tertiary sector should not be equated too closely with the control sector, which has a much more diffuse nature, but employment in some activities which fall quite clearly into the control sector, such as financial services and information networks, grew dramatically during the 1980s and, to that extent, the growth of the tertiary reflects the growth of the control sector. The severity of the shake-out in the tertiary sector in the recession of the early 1990s, notably in areas like financial services, suggests that the control sector in the UK in the 1980s became significantly overgrown.

It is also possible that, before the recession triggered the safety valve world-wide, the market mechanism was already seeking to relieve the pressure by exporting control, adding further fuel to the globalization of information businesses in the 1980s. That is to say that the involvement of industrial, commercial, financial and governmental entities in affairs beyond the borders of their home states may have relieved the pressure of an excessive control component in their domestic economies.

Such cross-border flows of control, where they go into countries with inadequate control sectors, may enhance productivity in the recipient countries to a sufficient degree that they are still, at a global level, generating increasing returns. It may be that the forces of the market are merely redistributing control capacity between the high-abstraction states, where the control economy has become too large for its physically productive base, and the low-abstraction states, where the size and efficiency of the productive base is inhibited by a lack of management and control. If so, then the process creates net gains and is beneficial for all concerned, but this kind of efficient factor redistribution is, in reality, only part of the picture and, even where the cross-border flows bring real benefits, they are typically associated with certain systemic difficulties.

People who manage information-driven businesses are, by definition, often aware at a very early stage of where profitable opportunities may exist and they usually act on the information quickly. In times of prosperity in the developed world, this can result in headlong rushes into putative growth businesses in economies which are already intensively managed by domestic operators. It is often the case, therefore, that resources are transferred from one high-abstraction state to another in pursuit of opportunities which may bring profits in the short term but which may be unsound in the longer term because the real economy of the recipient country is already nearly or actually control-saturated.

In developing countries, where the economy is very far from being saturated, the connotations of foreign management involvement in their affairs invoke in the minds of the governing classes the more sinister meaning of the word 'control' and governments typically seek to keep such foreign involvement at arm's length. The educated elites of developing nations also recognize the personal benefits of involvement in abstract rather than physical activities and seek to develop their own expertise in control economy specialisms. As the intellectual infrastructure in the developing world grows, there is accordingly likely to be increasing 'back pressure' in the export markets for control economy services, which will become even less internationally tradeable than they are now.

Even within the advanced domestic markets for control and information products and services, there are several types of back pressure working to constrain growth but, in recent years, these have been overwhelmed in a headlong drive towards computerization, office automation and informatization of all kinds – and all of this piled on top of what was already a highly developed information economy.

The major factor which has given rise to this rush has been the advent of powerful information technology. The enthusiasm with which it has been grasped is often attributed to an acute, and apparently logical, sense that those who fail to keep up in the application of new information technology would be committing competitive suicide. The doyens of the computer culture have certainly encouraged such ideas and there are areas of economic activity in which they are irrefutable. No airline of any size could survive without a computerized reservation system, no securities trader without sophisticated communications and information systems and, back in the manufacturing sector, few machine shops are properly competitive without numerically controlled equipment. These are open-and-shut cases but there are innumerable examples of massive and ill-conceived computerization projects which have wrought havoc in organizations and others where the benefits have been dubious at best. The appeal of the new technology has, in other words, sometimes proved to be meretricious.

To many senior managers in organizations of all kinds, managing information technology and coping with the proliferation of information sources, communications and value-added services presents major difficulties. Most senior executives in the early 1990s are ill-equipped by education and experience to deal with these problems; many of them were already in senior positions in their organizations when the first microprocessors, multiplexers and multi-purpose office software packages appeared on the scene. They shy away from information technology problems themselves and are often unable even to comprehend the advice offered by the specialists to which they delegate them. And yet the organizations over which they preside push relentlessly on with the process of informatization. The corporate culture holds that there is no alternative. They can't live with it but they can't live without it, and the picture is all too often one of fumbling decision takers, attracted by glittering opportunities, bewitched by technology but most of all goaded by fears of what will happen if they fall behind. These attitudes have fuelled a bubble in a wide range of information businesses.

In the culture which prevailed in the late 1970s and the 1980s, the motivation for informatization went far beyond short- and medium-term considerations of profit and wealth and, indeed, beyond meeting the needs created by the increased complexity of social and economic organization. The notion of post-industrialism, although somewhat beleaguered in academic circles, has established itself in the popular culture of the professional classes, particularly in the English-speaking world. The job content and life-style which it seems to offer to a large number of people is very attractive. Post-industrial jobs are safe, clean, interesting, lucrative, prestigious and generally agreeable. Having escaped from the dark satanic mills, a large segment of society in the developed world has no desire to return to them.

The particularly high levels of tertiary sector employment in the Anglo world perhaps reflect particular enthusiasm for the post-industrial notion within the English-speaking culture. The corollary of this enthusiasm, however, is a widespread belief that, in emphasizing the information sector of the economy, it is acceptable to de-emphasize manufacturing. Such beliefs can, however, have severely deleterious effects not only on manufacturing but on the mass of service and information businesses which surround any manufacturing activity. Where a factory closes down through inability to cope with foreign competition, it is not only the direct manufacturing revenues and jobs which are lost but also those in the mass of ancillary functions. Cohen and Zysman (1987) demonstrate that these linkages are widespread and very important to any economy and that the transition which should take place as a result of automation and the information revolution is not to a post-industrial economy but to a new kind of industrial economy.

Another problem with the post-industrial concept, particularly the high-tech idyll of the 'electronic cottage' variety, is that it is predicated on an assumption of a high level of general affluence – an affluence which has not yet been achieved in most parts of the world and which will be enjoyed only by a small portion of humanity for the foreseeable future. The competition among aspirants to even the centralized 'air-conditioned office block model' of the post-industrial state can only intensify as the symptoms of control saturation and ineptitude in management in the developed world worsen and new competitors, coming from unexpected corners and bearing superior mousetraps, start to make inroads into the existing information businesses themselves.

In the developed world, as mass media and communications businesses are confronted with saturated markets, convergence in information markets is increasingly likely to result in collisions, as hardware and software producers invade one another's territory and telecoms and media moguls slug it out on disputed ground. The competition will be both domestic and international and the political significance of the control elements in information businesses means that they will come increasingly under the scrutiny of national governments.

Progress towards a state in which the high ground of society and the economy is dominated by an intelligent and continuously informed group of high technology information-driven businesses and institutions is unlikely to be as smooth as the proponents of the post-industrial society imply. It is likely to be a highly competitive and rather messy affair, with bubbles in control economies being burst and havoc being wrought in tertiary sector labour markets – as it has been in the early 1990s. Although some countries and companies have a large head start in the race to the intelligent state, they will increasingly be forced to look to those elements in their own economies and institutions which will affect their competitive positions and to question the viability of large parts of what they had hitherto considered to be the ultimate growth sector. The role of education, consumer conservatism, the threat of unemployment, in particular of white-collar unemployment, and the potential complexities of info-politics are all problems which threaten to distort or inhibit the future development of the information sector. It could be a rough ride.

The Education Crunch

When examining the implications of the nature of a system of education for the creation and management of an infostructure it is perhaps natural for the observer to take an instrumental approach, and to regard education purely as a support function to the abstract business of the society. Education is in truth much more than this, as the ways in which a society educates its members are integral to its whole nature and a major part of the energies of any educational infrastructure is devoted to imbuing its students with the tenets and values of the culture, a particular view of history and the whole 'folk memory'. As a culture is, for the most part, a product of *ex post facto* adaptation to events, education systems seldom, if ever, anticipate change and, as products of social consensus, they tend even to lag behind society at large in response to it.

The apparatus of education is anyway too complex and cumbersome, and too set about with intellectual and moral debate, to adapt itself quickly to whatever technological or economic change seems to require. Education, which might be expected to be a driving force in infostructural change, tends therefore to be at best a neutral force and at worst a significant obstruction. In this sense, any changing society faces an education crunch of one kind or another and, the more rapid and thoroughgoing the change, the more resounding the crunch. On the face of it, the kinds of change which the technological and social forces described above are likely to unleash over the next decade or so are such that a whole series of educational crises seem inevitable.

Developed and developing countries are confronted with rather different types of actual or perceived educational crises. Bermuda and the USA will be affected by change differently than will Burkina Faso and India, which start from very different bases. It has been suggested here that developing nations have clear precedents, in the experiences of the developed world, to follow in the creation of their infostructures but, even with regard to such First World basics as literacy, these nations must choose when and how they should follow this path. Education and universal literacy may be part of the longer term solution to the problems which developing countries face but the costs of pursuing them may be unacceptable in the short term. It may be that, in the case of a country like India, an option of high urban literacy co-existing with a continuing high level of rural illiteracy is a pragmatic response to the nation's needs. The elite segments of the educational establishment in some Third World and developing countries, including India, have already produced many individuals who have proved capable of competing (as *émigrés*) at the highest levels of advanced information societies and there are clear signs that centres of excellence, such as Bangalore, within countries with otherwise low educational standards, are beginning to emerge as competitive participants in the international arena.

It is in the developed world, however, that the question of the educational response to the information revolution is generally perceived to be most pertinent and urgent, and this question usually forms part of the backdrop to discussions of the adequacy or otherwise of education. In such discussions, the characteristics of the education systems in various countries are often compared and contrasted and the shortcomings of the home teams highlighted. The British say that their system produces too few engineers, scientists and mathematicians, the Japanese criticize their schools for overworking their students and stifling creativity and Americans fret over student indiscipline and the downward track of those Scholastic Aptitude Test scores. Criticisms of the subject matter and methodology of schooling abound but, if the extent to which generally acclaimed improvements are ever achieved is anything to go by, the problems seem to be largely intractable.

One reason for this is that the way in which education actually operates in any country is, for the most part, culturally, and not systematically, determined. Whether schoolchildren do their homework, respect their teachers, are generally interested in learning French, fight in class or take drugs is seldom anything to do with the education system itself. Classroom violence in Japan has become a major problem in recent years and the authoritarian system which was held up as an exemplar by educational conservatives in other countries has proved incapable of doing anything to prevent it. The children of lawyers and engineers are often imbued with law and engineering from birth and some regard their parents as natural role models, reinforcing existing occupational and intellectual leanings. Such cultural and behavioural factors account for as much of the differences in orientation and performance between students internationally as do systemic differences.

It should be possible, in theory, for the educational authorities in a country to make strategic assessments of the required shape of the labour force in 10 or 15 years' time and to adjust the system to produce what is required. If such assessments can be made, countries where centralized planning and prescription takes place might be more successful in coping with such changes than a country like the USA, whose citizens resist such prescription.

Some countries do successfully emphasize certain subjects, as international studies have shown. The high scores achieved by Japanese and

Korean students, and the low scores recorded by Americans, in the 1986 comparative study of science studies conducted by the International Association for the Evaluation of Educational Achievement, excited much comment, particularly in the USA. The emphasis placed on particular subjects in particular countries, however, is more a reflection of what they choose to do than of how they choose to do it. If more Koreans and Japanese, for whatever reason, see the study of science as something which will benefit them, this is likely to be reflected in the shape of the curriculum and the results achieved. It does not necessarily say anything about the system as such.

In practice, cultural market forces usually subvert any high-handed, or even excessively far-sighted, official direction. Government initiatives to create more science and technology places at universities, for example, can result merely in excess capacity or very low entrance requirements and standards in these subjects, as students persist in their preference for social science or literature. The only way in which a government can really influence educational orientation is in some way to create an atmosphere in which the subjects which it wishes to emphasize are believed by the public to be important and interesting and then to provide the wherewithal for them to be studied to a high level by a significant portion of the population.

From a systemic point of view, there is only one developed country whose educational set-up seems to run on fundamentally different principles from the others and that is the USA. Education in most countries is managed in a more or less highly prescriptive fashion. In extreme cases, such as Japan, not only is a detailed national curriculum imposed but teaching methodology and timetabling are also prescribed. In less extreme cases, such as the UK, quite wide variations are permitted but a tightly-regulated national examination system sets standards and requires that anybody who wishes to leave the system clutching the desired qualifications must arrive at a similar academic destination, by whatever means. Europe and Japan have also continued to be concerned about the maintenance of absolute and objectively measurable standards. The education authorities thus attempt, with varying degrees of success, to prescribe not only what students will learn but the standards of learning which are deemed to be acceptable, the maintenance of standards being achieved by a process of attrition by examination.

In the USA, such centralized authoritarian prescription is deemed to be no more acceptable in education than it is in any other aspect of life.

There is no national curriculum, such national standard examinations as there are take the form of relative performance measurements, rather than pass/fail barriers, and it is up to the prospective employer or college to decide, on the basis of these scores, whether or not the students have achieved a standard sufficient for them to be taken on. There is, in other words, a much more open recognition that the forces of the market will determine the prospects of any student and that the market will determine what are acceptable standards. Similarly, the market is allowed to determine what shall be taught, insofar as any school can teach any course which its local governors approve and can issue its diplomas for the perusal of potential employers or higher educators of its graduating students. There is a heavy emphasis in most schools on elective and vocational subjects, which gives the whole system a very free-form, market-driven ethos.

Whether or not the extent to which *laissez faire* principles are applied to education in the USA is appropriate, or whether the more prescriptive approach taken by European governments is to be preferred, it is undeniably possible for governments to get their projections wrong and, in a complex area like labour force projection, such dangers are quite real. The educationalists' knee-jerk reaction to the information revolution is that we will need more mathematicians, scientists and engineers, and yet there is a large school of thought which holds that the high-tech parts of the information sector will employ rather few people and that the classic pattern of liberation-by-automation will result in a further shift to soft, 'wet', human occupations. And so, although it is probably right for education authorities to fight vigorously against declining standards in basic communication and numeracy skills, heavy-handed government action to reshape the curriculum in anticipation of the information revolution is probably inappropriate and unlikely to be successful.

The heavy emphasis which is commonly given to schooling as a determinant of a society's adaptability to infostructural change is anyway perhaps misplaced. The real differences in intellectual performance which will determine the relative success of nations in the race to the intelligent state are often determined more in the boardroom than in the classroom. The corporate sector has become increasingly dominant in research and development in the information sector and it is often forgotten that much of the basic learning which forms the foundation of this work also takes place within the corporate environment. The nature of in-house training and ongoing learning within companies is therefore probably at least as important for competitiveness as is formal school education and its efficacy is very much a product of corporate culture. The existence of a pool of knowledge and skills within a company, the (often lacking) commitment of the company to staff development and the continuity of employment of key staff are the main determinants of this learning culture.

The key expertise can be home-grown or head-hunted, the staff development can be formal or informal in its style and the typical period of tenure can vary widely, so that the learning styles even of highly successful organizations can be very different. Silicon Valley and Wall Street firms are well-known for head-hunting talent (often from abroad) which they allow to operate in a free-wheeling manner, adding to the corporate knowledge base and reputation before moving on to pastures new. Japanese companies, with their low labour turnover rates, prefer to hire the best products of the top Japanese universities, push them through a rigorous induction and on-the-job training regime which lasts many years and only let them loose on important decisions when they know their business inside-out. The corporate styles are thus set and the stereotypes of the quirky, creative American and the solid, developmental Japanese are perpetuated. Whatever style is adopted, however, it is clear that the responsibility for ensuring that appropriately educated people are directing the progress of the information sector will reside at least as much with managers as with teachers.

Dirigiste reform of education for the purposes of producing a labour force suitable for the furtherance of the information revolution, then, seems unlikely to make a crucial competitive difference and much of the important education and training must take place in the corporate sector, in which training has so often been the Cinderella of management disciplines. Both of these conclusions suggest that little can be done to circumvent the problems of shortage of suitably educated labour which are likely to impede progress in the information sector but if, in both cases, the problem lies in the culture, either the national culture or the corporate culture, it is logically here that solutions must be sought. Attitudes can be changed, provided that the message is put over loudly and clearly, and fertile cultures can be created over time. Japan and, particularly, the USA, have sizeable groups of enthusiasts in infostructurally relevant areas and some of them are accorded much kudos. America has its info-heroes and info-billionaires, such as Bill Gates of Microsoft, and a powerful subculture has grown up around them. Promotion of the popular images of such people will probably do more to encourage the kinds of educational change required to further the

information revolution than any amount of official policy pronouncements. It will be in places where not only the students but the teachers
and the employers have all become committed to the info-culture that
things can really change quickly.

It may be that progress in the information sector is somewhat
inhibited by the reactive, rather than proactive, nature of school education, but a more important and intractable education crunch may
become evident among those whom the infostructure is designed to
serve. It is possible, in other words, that the major intellectual constraint
on the sector will not be a shortage of suitably educated producers but
rather a lack of customers who readily understand or have a use for the
increasingly complex products. Many businesses have failed because
their proprietors incorrectly ascribed their own sentiments and enthusi-
asms to their customers (although substantial fortunes have been made,
notably in software, by getting such intuitive judgements very right) and
this danger is ever-present in the information sector.

Much effort is put into making technological products user-friendly
because it has long been recognized that the markets for unfriendly
products, however much functionality they may offer, evaporate very
quickly. Potential or actual customer resistance to complex products is
a constant cause of anxiety to makers of consumer electronics products
but an unfavourable functionality/complexity balance has not emerged
as a major problem in the information sector so far, because much of
the growth in information technology and information services has
gone into the corporate sector, where it is reasonable to expect people
to make the effort to understand the product. Designing cars, controlling machine tools or managing the company's balance sheet is, after
all, what the user is paid to do.

Parallels with consumer electronics are valid, however, because there
may well come a point at which the complexity of the products, the
sophistication or specialist segmentation of many of the services or the
sheer scale of the information overload may cause some information
businesses to be destroyed by the ignorance and indifference of the
customers, private and corporate alike. If this happens, it will reflect,
among other things, shortcomings in educational accomplishment and
attitudes, and it may be that this, rather than educational limitations on
the supply side of the sector, will prove to be the information sector's
ultimate education crunch.

The most effective competitors in the race to the intelligent state,
then, will be those who minimize the various effects of what is referred

to here as the education crunch, both on the supply and the demand side. They will maintain and improve standards in the learning of basic communication and numerate skills by children, their business corporations will be committed to the intellectual development of their employees and, above all, they will create large subcultures which work at the creation of an advanced infostructure with such energy that their enthusiasm spreads to their fellow citizens. This is a race between nation states and, ultimately, it will be their broader cultures, and not just their education systems, which make the crucial intellectual difference.

The User Shake-up

It is commonplace in commerce for groups of people who use different technologies and define their activities under different industrial categories to compete with one another to provide similar functionality to the public. Sustenance, energy, transport and communications are all provided in a variety of ways and the relative competitive positions of the various providers are determined by a complex of factors, including cost, custom, environmental and social impact, and appropriateness of technology. The combination of technology and human enterprise increases the range of options available and often allows choices to be made on the basis of ever more rigorous criteria. It is very unusual for a technology to emerge which achieves dominance so quickly that all alternatives are immediately abandoned and it is normal for competing technologies and modes of provision to co-exist, albeit in a dynamic and changing pattern.

Over time, however, conservative forces tend to be overcome and the most appropriate technologies and modes of delivery gain dominance. At the beginning of the twentieth century, horses, sails, steam, electricity and the internal combustion engine competed to provide motive power for the transportation of people and goods. By the middle of the century, electricity and the internal combustion engine dominated, the piston engine having not yet ceded hegemony in air transport to the gas turbine. In the process, the designs and methods of the providers converged towards agreed optimal standards which continued to evolve as smaller numbers of larger companies confronted the same developmental problems, armed with similar technological tools. Few people could say with any confidence that a newly unveiled car was a Peugeot, and not a Toyota or a Ford, if the marque's badges were left off. Users of maturing dominant technologies, in other words, tend to offer increasingly indistinguishable products which are ever more widely used; everybody drives cars and they all look much the same because their designers are all similarly constrained.

The broader information sector is nowhere near this stage of maturity, although the more narrowly defined information technology sector may be closer to it than is commonly realized. Mass and interpersonal communications needs are still served by a variety of competing media, whose relative competitive positions owe as much to the inertia of traditional alignments and practices as they do to their real functional characteristics. Broadcasters broadcast, telephone companies run telephone networks and newspapers fight circulation wars because that is what they always have done. The fact that new technology has made other arrangements possible, and perhaps desirable, has so far had little impact on these traditional activities.

In information technology, their still exists a mass of producers who struggle to differentiate themselves in the face of clear signs of technical and functional convergence. Notebook computers bearing hundreds of different brand names offer near identical functionality, while increasingly large shares of the software market are captured by the large, well-capitalized operators who have the accumulated expertise and can afford the man-centuries of development work which the writing of a new package requires. Commoditization and structural coagulation in some information electronics markets therefore seems inevitable and is likely to occur relatively soon.

Few observers of the information technology scene would dispute that the industry has still to go through some re-alignment before it is likely to settle down to the kind of relatively stable equilibrium which is typical of, for example, the automobile and steel industries. But it seems increasingly likely that the biggest upheavals in the broader information sector are yet to come and that they will be among the users, not the producers, of information technology.

The process by which this will happen can be described as a ripple effect. The emergence of enabling technologies creates opportunities which generate a wave of change, first in the industries which develop and package the technologies for practical purposes. In the initial stages, applications of the technologies are offered in a multiplicity of competing forms, most of which are suboptimal. Some combination of technical, commercial and political factors causes the industry to converge on products which are perceived to be optimal, and a dominant group of producers emerges in the process. The dominant group reinforces its position and the developmental stream is focused among its members. In the later stages of the progress of the technology wave through the industry, the products become standardized and are mass produced by the dominant group. Further technological change can destabilize the situation again but the dominant group usually has sufficient technological and organizational grasp to cope with change even if it does not initiate it. The information electronics industry is showing signs of entering this final stage and, although the waters are unlikely to subside to a millpond calm in the near future, there is no technological tsunami on the horizon which is likely to overturn any of the larger boats.

This may not be the case among those industries which are the major users of the end products. While the more or less stabilized technology companies can continue cheerfully to charge down developmental paths which take them towards ever more powerful machines, it is the users of the equipment, the organizations of which they are members, and the industries of which the organizations are parts, which will next be shaken up by the technology wave as it rolls on. The ground swell at the service end of the information sector is only just beginning to grow but it is already becoming apparent that some industries and professions will be profoundly affected by it. The examples described below are just two of countless instances in which upheaval could be seen across a broad segment of the global economy which has enjoyed a secular trend of growth for decades.

Collisions Along the Cable?

If any single technological image has symbolized the vision of the information society in the developed world in the early part of the twenty-first century it has been that of multi-purpose optical fibre or coaxial data connections into offices and homes from integrated broadband networks (IBNs). According to the purest form of the vision, the office or household could conduct all its information transactions, in cable television and audio (it could no longer be called radio), telephone, perhaps videophone, facsimile, teleconferencing, data communications and tele-shopping and banking, through the single data pipe. Terrestrial and satellite broadcast spectrum, in this scenario, would be used increasingly for mobile and emergency communications and for the provision of communications services to remote areas.

To all intents and purposes, IBNs are technically possible today, although their management and maintenance might prove formidable tasks if they were to exist on a large scale, and technological changes likely to appear soon (such as the digitalization of television, improved video signal compression techniques and the use of asynchronous transmission mode) would be likely to render any system established now obsolete in the near future. If IBNs are to be implemented, however, there are difficult problems to be resolved with regard to the related questions of who is to provide the various services which flow through the pipe and how it is all to be paid for.

Governments have long feared that the creation of IBNs, although it might eventually prove to have a compelling logic and be clearly in the public interest, might result in unacceptable monopoly powers for the common carriers. In the USA and the UK, cable television, whose networks offer a potential alternative multi-purpose broadband transmission medium, is widely diffused and the potential for conflict between the telephone and cable television companies is already well recognized. As long ago as 1970, the Federal Communications Commission adopted a rule banning cross-ownership of cable television companies by telephone companies which effectively prevents them from providing video services. In The UK, the public telecommunications operators are similarly banned from providing entertainment services on their networks until at least 2001.

The logic of these restrictions has been that the telephone companies should not be allowed to use their huge networks and their financial strength to swamp the cable television operators. It has further been argued that the provision of multiple services along a single cable creates opportunities for cross-subsidization which would be anti-competitive and invariably to the benefit of the telephone companies at the expense of the cable operators. Some studies suggest, however, that the economics of IBNs are such that not only is such a scenario unlikely but that the boot may well be on the other foot.

The costs of installing nation-wide IBNs are very high. It has been estimated, for example, that NTT's B-ISDN system would cost ¥60 trillion ($500 billion) and questions are often raised as to whether an IBN offers the best means of providing the information services which the Japanese people will want, and be prepared to pay for. Is the 'V', the visual part of NTT's 'V, I & P' strategy, for example, really necessary in a communications context? Teleconferencing and video-phones have their enthusiastic advocates but even some within the telecommunications companies, which officially enthuse about the concept, privately express fears that the appeal of video communications may be insufficient to justify the costly installation of broadband capacity.

One ostensibly logical solution, for a small and populous country like Japan, whose communications are at least potentially if not currently constrained by the limitations of terrestrial and satellite broadcast spectrum, might be to de-regulate the common carriers and give them access to the television market, a market which might justify the costs of installing the IBN in the medium term, in order that longer term benefits (whatever they may be) will not be lost. If, however, the common carriers were to be given the job of conveying signals which have in the past been broadcast by radio and television companies (Japan has only an embryonic cable television industry), the commercial basis upon which the broadcasting companies operate would be changed and the nature of the services which they provide could be affected in ways which they and the public might find unacceptable.

The economic issues relating to the provision of broadband services by the telephone companies and their principal competitors, the cable television companies, are easy to identify but more difficult to resolve. If the costs of construction of IBNs are so high, the comparative costs and merits of separate networks for video and data should be examined. Is it cheaper to provide everything through one pipe than through several? If it is more expensive, what new services would the single broadband pipe be capable of providing which might justify the higher cost? If the legal barriers which exist in most countries to the provision of television services by telecommunications companies were to be removed, would increased competition result or are the economies of scale of the provision of cable television services in an area sufficient that these companies are in fact natural monopolies?

The only functions which an IBN could provide which a combination of conventional cable television and telephone networks could not are switched video services of one kind and another. Video telephony and universal video conferencing capability would be provided by an IBN, as long as the consumers were willing to purchase the requisite terminal equipment, and video programming could be received 'on demand' from some huge video archive. This latter service would differ from that offered by conventional cable television in that, whereas cable television transmits a varied but limited stream of programme material at scheduled times, switched video on an IBN could provide any programme on demand at any time, analogously with a huge video rental store. The distinction between this kind of service and the 'pay-per-view' services being introduced by the cable television companies is merely in the range of material available. Switched entertainment video, provided by the telephone companies themselves or by third parties availing themselves of a 'video dial tone' facility, would be just another form of cable television and the cable operators in some markets have already moved to a position in which they can provide something very close to the service which a hypothetical IBN would offer.

By expanding their optical fibre trunk lines, the cable television companies in the USA have overcome the technical shortcomings of their traditional coaxial cable networks and now have the capacity to transmit a huge volume of data of all kinds. Because they already have coaxial cables running into more than half of American homes, and could easily connect up most of the rest, they have established a clear lead in the provision of broadband services to homes, which the telephone companies would find it very difficult and expensive to overturn.

Is it possible, then, that IBNs will exist in the early part of the next century but that they will be operated by cable television and not telephone companies? Certainly the regulatory environment in most countries has favoured the cable television companies and, in the USA, they have created the nearest thing to a broadband network which exists anywhere. They have already started to take advantage of this by offering database, videoconferencing, computer networking and other services which, until recently, would have been regarded the natural preserve of the telephone companies.

The telephone companies could, if deregulated, fight back strongly and it is also possible that hardware manufacturers might seek to enter the business. All of the telephone companies and many of the hardware makers are sufficiently wealthy that they might mount powerful attacks upon the cable television companies' position, but it is perhaps because the cable companies are most naturally involved in a business which justifies their installation of broadband capacity that they have forged ahead, while the telephone and computer companies, which can only point to some rather hypothetical future benefits of IBNs and whose current needs are easily met by conventional narrowband networks, have started to show signs of hesitancy. Without video, IBNs seem hard to justify in the shorter term and, as the most natural providers of video are the cable television companies, there is an appealing logic in their constructing the medium of delivery, however much this may fly in the face of conventional expectations.

The debate over broadband networks highlights several of the difficulties which will confront the information sector over the years to come. The process of structural and commercial re-alignment, which will result from the increasingly common trans-sectoral use of certain key technologies will be the cause of extensive debate, wasted effort, bankruptcies, frictional unemployment and consumer confusion. The market mechanism deals quite smoothly with minor adjustments in the allocation of scarce resources but the changes involved here are often such that significant disruption seems inevitable.

The technologies involved are available to a sufficiently wide range of companies that it will be difficult to predict, in the absence of legal regulations which prescribe who will do what, which types of companies will come to dominate certain types of information service. The precedents set in one country will not necessarily hold for other countries, where the established interests are different (where there is no cable television industry, for example) and where national planners are starting with something like a clean slate. The tendency of providers of the functions which the public requires here and now (i.e. cable television) to dominate the scene can be expected to continue for the time being, as will the difficulties of persuading potential consumers that a hypothetical functionality of which they have no experience and have difficulty in envisaging (i.e. a multi-functional broadband network) is worth paying for now. In the longer term, however, perhaps the most likely scenario to emerge is that, as the more general advantages of IBNs become more widely understood, public opinion will prevail on the regulators to remove operational and cross-ownership restrictions and digital networks will come under the semi-monopolistic control of the big telecommunications battalions.

If the telecommunications and entertainment video industries are already starting to be shaken up to a greater or lesser extent by the advent of rudimentary IBNs, what might be the longer term implications of the establishment of such networks in fully fledged form? Certainly, the installation of nation-wide IBNs would be likely to accelerate the transfer of classified advertisements and information directories to public electronic databases, with potentially dire effects on advertising agencies, travel agents, publishers, printers and local newspapers. When and how such effects will be felt can only be guessed at but it should be realized that IBNs have the potential to create a relatively perfect market in information and, by so doing, to make the markets for products and services much more efficient than they have ever been before and that this will eventually have implications for intermediaries of all kinds.

If the history of technology tells us anything, however, it is that, once a major industry (and, in this case, there are two major industries involved) has a particular technological bit in its teeth, there is no stopping it. It seems highly likely, therefore, that, by 2005, broadband information networks of one kind or another will be linking many of the workplaces and homes of the developed world. How we get from here to there is as yet unclear but a large number of companies and individuals, including a goodly number in the broadcasting industry, seem likely to sustain damage along the way and many more will feel the effects later.

The Securities Analyst – An Endangered Species?

When the world heard, at 04.57 GMT on Monday 19 August 1991, that Vice President Yanayev was taking over the Soviet presidency due to President Gorbachev's 'ill health', stock markets reacted immediately. The Far East markets were well into their business day when the story broke and Tokyo's Nikkei index fell almost 6 per cent, with traded volume sharply higher than that of the previous Friday. Hong Kong also saw feverish activity and the Hang Seng fell by nearly 8.5 per cent on the day. At the same time, the US dollar, a traditional haven in times of anxiety, soared on the foreign exchange markets. By the end of trading on Wall Street, however, the likelihood of the coup being made to stick was being questioned and markets began to recover. Three days later it was all over.

The Reuters news agency claimed to have delivered the initial news of the coup to the world 3 minutes 42 seconds ahead of its competitors – a claim which it subsequently used in its advertising. This emphasis on, and pride in, extreme timeliness reflects the extent to which Reuters as an organization focuses its marketing on the financial services sector. It is only financial markets, and some commodity markets, which react so quickly, sometimes violently, to such news and it is only really the financial sector which reacts to so much of the wide range of information inputs which the news services provide. When an event such as the 1991 Soviet coup occurs, traders in financial markets not only need to know but need to know as soon as their competitors do. The Reuters advertisement was intended to illustrate just how dangerous it could be for traders to be without a Reuters monitor on their desk and how none of the competing products is really quite the same. The liquidity of financial markets is such that it is possible to lose a great deal of money in 3 minutes and 42 seconds, if your competitors know something which you do not, or to make a killing if you alone are in the know.

Traders in the financial sector have long been accustomed to using news services to monitor breaking stories which might influence their business but the range of information which the Reuters information system and its competitors provide to the financial sector stretches far beyond the confines of breaking world news. Security and commodity prices are displayed in real time, announcements made by companies appear on screens almost as soon as they break and news of all kinds is available, including constant updates on particular topics. All of this is usually delivered to the customer through a dedicated terminal with a special keyboard. Bloomberg, Bridge Data, Datastream, Knight Ridder, Quick, Quotron and a number of other services compete with Reuters, either globally or in specialist markets, and the range of services provided by such vendors has grown apace. The real-time terminal now provides not only information but software for its analysis. Users can tabulate, compare, contrast and plot data at will and can access not only current but also historical data for analytical purposes.

These services are used, for their various purposes, by traders, salesmen, analysts, fund managers, settlement staff and accountants and the nature of some of these occupations has been profoundly affected by the proliferation of the electronic information systems which they use. Indeed, such is the degree of functional convergence between the roles of the real-time information vendors and their customers that substantial re-alignment in the financial information complex seems inevitable in the longer run. The economic pressures for re-alignment are growing and nowhere more so than in the field of equity research.

The research departments of the securities houses and investment banks of the world's financial centres, particularly those in the rich English-speaking nations, employ people who are among the most prominent in the financial services industry. These professional pundits, the financial analysts, devote their professional lives to the in-depth study of the companies which make up the industries in which they specialize. Analysts come from varied backgrounds and bring different skills to the task but their common purpose is to analyse the forces which affect the profitability and worth of the companies and to predict the likely trajectory of their share prices.

A good analyst should be able to comment knowledgeably on the structure of a company, its competitive position, the technology which it uses, the nature of its products, changes in the market for those products, the company's financial position, the attitudes of investors to the company and the likely course of corporate earnings. Indeed the analysts, collectively, are perhaps the most respected sources of this kind of information and are often sought out by journalists and others who are seeking an independent and authoritative view on a company or industry and the analysts' consensus forecasts (where there is consensus) are a major plank of the basis for the valuation of the companies' shares in the market.

Analysts in the major financial centres, particularly on Wall Street and in the City of London, often enjoy celebrity status, are much sought-after by competing firms and are paid very high salaries. The basis of this celebrity, however, is being undermined by a complex of factors, most of which derive from the onward march of information technology, but some of which relate to the peculiar nature of information businesses in general.

There was a time when financial analysts were, in an important sense, purveyors of information; they were able to supply their customers with information which was not easily or promptly available elsewhere. Collectively, the analysts represented a major source of raw information regarding industries, as well as offering insights regarding the relevance of the raw information. This function has become much less important as the legal strictures concerning insider trading have tightened and as the specialist press and wire services have expanded their activities in this direction. Such was the expansion of stockbroking in London in the 1980s that the major pharmaceutical companies which, for unfathomable reasons, found themselves in the most intensively analysed sector of industry, found that their information meetings were being attended by as many as 150 analysts. The logistical and political task of managing flows of share price-sensitive information through such a mass created considerable difficulties for the companies, which increasingly used the specialist press and wire services as preferred conduits, knowing that all the analysts would be informed simultaneously through such a route. It is now generally the case, therefore, that the analysts hear important corporate news at exactly the same time as their clients do.

The specialist and semi-specialist press, ever conscious of the chang-ing needs of its readership, and itself under pressure from television and the real-time information vendors in the breaking news area, has also moved towards the provision of more considered and sophisticated analysis of the political, industrial and technological trends which affect stock markets. The role of the specialist journalist thus increasingly overlaps with that of the financial analyst in the provision of these technical views and the two are often important sources of information for one another.

As a result of this overcrowding in the industrial and corporate information markets, the analysts have retreated towards the area in which they are least vulnerable, towards a heavier emphasis on the detailed financial analysis of companies and financial forecasting. This analysis is now highly computerized and increasingly sophisticated, reflecting the increased complexity of companies' finances but it is also highly dependent upon the financial data which the companies disclose. As corporate disclosure is becoming increasingly uniform and consistent and as the techniques for analysing it become increasingly standardized, the day when this function becomes very susceptible to the expert systems approach cannot be far away.

If analysts in the next few years finds themselves hemmed in on all sides by wire services, specialist journalists and expert systems, it is likely that they will still be able to provide a valuable service by being a 'one-stop shop' to their clients, purveying everything that anybody might reasonably want to know on a particular company or industry. But there is yet another technology-driven threat to the position of conventional investment analysis. This is the technique known as passive investment management. This approach to investment, which has grown rapidly in popularity in recent years, is founded on the belief that the selection of a portfolio of investments on the basis of detailed analysis and evaluation of the companies concerned, with all the effort and expense which this activity entails, seldom produces higher returns or less risk than does a strategy of diversified investment across the breadth of the market. In its simplest form, this type of strategy involves 'indexation' of portfolios, so that they reflect as closely as possible the characteristics and performance of the whole market. There are many variations on the passive management theme but all are abstract and quantitative in their focus and are not dependent upon input from the mainstream financial analysts to any significant degree. The 'quant' specialists typically have mathematics, statistics and computer science training and are heavily dependent upon their computer systems.

The position of the traditional analyst has thus been undermined significantly by competing sources of information and analysis and it is not surprising that the economics of the business have begun to reflect this fact. In the days prior to 'May Day' in 1975 in the USA and 'Big Bang' in the UK in 1986, when commissions paid to stockbrokers were deregulated, the fixed commission environment in which stockbrokers operated provided a clear financial justification for the provision of research to their clients, although there was never any direct contractual link between the service provided and the commission paid. Commission was always nominally a payment for the execution of a transaction and research was provided on a goodwill basis in order to induce the client to deal through the broker who supplied it, as a kind of loss-leader. As such, it was very effective but, as alternative sources of information and analysis proliferated and brokers' research was often either ignored or taken for granted, institutional investors realized that they could extract more from the brokers in return for their commission dollars than just research and the execution of transactions.

This devaluation of the research service in relation to the commission flows available to pay for it gave rise to the practice of 'softing'. In a 'soft' commission arrangement, an investor contracts with a broker or an intermediary to pay to a broker an agreed multiple of the cost of a third party service in the form of dealing commission. The broker agrees to pay for the third party service which the investor receives and retains the residual revenue as payment for the execution of the deals and the other services, including research, which he provides to the investor. The bodies which regulate financial services recognize this practice, although they seek to control the effective commissions paid and the types of third party service which can be purchased through such arrangements.

Easily the most common type of third party service to be purchased in this manner is the real-time information service, and the archetypal soft deal is one where a broker pays the full cost of a Reuters terminal on a fund manager's desk and receives, say, 1.5 times the amount disbursed in pledged broking commission. The net effect of such arrangements is a heavy discounting of nominal commissions, of which a part was always tacitly or explicitly recognized to be in part a payment for research.

Investors still generally value the research services which they receive from brokers and implicitly recognize this insofar as they continue to use, and to remunerate 'full service' brokers at commission rates which are higher than they would pay to 'execution only' brokers, who provide no research. The erosion of the position of brokers' research in relation to the services provided by Reuters, Bloomberg and the rest is, however, clear and is quite explicitly recognized in the 'softing' arrangements.

The providers of real-time and other on-line information services regard financial analysts as being some of their more important customers and would, for the most part, derive no immediate benefit from seeking to compete with them. But, should they decide, as their existing business matures, to seek to add value by crossing the border into the territory currently occupied by the brokers, there should be no doubt that Reuters, Knight Ridder, Quick and the rest, with their extensive networks and widespread, and sometimes privileged, access to information, their systems expertise, their very large installed base of terminals and, in some cases, substantial financial reserves, would be formidable competitors to the brokers' analysts.

The on-line information business represents a kind of 'food chain' and companies such as Reuters have expanded their activities to occupy several parts of the chain. The Reuters correspondents around the world act as a primary source of information but they are not by any means the only source upon which the system draws. Data consolidation, the packaging of information from a variety of primary sources, is a function which the company also performs, transmitting this information alongside that from Reuters sources. The information is transported in a convenient electronic form up the food chain towards the end-user and, although some major securities companies have provided clients with terminals dedicated to the provision of their own proprietary research services, it is companies such as Reuters, which provide consolidated multi-sourced information down a single pipe, which have come to dominate this delivery function as well.

This is where the on-line information service used to end but, in recent years, the vendors have started to provide sophisticated software tools for the analysis of much the information which is delivered through the system. This is where the vendor–customer divide currently exists but it should be remembered that many of the existing customers are but parts of the information food chain and are not the ultimate customers. Institutional fund managers, individual investors, and corporate and local government treasurers represent the nearest thing currently imaginable to ultimate customers but there remain at least two links in the food chain between Reuters and these groups of people – links which might come under severe strain.

The erosion of the analyst's position which has taken place so far suggests that the food chain might be shortened as a result of this kind of functional convergence and of the computerization of some of the functions which were previously performed by groups of people who purported to add value and who were paid for doing so. The overall functionality of the chain, in other words, is subject to revision as some of the companies operating in it become more or less capable of adding appropriate value. If the introduction of technology which enhances productivity in the various functions in the chain can be expected to add meaningful new functionality, by enabling the existing participants to make genuinely improved decisions, then it may be that the length, and even the shape, of the chain will remain essentially unaltered. If, however, as seems more likely, the assembly of powerful information systems and analytical tools enables better decisions to be taken by far fewer people, and possibly different people, then some links in the chain may well be removed.

Neo-Luddism or a New Creativity?

The shake-up of the relationship between telephone companies and broadcasters and the potential erosion of the position of the financial analyst by the expanded role of on-line information providers are but two examples of the kind of pressures which technology-driven functional convergence is likely to exert on existing institutions in the information sector over the next few years. These pressures will cause problems which may be 'frictional' or longer term in their impact. Companies and whole sections of industry which have invested considerable effort and resources in their attempts to create new businesses may be driven to the wall by competition from unexpected quarters and, as sophisticated information technologies usurp functions which could previously only be performed by people and perform them better than people ever could, some professional groupings will shrink and there is considerable potential for unemployment.

Technological unemployment is a spectre which has haunted the thinking of economists since Ricardo but it has never in the past been a problem which was associated with workers in what we have here referred to as the 'control sector'. Nor, indeed, is it a question which has ever satisfactorily been resolved in relation to manual or manufacturing workers. As Whitley and Wilson (1991), the authors of a research report of the Institute for Employment Research of the University of Warwick, put it:

> The kernel of the debate concerns the extent to which the initial impact of technical change in terms of job displacement may be compensated for by endogenous and exogenous factors which tend to increase employment in other ways. The results of over 250 years of scholarly effort and research have greatly improved our understanding of the nature of this balance, but the complexity of the political, economic and social inter-relationships involved has defeated all attempts at providing a final answer to this question (p. 1).

As far as the application of technology to manufacturing is concerned, the productivity gains which have been achieved in, for example, the UK over the last 20 years or so have resulted in a marked decline in manufacturing employment which suggests that any 'endogenous and exogenous factors' which might be compensating for displacement are not, at least, being felt in the manufacturing sector. The steady increase in the services sector and in managerial and professional occupations suggests that such factors might be at work elsewhere but there is at least a *prima facie* case for suggesting that the net impact of information technology on employment may turn out to be substantially negative, once information technology-driven productivity gains similar to those seen in manufacturing are replicated in the control sector.

The Warwick study, which attempts to project the impact on employment in the UK of information technology in general and micro-electronics in particular, uses a macro-economic model which is 'bent' to reflect different assumptions. In the data used to create the model for what the authors refer to as their 'base run', it is assumed that certain factors will compensate for technological displacement. One of these assumptions is that the introduction of information technology into various sectors of the economy will be slow and evolutionary, rather that rapid and revolutionary.

The scale of the investments in capital equipment and training necessary before widespread adoption of productivity-enhancing technology is cited as a reason why such technology is diffused only slowly and, given this slow implementation, the study argues, the productivity effects of the introduction of any particular technology become indistinguishable from the general trend of productivity increase.

Both of the above observations lead to the suggestion that the effects on employment of the introduction of technology may be less dramatic than has been feared or that they will be felt sufficiently slowly that they can be absorbed without difficulty. Where the possibility of substantial increases in productivity resulting from the introduction of information technology is admitted, the only compensating factor offered is increased output. That is to say that more may be produced by a similar number of people, rather than a similar amount being produced by a smaller number of people. Where improved productivity is in offices, suggests the study, this may be reflected in qualitative, rather than quantitative, improvements. The example cited is of a government White Paper whose quality is improved because the replacement of typewriters with word processors has allowed more drafts to be produced.

There can be little doubt that many of the productivity improvements which result from the introduction of information technology are qualitative and that it is indeed the improved quality of decision making and control which is the principal intended benefit. There is equally no doubt that many clerical processes are analogous to production line processes and the numbers of staff required to handle any given number of accounts or transactions, for example, may be reduced greatly as a result of computerization. The Warwick study recognizes this problem and, in the simulation in which the authors assumed a more rapid diffusion of information technology in service industries:

> ... the productivity gains in service industries, as a result of the assumed acceleration in the rate of diffusion of information technology, lead to a large loss of jobs. [And] ... there are only relatively modest offsets due to investments compared with the manufacturing simulation.

The fact that many of the productivity gains which result from the use of technology in office jobs are in non-traded sectors, such as public sector accounting, is cited as one major reason why the employment offsets which might otherwise result from increased competitiveness are absent in this case.

The prognosis of the Warwick report for overall employment levels is comparatively optimistic but the potential implications for white collar employment, if the results of the accelerated diffusion simulation are to believed, are disturbing. And the Warwick model deals only with productivity displacement at the micro level; if the kind of strategic erosion of whole professions and industry segments referred to above is taken into consideration, the picture could be much worse.

If, painting gloom upon gloom, the worst-case scenario were to be drawn, it may be that micro-level displacement in the strategically better placed sectors could combine with the larger scale displacement resulting from the demise of whole subsectors whose functional purpose had been usurped to create large pools of white collar unemployment. If, additionally, there is a significantly uneven international distribution of those industries in which the compensating growth is taking place, the technological unemployment problem in some countries could become particularly acute, occasioning significant social and political difficulties.

Such a prognosis is sharply at odds with the much more optimistic visions of the post-industrial information society offered by many futurologists, who recognize that technological displacement will give rise to problems but take a much more sanguine view of the employment-creating opportunities which the technology will generate. It is notoriously difficult to isolate the effects of technology shifts from the overall cyclical movements of economies and even more difficult, as Whitley and Wilson rightly note, to predict what the effects will be, either for the total world economy or for that of any individual country.

The Luddites broke machines in the East Midlands and Yorkshire in the early part of the nineteenth century in a reactionary attempt to save jobs which had been rendered obsolete by textile technology. The British printing unions fought a similarly-motivated campaign in the 1970s and 1980s but there has been no example of white collar or managerial workers staging such action – so far at least. Although widespread outbreaks of computer-breaking seem unlikely, reactionary pressures of a more insidious nature are perhaps more plausible. Meaningless jobs might be artificially preserved by managers who saw more merit in solidarity with their colleagues than in cost reduction for their employers and progressive change might otherwise be subtly but stubbornly resisted. Neo-Luddism, should such a phenomenon emerge, is unlikely often to be as conspicuous as the original version was.

If passive or active resistance to change were to be the reaction to the threat of white collar unemployment, it is likely that the protesters would have a far more effective political voice, in virtually any society, than displaced manual workers ever have. It is one thing for technology to impact the jobs of the controlled; it is quite another when the livelihoods of the controllers themselves are under threat. At the very least, the question of technological innovation in the control sector could, under any of the gloomier employment scenarios, pose a major dilemma for the managerial classes and it could become a major political issue.

If a more sanguine view is taken of the compensating employment opportunities offered by the advent of information technology, it is not inconceivable that, in the long run, as many people as are displaced by the technology could be employed in much more amenable jobs which did not exist before. This, in essence, is the ideal vision of the information society but, if this scenario is to become a reality, it is likely that the new jobs created will often be for different types of people in different industries and even in different countries. In the long run, a happy new equilibrium could be arrived at but not before substantial changes in corporate, regional and national cultures have taken place. A new creativity could well emerge in a depressed basic manufacturing area or one in which, for example, several large insurance companies had merged, shedding hundreds of clerical jobs and, given something approximating to the economists' perfect market, there would be economic forces at work which might encourage this to happen. The reality, however, is that such changes take time and that socio-economic inertia usually causes employment opportunities and pockets of unemployment to be inefficiently, and sometimes painfully, concentrated.

In the long run it is to be hoped that a new creativity will rise from the ashes of the jobs which information technology destroys but concentrated economic pain has in the past caused Luddites to break machines, Jarrow shipbuilders (peaceably) to march on London, Detroit autoworkers to take sledgehammers to Toyotas and entrepreneurs everywhere to seek government protection from their competitors. Such actions invariably evoke political responses of one kind or another and it would be unreasonable to expect upheavals of the kind which can be predicted over the next decade not to result in some political storms.

6

THE INFORMATION
WORLD IN 2005

A large portion of this book has been devoted to a discussion of the enabling technology of the information world, an emphasis which signifies an implicit recognition of its pivotal importance in the changes which are taking place around us. It has also been suggested that technology is the most predictable element in the development of the world's information infrastructure, although its application has so often been seen to occasion unpredictable patterns of change. That is to say that the general pattern of technological change can be predicted more easily than can its effects.

Technological change is normally propelled by competitive dynamics whose focus is quite particular. This is almost invariably the case where there is no Kuhnian paradigm shift involved and sometimes even holds true where there is. The inventors of the atomic bomb were motivated by a competitive dynamic of a specific kind – the desire to win a particular war – but their invention had implications for politics and world society far beyond the resolution of that conflict. This analogy is pertinent to the dynamic of technology in the information sector, where innovation usually occurs because companies are striving to enhance specific products in relation to those of their competitors for the specific purpose of making profits. It is not for the management of these companies to question the desirability or otherwise of the innovations which they are introducing beyond the scope of their own segment of the market economy. The development of known technologies for specific purposes by individual companies is meticulously planned; the manner in which those technologies will eventually fuse into major systems, the ways in which the major systems will be used and to what effect, is not.

Another important characteristic of the process of technological change is that what has been learnt cannot be unlearnt and, once momentum in a particular direction has been established, the near-focused competitive drive and the economic interests of those directly involved tend to keep it going.

The technologies of the information sector are very powerful and have great economic and social significance but, if we are to attempt to predict even the general nature of the information environment and economy in our horizon year, it is not sufficient merely to consider what the technologies are intended to achieve. Rather, we must attempt to assess their combined effects two or three steps beyond the points at which their promoters intend them to impact.

At the end of chapter 3, some aspects of the likely technological environment in 2005 were listed. The emphasis here was, by implication, on the kinds of changes which technology would bring to the information environment of the developed world over that period and much of the discussion which followed focused on the likely positive and negative impact on the richer nations with more advanced infostructures. It should also be remembered, however, that much of the influence which modern information technology will have on the global economy will come from technologies which are already established, mature and even, to citizens of the developed world, passé.

The effects of the spread of several generations of information technologies in India and Thailand were described in chapter 2 and, although the use made in those countries of very advanced technologies was mentioned, it should be clear from the description that the infostructural technologies which have had the greatest impact on the development of those countries have often been quite basic or mature. The continued spread of literacy, radio and television in the developing world is, after all, likely to have a greater influence on the nature of the global society than the spread of broadband digital data networks in the developed world.

It can be assumed that much of the impact of mature information technologies on the nations of the developed world has already been felt. The high diffusion rates of newspapers, radio, television and simple telephones in the rich countries suggest that the life-style changes brought about these things have already taken place in these nations. The questions outstanding in the rich countries relate to how advanced technologies will change things.

In the developing world, both mature and advanced technologies have the potential to bring about change, often of a dramatic nature. Not only is the scope for development much greater in a country with a primitive infostructure but the potential pace of change is also much faster. As the developed world gropes for direction in infostructural enhancement, the poorer countries can see exactly where they want to go and are usually constrained solely or mainly by economic considerations.

The potential for the technological changes which are already well in train to bring about a restructuring of the geopolitical balance of the total world infostructure is colossal. Information technology, in its broadest sense, has begun an irreversible process of globalization. The important part of this process is not the part which allows the nations of the developed world to commune more fully; it has little to do with the further globalization of financial markets or the ability of people in New York and Hong Kong to converse on their pocket-size mobile telephones. Modern information technology, whose most powerful manifestation is still the humble television, will, by 2005, have created a global culture which will be more homogeneous and will extend more widely than ever before.

This is not to suggest that Daniel Lerner's 'Traditional Society' will finally pass away, but whole nations will see their cultures changing dramatically as at least large minorities of their people subscribe to the increasingly international media and information society. This can already be seen, in different ways, in India and in Thailand. The mass media and modern communications are already changing the collective psyche of the Thai people and the whole nation is undergoing dramatic politico-economic change. India as a whole is not changing as Thailand is, but there are popular Indian rap singers appearing on MTV in Bombay and across Asia and a whole new class of Indian technocrats is shuttling between Silicon Valley and Bangalore.

The cost of the basic hardware of the information revolution, both capital and consumer goods, is plummeting and, as incomes in the developing world rise, incomes and prices will converge to make information access affordable to millions who have hitherto had little or no awareness of the world scene. It can be predicted with some confidence that a redrawing of our Information Access Index in 2005 will show a considerable narrowing of the spread between the highest and lowest scores.

If the universal mass culture has an impact on the traditional lifestyles in the Third World at an accelerating rate, it may well be spearheaded more by the likes of Sony, CNN, MTV and Nintendo than by the worthy efforts of extension workers and developmental programming like *Krishi Darshan*. The recognition of alternative, and apparently desirable, life-styles seems likely to alter the collective consciousness and to spur changes in education in developing countries. Literacy, and the other tools of the information world could suddenly start to seem much more useful to millions of people who formerly regarded them as troublesome irrelevancies.

The increased affordability not only of the basics of the information infrastructure but also of the productivity-enhancing information tools which have already transformed the efficiency of manufacturing and distribution in the developed world is likely to combine with changes in the collective consciousness, improved educational standards and rising incomes to spark economic growth in an increasing number of parts of the developing world. The NICs will continue to grow rapidly, with the process embracing all of their citizens, but it is also likely that nations whose sheer size and/or economic problems render them incapable of transforming themselves in this manner will adopt the kind of technopolis strategy exemplified by Bangalore and a sizeable intellectual middle-class minority will represent them in the global information society.

In the redeveloping former communist world, the new relatively free transferability of information technology, and information itself, from the West should prove to be of great value to the emergent market economies. The educational and intellectual infrastructures of some of these countries are very strong indeed and it can only be a matter of time before the greatly increased mobility of people and ideas into and out of them starts to have a marked impact on their fortunes and on the advanced sector of the global infostructure.

Native brain-power is evenly distributed throughout the world's population and the emergence of an international information subculture in most countries, the increased ease of travel and the greatly enhanced flow of information is already releasing this. In the past, where highly educated migrants left their homes in search of opportunities, the trip was one-way but more and more are now returning to their native lands with technical knowledge and with the wealth and determination necessary to turn it to economic advantage. Migrants are very prominent in the leading technological centres of the world and returnees have already changed the economic landscapes of countries like Taiwan, Korea and Thailand.

This rather up-beat assessment of the prospects for infostructural development in the developing world and of the effects that it will have must inevitably be accompanied by caveats. It would be wholly unreasonable to expect Burundi or Burkina Faso to be much influenced by these forces in the foreseeable future, and certainly not before 2005; even the pre-conditions to the pre-conditions of such changes do not exist in these countries. Wherever the pre-conditions do exist, however, and where there is sufficient political and economic stability for people to focus on the potential for change, the globalization of the information society will greatly accelerate the change.

There is also the risk that, if the free flow of people and ideas is impeded for any reason, the information revolution in the developing world could stall. The flow of technology and information from the developed world might be constricted if the citizens of the developed world fear the effects of growth in the developing countries. It would be naive to expect the developed nations to give away their hard-won technological advantage to a host of potential competitors and a growing world trade in abstractions could well result in the emergence of some forms of info-protectionism. This may be triggered by unscrupulous behaviour in the developing countries as they go through their industrial adolescence. The cavalier treatment of software copyright and other intellectual property rights might, for example, result in the developed world imposing sanctions.

One of the main hypotheses offered in this book, however, is that, whereas talk of the information revolution has centred upon the sharp edge of technology applications in the developed world, on the digitalization of everything, on the electronic cottage and the infonauts, there are good reasons to believe that the positive effects of the phenomenon will be far more noticeable in the developing world. There are many emerging infostructures and they are likely to be some of the major bright spots of world economic growth over the next decade or so. These nations have seen the effects which strong infostructures have had in the rich countries and are seeking to build their own as quickly as possible, running the whole gamut of information media. Newspapers, magazines and general publishing companies, film and video production groups, broadcasters, advertising agencies, cram-schools, software vendors, electronics companies, telephone utilities and all their related ancillaries will become growth businesses in growth economies.

Change in the advanced infostructures of the developed world will be driven by the same factors as will shape the emerging infostructures of the developing nations. The technological, commercial, political and human forces will, however, interact in different ways to produce very different results.

The basic instincts which propel technological competition in the developed world – a profound belief in the power of science and technology and the pursuit of profit – are unlikely to change much before our horizon year of 2005 but the competitive dynamic may be influenced by other factors. The most significant of these is likely to be the enormous cost involved in the implementation of the latest enabling technologies. It has for a long time been true that the management of some of the smaller companies in the electronics industry have staked the whole future of the company on each new product. The costs of development and manufacture of these complex products is now so high that companies simply cannot afford for them to be commercial failures.

As the design rules in integrated circuits start to test the theoretical physical limits of silicon, the capital cost of each part of the production chain will expand to a point at which even the largest manufacturers will blanch at the thought of a commercial failure. It is therefore likely that the number of companies actively involved at the sharp edge of the technology will decline and that those which remain will adopt a more co-operative attitude towards one another. IBM and Hitachi, Intel and NEC are likely to behave more like Boeing and Airbus Industrie, General Electric and Rolls Royce because it is becoming as difficult and expensive to design and create the equipment needed to make a state-of-the-art integrated circuit as it is to build a new airframe or turbofan and soon few, if any, will be able to go it alone.

If the competitive dynamic is thus subtly altered, its effects, in terms of the technologies which will be pushed down the path of commercialization, will not change. The key enabling technologies mentioned in chapter 3 all have a good deal of momentum and, although there is always a slight possibility that some scientific upheaval will change everything, it is, on the whole, unlikely that anything will happen by 2005 to alter the picture radically. It should be remembered, however, that these technologies, however seminal their more advanced manifestations may prove to be, will not wholly displace more mature technologies overnight. Mature technologies, even where their functionality is completely interchangeable with that of the new technology, have a habit of surviving for far longer than might be imagined, particularly if they are cheap, robust and familiar. Thus it is unlikely, for example, that optical mass storage media, however superior they may prove to be in the long run, will have completely ousted the venerable Winchester disk by 2005.

Similarly, some information delivery media, however mature they may be, have a residual functionality which new media cannot easily replicate. Books and newspapers, for example, have certain clear advantages over their potential competitors. A broadsheet newspaper may be a primitive, and ultimately untimely, way of conveying news but (with a little skill in that particular form of origami in which commuters are so adept) it can be read on a crowded train and can quickly be personalized or 'editionized' by the readers, who scan the headlines and quickly read only those parts which interest them. No electronic medium offers this capability in such a cheap and elegant form. The new media, therefore, will be absorbed into a world of existing media and, however great an impact they may have, it is likely to be incremental rather than substitutional, over this time-span at least.

Conversely, the proliferation of electronic gadgetry in both domestic and commercial life is likely to be running against an increasingly strong current of consumer apathy and scepticism. In 2005 the microelectronics industry will turn 40 years old and its customers will have had 40 years' experience of the somewhat speculative manner in which many of its end products are marketed. In the early years, curiosity and naiveté caused private consumers and corporate purchasers alike to buy products which were ill-conceived and offered little real benefit to their users. By 2005 purchasers will be much more circumspect; they will better understand what they are buying and they will only buy what they understand. Functionality and standardization will be essential elements in successful information technology products across the spectrum and the days when a group of youths could develop a superior mousetrap in a garage and take the world by storm are probably over.

In short, the information electronics industry, which is already showing signs of maturity, will be palpably mature by 2005. Certainly its products will be wonderfully capable by comparison with those of today and, insofar as the pace of functional enhancement generates obsolescence, it will prosper on the back of its continued cleverness. But it seems inevitable that a far greater proportion of the electronics market in 2005 will be a replacement market than is the case today and the image of the industry is likely to have changed from one of futuristic promise to one of established power in the industrial and commercial world.

Most of the information technology themes current in the early 1990s will by 2005 be regarded as old hat. If the predictive process is thrown into reverse and we look back a dozen years instead of forward, the likely nature and flavour of the development process might be intuited. In 1981, few offices had facsimile machines, the CD was a curiosity, the mark one Sony Walkman was a new product, most word processing was done on dedicated machines and the latest PCs were lumpy 8 bit desk-top models without Winchester disks, attached to bulky dot-matrix printers and running *Visicalc* and the original *Wordstar*. At that time, telephone networks contained few, if any, digital switches, the whole system being based on Strowger and Crossbar electro-mechanical re-lays, optical fibre was being made in pilot plants and cellular networks did not exist. Industry analysts had, however, identified what the main technical issues of the decade were going to be and few would have been too surprised if they had been allowed a time-machine preview of the technical state of affairs at the end of 1992.

Projecting out to 2005 in this spirit, the most significant change will probably be that, by then, most households and virtually all offices in the developed world will be connected to an integrated digital broadband wide area public network of some kind. Cross-ownership rules will have been relaxed to allow telephone and cable television companies to merge and these new entities will be experimenting with new bandwidth-hungry services. Video conferencing will be commonplace and the range of information available over networks will be incomparably wider than it is today. Mobile personal communications equipment will be common-place, with perhaps one-third of the population of the developed world carrying mobile telephones, and user-friendly PCs with a range of input modes will be networked around the globe. It goes without saying that, if these predictions prove to be correct, all of this will be taken for granted.

The things which the interested observers of technology in 2005 will probably not be taking for granted, the themes which will define the technological frontier of the day, will probably cluster around network-ing and machine intelligence. It may well be that expert systems will have become such a familiar feature of the landscape by then that the sense of intellectual agoraphobia which often accompanies discussions of machine intelligence may have been dispelled and that the develop-ment of a new man–machine intelligence complex may have become a widely accepted social objective. An information revolution of sorts is likely to have run its course by 2005 and an intellectual revolution might be built upon the foundations which it creates. The tools of conventional scholarship and thought may quietly be transformed over the next decade or so but the quantum leap in intellectual life which machine intelligence might bring is unlikely to be seen until some time well beyond the chronological purview of this book.

It has been suggested here that the developing world will have little trouble in coping with its information revolution but that the developed world may face difficulties, as the effects of the changes in the info-structure make themselves felt in commercial and institutional structures and begin to have a significant impact on the structure of employment. The structural re-alignments necessary to cope with what is referred to here as 'the user shake-up' in the developed world are likely to continue into the next century.

The thesis offered here is a simple one. It has become the conventional wisdom in the developed world, and in the English-speaking world in particular, that the information-based service sector of economy will, and should, grow as a proportion of the total economy into the foreseeable future. As the secondary sector displaced the primary as the major employer of people and resources, runs the argument, so inevitably will the tertiary displace the secondary. Insofar as the tertiary sectors of the Anglo-bloc countries now employ around three times as many people as do their manufacturing sectors and insofar as the secular trend in the other developed countries is in the same direction, this can be seen to have happened already. But the notion that this trend can continue indefinitely towards a post-industrial information society, in which virtually everybody becomes a knowledge worker, is seriously flawed.

The trends likely to be seen in the next decade or so in the infostructures of the world's two information superpowers, the USA and Japan, have been described here and, although they share many characteristics, they have diverged and are, by implication, officially forecast to continue to diverge, in one important respect. Manufacturing in the USA (and in Canada, Australia and the UK) employs a far smaller proportion of the population than it does in Japan (or Germany or Korea). However productive workers in the tertiary sector may be, the services which they provide are less tradeable internationally than are goods which can be put into boxes and loaded onto ships or aeroplanes. Tertiary sector people, and those in the information and control sectors in particular, are highly paid and the demand which they generate tends to draw in imports of physical goods. It is no coincidence that it is those developed countries in which the concept of the post-industrial state is most strongly established which tend to have chronic balance of trade deficits or that the rapid growth of the tertiary sectors in these countries has often coincided with the problem becoming entrenched.

Such structural imbalances might be defensible were the outsized tertiary sectors to be balanced by manufacturing sectors which were sufficiently competitive internationally as to offset the structural disposition towards imports which this produces but, because the likes of Japan, Korea and Germany have manufacturing bases which are not only proportionally large but also among the most efficient in the world, this has not been the case.

A wave of computer-based technology has rolled through much of the manufacturing sector in the developed world, greatly increasing output and decreasing the numbers of people employed. The result has been a massive shift of employment into the tertiary sector and into the control segments of all sectors of the economy. As the computerization wave has rolled on into white collar work, the roles of previously distinct occupational groups have become blurred, bringing structural pressures to bear on a labour market which is anyway certain to experience a process of compression similar to that previously seen in manufacturing. As the flood of technology advanced through the primary and secondary sectors, people moved into the tertiary. The tertiary and control sectors are now so awash with productivity-enhancing technology that over-employment in them can no longer be ignored and a process of re-structuring is probably already under way.

It should be emphasized that this seems to be primarily a problem of the Anglo bloc, and of the USA and the UK in particular. The Japanese, as we have seen, are gradually moving towards a higher service and control component in their economy but this is in response to observable demographic trends and predictable social needs and there are no signs that they will soon fall prey to the kind of imbalance which has crept up on the Americans and the British.

Equilibrium will probably be re-established as a result of three emerging trends. In the first place, the not inconsiderable new functionality which information technology is generating will be unlocked by the growth of businesses which offer either something which has never existed before or greatly improved ways of dealing with old problems. Some of the new goods and services offered will undoubtedly be in the electronic cottage or infonaut mould but more mundane, mass-market applications of information technology will solve problems and generate revenue and jobs.

Combating the rise of crime in the developed world could, for example, prove to be a major growth area within what we have referred to here as the control sector, creating markets for both hardware and services. It may well be that the cars of 2005 will be virtually unstealable, or instantly traceable and that intruder surveillance equipment will by then have become so efficient and affordable that burglary goes out of fashion. Other identifiable problem areas, from traffic control to environmental rehabilitation could be addressed using the new technology and have similarly beneficial economic effects.

The second trend which is likely to have a beneficial effect is the growing realization that consumption patterns are likely to shift from their past emphasis on tangible physical goods to social goods, such as health care, social services and care for the aged. The deflation of over-resourced control sectors and the resuscitation of under-resourced care sectors is likely to bring real benefits here. This trend is clearly flagged in both American and Japanese labour market projections for 2005.

The third, and perhaps most essential shift, however, is towards a re-emphasis of manufacturing in those countries where its relative weight has been allowed to shrink too much. The traditional response to this problem has been to resort to protectionism of one kind or another. This has been successful where it has given a brief respite to industries which have subsequently revitalized themselves but is a process which is generally undesirable. A much more promising trend is the growth of transnational manufacturing businesses which are producing an increased proportion of their goods in overseas plants. The British, for example, have become so accustomed to the presence of American manufacturers on their soil that they no longer think of them as anything but British. The signs are that they will soon start to think of Nissan, Sony and Hyundai in the same way as they do of Ford or Mars.

For the purposes of re-establishing the balance of the economy, the most important point is not the ownership of the manufacturing plant but rather its location. Over time, the manufacturing heavyweights will not only be opening plants overseas, they will also be closing down plants at home. Certainly they will only be able to manufacture where the host country is capable of providing an adequate pool of skilled labour but the advance of information technology has made it much easier to export complex manufacturing know-how on a systematic basis than it has ever been before and the problem of inadequate productivity in offshore plants, relative to that in the home country, will soon be a thing of the past. This is perhaps the most powerful mechanism through which the balance of national economies and an easier equilibrium in international trade will be achieved.

When the information revolution is viewed with a sufficient degree of detachment that the enabling technologies can be seen in their proper perspective, as nothing more than rather intriguing tools of change, the whole process can be seen as one of the demolition of barriers. In 2005 the level of wider world consciousness in parts of the developing world will have risen dramatically and this heightened understanding will have stimulated rapid social and economic change. The infostructure of the developed world will have changed perceptibly, but probably not dramatically, and those countries which have rushed prematurely down the post-industrial road may have understood some of their problems more clearly and be taking steps to address them. The world will shrink still further and a larger and culturally richer international society, in the sense of a highly mobile subculture, will continue to grow. The removal of barriers will inevitably result in feelings of intellectual and political agoraphobia which could pose major threats to stability and it can only be hoped that understanding and co-operation will prevail over fear and loathing.

The developed world, at any rate, should be awash with information by 2005 and, perhaps for a majority of its citizens, the information revolution may have run its course. However, the race to the intelligent state, as the figurative use of the word implies, is a competitive process and the techno-commercial dynamic is likely to ensure that, like dogs chasing an electric hare, we all continue to pursue some ever-receding ideal state of physical and spiritual well-being. The new tools which will be available to us in 2005 may just be opening the door to an intellectual revolution which will enable us to make use of all that information. What a race that could turn out to be.

APPENDIX:
THE INFORMATION
ACCESS INDEX

Country	Rank	Index*	Literacy (%)	News-papers per '000	Radio sets per '000	TV sets per '000	Tele-phones per '000
Bermuda	1	373	98	321	1,379	948	1,025
USA	2	326	100	259	2,122	814	510
Switzerland	3	304	99	504	851	406	924
Japan	4	297	100	572	1,234	610	422
Denmark	5	295	99	359	1,012	528	855
Sweden	6	286	99	526	885	471	666
Finland	7	281	99	547	998	488	534
Norway	8	261	100	551	796	423	504
Canada	9	255	99	231	1,023	626	592
New Zealand	10	253	99	327	922	372	728
UK	11	252	99	414	1,145	435	454
Germany**	12	248	99	331	949	506	545
Hong Kong	13	242	77	574	642	260	588
Iceland	14	241	100	500	785	319	508
Australia	15	236	100	252	1,262	484	431
Netherlands	16	230	99	311	902	485	460
Malta	17	225	84	195	524	741	537
Austria	18	217	98	362	622	475	413
Belgium	19	211	98	219	776	447	514
France	20	204	99	212	895	400	452
Luxembourg	21	202	100	395	623	252	442
Netherlands Antilles	22	194	94	228	1,099	332	330
USSR	23	189	98	474	685	323	140
Czechoslovakia	24	187	99	345	583	410	263
Italy	25	185	97	105	794	423	465

Information Access Index (contd)

Country	Rank	Index*	Literacy (%)	News-papers per '000	Radio sets per '000	TV sets per '000	Tele-phones per '000
Singapore	26	183	83	289	306	372	491
Qatar	27	177	76	206	510	514	348
Macao	28	169	79	620	246	65	257
Barbados	29	165	99	158	878	263	332
Israel	30	159	96	208	468	266	390
Puerto Rico	31	156	89	185	720	266	306
Hungary	32	156	99	273	592	409	88
Bahamas	33	155	93	138	538	225	467
Bulgaria	34	153	95	267	436	249	293
Ireland	35	152	99	205	583	271	279
Spain	36	145	96	82	304	389	399
Korea	37	141	88	197	1,003	207	98
Greece	38	139	90	107	419	195	458
Brunei	39	137	78	346	234	225	208
Uruguay	40	137	95	267	600	228	109
Oman	41	135	20	45	645	762	50
Bahrain	42	132	79	61	527	402	247
Kuwait	43	126	75	209	337	281	205
Taiwan	44	123	89	99	314	272	309
Lebanon	45	122	80	97	834	327	52
Argentina	46	121	94	154	673	219	99
Poland	47	121	99	184	428	292	87
Malaysia	48	118	70	323	428	144	89
Cyprus	49	118	94	125	289	141	350
Trinidad & Tobago	50	117	95	108	460	301	147
Andorra	51	114	100	122	219	149	332
UAE	52	99	55	200	322	109	199
Yugoslavia	53	98	90	100	245	197	194
Venezuela	54	96	85	164	432	156	61
Romania	55	93	98	159	195	194	85
Martinique	56	93	93	95	207	137	228
Surinam	57	91	65	102	633	133	87
Cuba	58	90	96	129	343	203	29
Portugal	59	88	79	54	216	176	230
Belize	60	85	90	18	580	165	82

Information Access Index (contd)

Country	Rank	Index*	Literacy (%)	News-papers per '000	Radio sets per '000	TV sets per '000	Tele-phones per '000
Mauritius	61	84	83	69	354	215	69
Brazil	62	81	76	48	373	204	90
Chile	63	80	91	67	340	201	44
Mexico	64	80	83	127	242	127	90
Jamaica	65	79	96	59	409	124	74
Costa Rica	66	79	93	86	259	136	96
Panama	67	76	86	69	222	165	104
South Africa	68	74	62	48	324	101	179
Turkey	69	71	76	55	161	174	122
Bolivia	70	71	63	50	597	98	32
Saudi Arabia	71	70	51	11	280	277	79
Colombia	72	62	85	53	167	108	77
Ecuador	73	61	84	51	314	82	35
Thailand	74	61	88	87	182	109	10
El Salvador	75	58	67	45	403	87	18
Jordan	76	57	67	53	252	77	75
Mongolia	77	56	100	85	131	38	31
Peru	78	55	82	31	251	95	34
Honduras	79	51	57	41	384	70	15
Iraq	80	50	89	22	202	68	35
Nicaragua	81	48	58	69	247	61	12
Egypt	82	47	45	78	247	80	11
Paraguay	83	46	88	34	169	48	21
Dominican Republic	84	46	69	42	168	82	24
Sri Lanka	85	44	87	35	194	32	7
Syria	86	44	60	15	248	59	45
Iran	87	42	52	22	245	66	38
Tunisia	88	42	51	44	188	75	27
Algeria	89	41	50	21	232	73	30
Swaziland	90	40	55	68	154	16	36
Ghana	91	39	60	33	295	15	5
North Korea	92	38	99	20	117	14	1
Libya	93	38	67	11	139	65	25
Philippines	94	37	56	56	136	41	9

Information Access Index (contd)

Country	Rank	Index*	Literacy (%)	News-papers per '000	Radio sets per '000	TV sets per '000	Tele-phones per '000
China	95	36	71	19	184	27	9
Madagascar	96	36	80	6	198	20	3
Zimbabwe	97	36	78	24	85	27	26
Indonesia	98	35	63	21	144	55	6
Zambia	99	34	73	11	150	25	9
South Yemen	100	34	49	10	155	62	30
Togo	101	32	71	3	210	6	3
Morocco	102	32	30	21	209	70	17
Gabon	103	32	62	14	138	36	10
Laos	104	31	84	3	124	5	2
Ivory Coast	105	31	54	9	139	59	7
Guatemala	106	29	46	39	64	45	20
Kenya	107	29	69	13	95	9	15
Sudan	108	29	31	6	235	61	3
Nigeria	109	28	51	9	171	29	8
Burma (Myanmar)	110	28	79	10	81	2	2
Ethiopia	111	28	62	1	188	2	4
Namibia	112	27	30	17	133	16	66
Zaire	113	27	72	9	101	1	1
Sierra Leone	114	25	21	3	220	10	53
Pakistan	115	24	26	64	86	16	8
India	116	23	41	28	78	27	5
Congo	117	23	57	1	109	5	8
Senegal	118	22	38	8	113	35	7
Cameroon	119	22	42	6	131	22	4
Liberia	120	21	20	6	225	18	4
Uganda	121	20	48	2	99	8	3
North Yemen	122	17	27	16	33	17	30
Angola	123	17	41	12	53	6	4
Tanzania	124	15	46	7	21	1	3
Afghanistan	125	15	28	4	104	8	2
Mauritania	126	15	17	0	143	23	2
Burundi	127	14	38	4	57	1	1
Haiti	128	14	35	7	42	5	6

Information Access Index (contd)

Country	Rank	Index*	Literacy (%)	News-papers per '000	Radio sets per '000	TV sets per '000	Tele-phones per '000
Bangladesh	129	12	29	10	41	4	2
Niger	130	12	28	1	59	4	2
Mozambique	131	11	28	5	41	2	4
Benin	132	10	17	0	89	5	2
Nepal	133	8	21	3	33	2	1
Central Africa	134	7	12	0	61	3	2
Mali	135	5	9	5	39	0	1
Burkina Faso	136	5	9	1	26	5	2
Averages		**100**	**72**	**128**	**390**	**183**	**169**

* Index calculated by indexing raw scores for literacy, newspaper, radio, television and telephone diffusion for each country against the average score for the item, then totalling the scores for all items and indexing the total against the average of all countries' total scores.

** Estimated figures for unified Germany.

GLOSSARY

AM (Amplitude Modulation) The process of varying the amplitude of one (the carrier) signal according to the pattern of another. Seldom used in data communications but widely used in low-fidelity radio broadcasting. (See also, FM.)

Analog (US and computer industry preferred spelling of analogue) Variable wave form of transmission or data handling – often used to mimic other physically measurable forces (e.g. sound).

ATM (Asynchronous transmission mode) A form of data packet switching which utilizes a standard packet 53 bytes in length, regarded as a key technology in merging telephone and data communications networks.

Bandwidth Range of frequencies which can be conveyed via a particular medium. Usually expressed in hertz (cycles per second), it is the difference between the highest and lowest frequency simultaneously passed by the channel.

Binary Number system, using base 2, most commonly used in computers and related systems.

Bit (Binary digit) Either 0 or 1, recorded or transmitted in media in which two states can be created and detected, to signify the presence (1) or absence (0) of a signal.

Broadband Term used to describe a medium which has large bandwidth value and can therefore convey complex data streams. (See also, bandwidth.)

Byte Unit of data consisting of eight bits or binary digits. (See also, bit.)

CAD (Computer-aided design) A technique which enables designers to produce, assess and modify designs (for anything from system kitchens to aircraft subsystems) with great speed and accuracy. In many cases it avoids the need for physical modelling and mock-ups.

CATV (Community Antenna television) Television system in which subscribers are linked by cable to a shared antenna system. The term is sometimes used to signify cable television of any kind.

CD ROM (Compact disk read-only memory) Optical disk of the same format as the audio CD but used to store up to 600 megabytes of data. Often used to store commercial databases and used in lieu of on-line services.

Cellular communications System of mobile communications in which a geographical area is divided into small areas or 'cells' in which communication takes place between very low powered radio transmitters and receivers and routed through the main telephone network. The small size of the cells ensures that a sufficient number of differentiated transmission frequencies is available in each, within the limits of the available spectrum, to satisfy the number of users likely to be in the area. To avoid interference, the same frequencies are not used in adjacent cells. Computers allocate the frequencies and ensure smooth transfer to a new frequency as the user moves from one cell to the next.

Coaxial cable Large capacity cable used for radio frequency transmission and consisting of a central insulated core surrounded by an insulated wire braid. Most familiar as antenna leads for television receivers.

Coherent light Light having a single frequency, typically produced by lasers.

CPU (Central processing unit) The central logic processing unit of a computer system, usually an integrated circuit microprocessor. When combined with primary memory, forms basis of the standard Von Neumann architecture.

Crossbar Obsolete electro-mechanical system for switching in telephone networks. (See also, Strowger.)

Curie Temperature The temperature at which a the magnetic characteristics of a material change from ferromagnetic to paramagnetic.

Decibel (dB) Unit of measurement indicating the intensity of a sound or the difference between two voltages, currents or power levels. Has logarithmic relationship to some reference value, such as lowest audible note in the frequency.

Design rules Principles of design and manufacture required in integrated circuits of a particular degree of integration, determined by line-widths and separation.

Diffusion furnace Furnace used in the processing of integrated circuits, in which molecules of selected elements are diffused into the exposed areas of pure silicon.

Digital A system in which data is processed, transmitted or stored in discrete quantities which represent binary digits. (See also, analog.)

Discrete device A single electronic component (e.g. transistor, resistor, capacitor) as opposed to an integrated circuit. A transistor, for example, is a discrete semiconductor, although the term 'semiconductor' is generally used to signify an integrated circuit.

DRAM (Dynamic random access memory) A common form of integrated circuit memory, in which the memory is stored only when current is applied (hence dynamic). Static random access memories (SRAMs) have a more complex structure but retain data in the absence of current (hence static).

DTP (Desk-top publishing) A sophisticated form of word processing and graphical representation which, utilizing small computers, enables documents to be produced which incorporate features previously only available using professional typesetting equipment.

Dumb terminal A simple computer terminal used purely as a link to another computer system, in which all intelligence resides and in which all data processing takes place.

EDI (Electronic data interchange) Generic term used to describe data communications standards such as OSI.

Firmware Software embedded in, and an integral part of, an integrated circuit.

Flash memory A high-density integrated circuit memory, a form of EPROM (electronically programmable read-only memory).

FLOPS (Floating-point operations per second) A measure of speed in supercomputers, usually counted in millions of FLOPS or megaflops.

Fly-by-wire Control system in aircraft in which mechanical and hydraulic linkages are replaced by electronic networks which activate servo controls. Greatly enhances stability and control and saves weight.

FM (Frequency modulation) The process of varying the frequency of the carrier signal according to the pattern of another signal. Widely used in data communications and high-fidelity radio broadcasting. (See also, AM.)

Footprint Area covered by the signal transmitted earthwards from a satellite.

Giga- Numerical prefix denoting 10^9 – a thousand million (UK), a billion (USA).

HDTV (High-definition television) A television system in which the conventional 405 (NTSC system) or 625 (PAL system) scan-lines on the screen are replaced with a much higher number (1125 or more) to give a much clearer, sharper picture.

Hertz A measure of frequency – one cycle per second. Thus one kilohertz (kHz) equals one thousand cycles per second, one megahertz (MHz) equals one million cycles per second and so on.

Icon Small graphic representation on a computer screen used to indicate particular functions. Usually used in conjunction with touch-screens and 'mouse' pointing devices.

INS (Information Network System) A proprietary data communications network established by NTT in Japan.

ISDN (Integrated Services Digital Network) A system proposed by the postal telegraph and telephone administrations (PTTs) for the delivery of all forms of signal traffic on a single digital network.

Josephson Junction A very high speed experimental form of integrated circuit junction which utilizes superconductivity.

Kerr effect Sometimes called the electro-optical or magneto-optical effect, this is the production of optical refraction effects by the application of magnetic fields.

LAN (Local-area network) A small computer network in a single location, usually linked by twisted pair or coaxial cable.

Laser Originally an acronym (Light Amplification by Stimulated Emission of Radiation), this is a device which converts mixed frequency light into a narrow focused beam of coherent light.

LED (Light-emitting diode) A semiconductor diode which emits light (usually red) when current is applied to it.

LSI Large-scale integration: A level of integration in integrated circuits in which at least 10,000 transistors are integrated on the chip.

Luggable Portable, but with some difficulty – used of computer equipment.

Magneto-optical See, Kerr effect.

Mask aligner A high precision device used to align photomasks over semiconductor wafers during the photolithographic processes of integrated circuit manufacture.

Mask ROM (Mask read-only memory) An integrated circuit in which memory is permanently stored via the design of the final photomask in an otherwise common set. Commonly used to store software for computer games.

Mega- Numerical prefix denoting 10^6, a million.

Micron 10^{-6} metres or one thousandth of a millimetre.

Microprocessor A semiconductor chip set or, more often, a single chip which incorporates at least an arithmetic and logic unit and a control unit. Used as the central processing units of microcomputer systems.

Microwave Electromagnetic radiation in the 0.3 to 0.001 metres wavelength (1–300 GHz frequency) part of the spectrum, used in radar and some forms of telecommunications transmission.

MIPS (Millions of instructions per second) A measure of processing speed.

Multiplexing The process of transmitting multiple signals simultaneously through the same transmission medium.

Nano- Numerical prefix denoting 10^9 or one thousand millionth (UK)/one billionth (US) part.

OCR (Optical character recognition) A system in which written or printed documents are scanned optically and the printed characters compared with characters held in the machine's memory. Where a match is made, the character is recognized and reproduced as a processing input by the machine.

OSI (Open systems interconnect) A series of rules for data communications suggested by the International Standards Organization (ISO).

PCM (Pulse code modulation) A technique for converting analog signals into digital bit streams by sampling the amplitude of the analog signal at high frequency and ascribing arithmetic values to the readings. The process can be reversed to reproduce, with high fidelity, the analog signal at the receiving end. Used, for example, in digital audio systems.

Photolithography   A process for printing high precision patterns on treated silicon wafers for the purpose of manufacturing integrated circuits.

Photomask   A kind of optical 'stencil' used in photolithography.

Pico-   Numerical prefix denoting 10^{-12} or one billionth (UK)/one trillionth (US) part.

POS   (Point of sales equipment) A kind of computer system used in retailing to record sales, monitor inventory levels and automatically re-order goods.

Qwerty keyboard   Standard alphanumeric keyboard, named for the first six letters of the top line of the letter keys.

RISC   (Reduced instruction set computing) Refers to a type of central processing unit which is designed to process a limited range of simple instructions at very high speed.

Silicon Foundry   A fabrication-only subcontracting facility for integrated circuit manufacture.

Spectrum   Common parlance for the electromagnetic spectrum but also often used to signify bandwidth. (See also, bandwidth.)

Stepper   Deriving from 'step and repeat', a machine functionally similar to a mask aligner in which the pattern projected onto the silicon wafer is optically reduced and the whole wafer exposed in a number of steps, rather than just one.

Strowger   Obsolete electro-mechanical system for switching in telephone networks. (See also, Crossbar.)

Substrate   Chip of pure silicon, or other semiconductor material, on which an integrated circuit is fabricated.

Teletext   A system for broadcasting information, with text and basic graphics, using spare capacity in television transmission. Interactive only insofar as the user can select data from a menu using a keypad.

Tera-   Numerical prefix denoting 10^{12} – a million million or a US trillion.

Transceiver   A combined transmitter and receiver.

Transistor   A semiconductor device which can be used to amplify a current or voltage or act as a switch in circuits. An invention of seminal importance in modern electronics.

Transponder   A device incorporated in a satellite which receives and re-transmits signals.

Videotex   An interactive data service utilizing a keyboard and telephone receiver. Examples include Captain in Japan, Prestel in the UK and Qube in the USA.

VLSI   (Very large-scale integration) A level of integration in integrated circuits in which at least 100,000 transistors are integrated on the chip.

Von Neumann Architecture   Standard architecture of the vast majority of existing computers. Based on separate logic, control and memory functions and stored programs in which the instructions are read sequentially.

VSAT   (Very small aperture terminal) A small, low-cost satellite earth station. Widely used to bring substantial communications capability to remote areas.

Wafer   Polished circular slice of an ingot of silicon or other semiconductor material on which integrated circuit chips are fabricated.

Wafer fab   Abbreviation for wafer fabrication, the central processes in semiconductor manufacture.

WAN   (Wide-area network) A large computer network, usually formed by linking local area networks through public communications media.

Winchester Disk   (a.k.a. hard disk) A large-capacity magnetic data storage disk utilizing a solid platter. A standard data storage medium in most computers.

Workstation   In general terms, any intelligent (as opposed to dumb) terminal or personal computer. The term is often used colloquially, however, to refer to RISC computers which use the UNIX operating system, are similar in function to, and compete with, personal computers.

WORM   (Write once - read many (times)) Large capacity optical data storage disk on which data can be recorded but not erased.

BIBLIOGRAPHY

Adair, Jay (1991) 'Leading the way towards deregulation', *World Broadcast News*, October.

Andersen Consulting (1992) *Trends in Information Technology* (2nd edn). McGraw Hill.

Beniger, James R. (1986) *The Control Revolution*. Harvard University Press.

Brown, D. A. (1986) 'Aerospace in India', *Aviation Week*, May.

Cahill, Kevin (1986) *Trade Wars – The High Technology Scandal of the 1980s*. W. H. Allen.

Campbell, Jeremy (1989) *The Improbable Machine*. Simon & Schuster.

Carey, Max L. and Franklin, James C. (1991) 'Industry and job growth continues slow into next century', *Monthly Labor Review*, November.

Central Statistical Office, *Annual Abstract of Statistics* (1970–89 editions). HMSO.

Central Statistical Office, *Blue Book – National Income and Expenditure Accounts 1991*. HMSO.

Chandra, P. (1987) 'Satellite Link for Indian Broadcasting' *Asia-Pacific Broadcasting & Telecommunications*, April.

Clark, Grahame and Piggott, Stuart (1970) *Prehistoric Societies*. Pelican.

Clarke, Arthur C. (1992) *How the World Was One*. Victor Gollancz.

Cohen, Stephen S. and Zysman, John (1987) *Manufacturing Matters – the Myth of the Post-industrial Economy*. Basic Books.

Corcoran, Elizabeth (1992) 'Storage Space', *Scientific American*, October.

Croucher, Phil (1989) *Communications and Networks*. Sigma.

Datapro (1991) *Datapro Reports on International Telecommunications*. McGraw Hill.

Downing, John, Mohammadi, Ali and Sreberny-Mohammadi, Annabelle (1990) *Questioning the Media*. Sage.

Economic Planning Agency (1990) *Shimyureishon; 2010-nen no Sangyo Keizai (Simulation – the industrial economy of 2010)*. Keizai Kikaku-cho.

Economic Planning Agency (1992) *2010-nen Gijitsu Yosoku* (*A technological forecast for 2010*). Keizai Kikaku-cho.

Economist, 'Set for a fall', 13 December 1986.

Economist, 'Sam, Sam, the switching man', 28 November 1987.

Economist, 'Forward into the past', 23 May 1992.

Economist, 'Thailand, the generals and the king', 23 May 1992.

Economist, ' Thailand licks its wounds', 30 May 1992.

Economist, 'Military Trim', 11 July 1992.

Economist Intelligence Unit (1992) *Thailand – Second Quarter 1992*. Economist Group.

Egan, Bruce L. (1990) 'Public policy for fibre-to-the-home' *Telecommunications Policy*, December.

Europa World Yearbook (1960–92 editions). Europa Publications.

Freeman, Christopher (1987) *Technology Policy and Economic Performance*. Pinter.

Friedland, Jonathan (1992) 'Cost of a Crisis', *Far East Economic Review*, 4 June.

Fullerton, Howard N. Jr. (1991) 'Labor Force projections, the baby boom moves on', *Monthly Labor Review*, November.

Gastil, Raymond (1986) *Freedom in the World*. Greenwood Press.

Gilder, George (1992) *Life After Television – the coming transformation of media and American life*. W. W. Norton.

Gupta, V.S. (1987) 'Rural Press Development in India', *Media Asia*, Vol. 14 No. 2.

Hadlock, Paul, Hecker, Daniel and Gannon, Joseph (1991) 'High technology employment: another view', *Monthly Labor Review*, July.

Hall, Peter (ed.) (1986) *Technology Innovation and Economic Policy*. Philip Allan.

Hamlin, Kevin (1992) 'On the beat', *BZW Pacific*, February.

Handley, Paul (1991) 'Cutting Edge', *Far East Economic Review*, 29 August.

Handley, Paul (1992) 'Wired for export', *Far East Economic Review*, 30 January.

Haque, Mazharul (1991) 'Information and Media and the Third World', *Media Asia*, 4.

Hardaker, Mike (1992) 'Back to the Future', *Windows User*, July.

Harth, Erich (1991) *Dawn of a Millennium*. Penguin.

Harvey, David A. (1990) 'State of the Media', *Byte*, November.

Hashimoto Takashi (1991) *ISDN Kakumei no Subete Wakaru Hon* (*All you need to know about the ISDN revolution*). HBJ Shuppankyoku.

Hivek, Christopher J. and Burn, Barbara B. (1982) *An Analytic Comparison of Education Systems*. National Commission on Excellence in Education.

Hof, Robert D. (1992) 'Inside Intel', *Business Week*, 1 June.

Holmes, Deborah (1986) *Governing the Press*. Westview Press.

Horsley, W. and Buckley R. (1990) *Nippon – New Superpower*. BBC.

ICOT-JIPDEC AI Centre (1991) *AI Hakusho (AI White Paper)*. Nihon Joho Shori Kaihatsu Kyokai.

Imai, Kenichi (1990) *Joho Nettowaku Shakai no Tenkai (The evolution of the information network society)*. Chikuma Shobo.

International Association for the Evaluation of Educational Achievement (1988) *Science Achievement in Seventeen Countries*. Pergamon Press.

International Committee Against Censorship (1991–2) *Article 19 Bulletin*, Issues 13–14. ICAC.

International Labour Office, *Yearbook of Labour Statistics* (1968–91 editions), International Labour Office.

Irvine, John, Martin, Ben R. and Isard, Phoebe (1990) *Investing in the Future*. Elgar.

Jain, M. (1990) 'A Burst of Colour', *India Today*, 15 January.

Johnson, Leland L. and Reed, David P. (1992) 'Telephone company entry into cable television', *Telecommunications Policy*, March.

Jolly, David (1992) 'Phone funk', *Far East Economic Review*, 16 July.

Kamal, S. S. (1990) 'Advanced Telecommunications for Rural Applications', *Satellite Communications*, October.

Karnik, K. (1981) 'Developmental Television in India', *Educational Broadcasting International*, September.

Kokusai Chiiki Kenkyu Centre (1987) *Sekai no Medeia (World Media)*. Kyoikusha.

Krishnatray, P. (1986) 'Management of Communications in Developing Countries: The Indian Case', *Media Asia*, 13, 3.

Kuhn, Thomas S. (1970) *The Structure of Scientific Revolutions*. Chicago University Press.

Kutscher, Ronald E. (1991) 'New BLS projections: findings and implications', *Monthly Labor Review*, November.

Lee, Simon (1991) *The Cost of Free Speech*. Faber & Faber.

Lerner, Daniel (1958) *The Passing of Traditional Society*. Free Press.

Levin, Stanford L. and Meisel, John B. (1991) 'Cable television and competition', *Telecommunications Policy*, December.

Lyons, Nick (1976) *The Sony Vision*. Crown.

McCluhan, Marshall (1964) *Understanding Media – The extension of man*. Ark Paperbacks.

McCluhan, Marshall and McCluhan, Eric (1988) *Laws of Media – The new science*. University of Toronto Press.

McCluhan, Marshall and Powers, Bruce R. (1989) *The Global Village – Transformations in world life and media in the 21st century*. Oxford University Press.

Macmillan *The Statesman's Yearbook 1991*. Macmillan.

Marsh, Peter (1985) *The Space Business*. Pelican.

Melkote, Srinivas R. (1991) *Communication for Development in the Third World*. Sage.

Messadie, Gerald A. *Great Modern Inventions*. W & R Chambers.

Menon, V. (1989) 'The Case of India'. In Jussawalla M., Okuma T. and Araki T. (eds), *Information Technology and Global Interdependence*. Greenwood.

Ministry of Labour, *Yearbook of Labour Statistics* (1960–1990 editions). Rodosho.

Ministry of Posts and Telecommunications (1991) *Eisei Tsushin Bijinesu* (*Satellite Communications Business*). Diamondo-sha.

Mohan C. V. (1983) 'INSAT and India's space programme', *Science Today*, January.

Mulgan, G. J. (1991) *Communication and Control*. Polity Press.

Nadeau, Robert L. (1990) *Mind, Machine and Human Consciousness*. Contemporary Books.

National Research Council (1982) *Outlook for Science and Technology*. W. H. Freeman.

Neuman, W. Russell (1991) *The Future of the Mass Audience*. Cambridge University Press.

Nippon Shimbun Kyokai (1992) *Zenkoku Shimbun Gaido* (*All-Japan Newspaper Guide*). Nippon Shimbun Kyokai.

Norris, Paul and Lewis, Jonathan (1991) *Reuters*. Investment report published by Barclays de Zoete Wedd Securities, November 1991.

NTIA (1988) *Telecom 2000*. National Telecommunications and Information Administration, US Department of Commerce.

NTT Mirai Yosoku Kenkyukai (1991) *2005-nen no Shakai to Joho Tsushin* (*Society and Data Communications in 2005*). NTT Shuppan.

NTT Mirai Yosoku Kenkyukai (1991) *2005-nen no Joho Tsushin Gijitsu* (*Data Communications Technology in 2005*). NTT Shuppan.

Pientam, Olarn (1992) *Thailand's National Strategy: Planning for Telecommunications Needs in the Future*. Telephone Organization of Thailand, June 1992.

Pendakur, M. (1991) 'A Political Economy of Television in India'. In Sussman, G. and Lent, J. A. (eds), *Transnational Communications*. Sage.

Pirard, T. (1986) 'India: Rich in Telecommunications', *Satellite Communications*, May.

Piriyapoksombut, Patra (1992) 'Getting past slow', *BZW Pacific*, April.

Poster, Mark (1990) *The Mode of Information – Poststructuralism and Social Context*. Polity Press.

Pratt, Vernon (1987) *Thinking Machines – The Evolution of Artificial Intelligence*. Basil Blackwell.

Raghavan, G. (1979) 'Communication and Development: The Indian Case', *Communicator*, April.

Rahman, S. A. and Rampal, K. R. (1984) 'Adversary vs. Developmental Journalism: Indian mass media at the crossroads', *International Journal for Mass Communications Studies*, 34.

Rheingold, Howard (1991) *Virtual Reality*. Secker & Warburg.

Rogers, E. M., Singhal, A. and Doshi, J. K. (1988) 'The Diffusion of Television in India', *Media Asia*, 15, 4.

Rosenberg, Nathan (1986) *Inside the Black Box – Technology and Economics*. Cambridge University Press.

Saatchi & Saatchi (1992) *Market and Media Facts 1992*. Saatchi & Saatchi Advertising (Thailand).

Shallis, Michael (1985) *The Silicon Idol*. Oxford University Press.

Silvestri, George and Lukasiewicz, John (1991) 'Occupational employment projections', *Monthly Labor Review*, November.

Singhal, A and Rogers E. M. (1989) *India's Information Revolution*. Sage.

Sommerlad L. (1980) 'Broadcasting serves a complex culture', *World Broadcast News*, April.

Stephens, Guy M. (1990) 'The Third World: Leaping Telecommunications Hurdles', *Satellite Communications*, May.

Stonier, Tom (1992) *Beyond Information*. Springer Verlag.

Sturgess, Brian (1984) 'Telecommunications and Mass Media'. In *People, Science and Technology*. Wheatsheaf.

Sussman, Gerald and Lent, John A. (1991) *Transnational Communications*. Sage.

Takeuchi, Ikuo, Kajima, Kazuto and Kawamoto, Masaru (1990) *Niyu Medeiya to Shakai Seikatsu* (*New Media and Social Life*). Tokyo Daigaku Shuppankai.

Television Information Office (1990) 'Monitoring Media Attitudes', *The American Enterprise*, July/August.

Toffler, Alvin (1981) *The Third Wave*. Pan.

TRC (1990) *TRC Marketfile*. TRC.

UNESCO (1991) *The UNESCO Statistical Yearbook* UNESCO.

Wagner, Daniel A. (1987) *The Future of Literacy in a Changing World*. Pergamon Press.

Wallis, Roger and Baran, Stanley (1990) *The Known World of Broadcast News*. Routledge.

Weizenbaum, Joseph (1984) *Computer Power and Human Reason*. Pelican.

White, Lynn Jr. (1978) *Medieval Religion and Technology*. University of California Press.

Whitley, J. D. and Wilson, R. A. (1986) *Information Technology and Employment: Quantifying the Impact Using a Macroeconomic Model*. University of Warwick.

Yadava J. S. (1991) 'Press System in India'. *Media Asia*, 18, 3.

Yamaguchi, Haruo (1990) *Telecommunications – NTT's Vision of the Future* (translated by Norman Havens). NTT.

Yoshida, Jun (1983) *Development of Television and Changes in TV Viewing Habits in Japan*. NHK.

INDEX